# MILITARY AND SCIENTIFIC ENGLISH FOR THE NAVY

# 海军军事与科技英语

## （第二版）

杨海英　王红霞　任　远　主编

北京大学出版社
PEKING UNIVERSITY PRESS

**图书在版编目（CIP）数据**

海军军事与科技英语 / 杨海英，王红霞，任远主编. —2版. —北京 ： 北京大学出版社，2022.8

ISBN 978-7-301-33143-9

Ⅰ.①海… Ⅱ.①杨… ②王… ③任… Ⅲ.①海军–英语–军事院校–教材 Ⅳ.① E153

中国版本图书馆 CIP 数据核字（2022）第 119885 号

| | |
|---|---|
| 书　　　　名 | 海军军事与科技英语（第二版） |
| | HAIJUN JUNSHI YU KEJI YINGYU (DI-ER BAN) |
| 著作责任者 | 杨海英　王红霞　任 远 主编 |
| 责 任 编 辑 | 郝妮娜 |
| 标 准 书 号 | ISBN 978-7-301-33143-9 |
| 出 版 发 行 | 北京大学出版社 |
| 地　　　　址 | 北京市海淀区成府路 205 号　100871 |
| 网　　　　址 | http://www.pup.cn　　新浪微博：@ 北京大学出版社 |
| 电 子 信 箱 | bdhnn 2011@126.com |
| 电　　　　话 | 邮购部 010-62752015　发行部 010-62750672　编辑部 010-62759634 |
| 印 刷 者 | 北京溢漾印刷有限公司 |
| 经 销 者 | 新华书店 |
| | 787 毫米 ×1092 毫米　16 开本　21.25 印张　660 千字 |
| | 2013 年 1 月第 1 版 |
| | 2022 年 8 月第 2 版　2022 年 8 月第 1 次印刷 |
| 定　　　　价 | 78.00 元 |

# 编委会

# 前　言

在新时代军事教育方针和海军转型建设思想的指导下，海军军事英语教学在海军院校的学历教育和军官任职教育中的地位日益突出，在培养高素质新型海军军事人才和做好军事斗争准备方面的作用越发明显。

《海军军事与科技英语》第一版正式出版使用近10年。近年来，为适应世界新军事革命发展趋势和国家安全需求，我军全面深化国防和军队改革，领导指挥体制、作战编成、军兵种、军事政策制度等都经历了深化改革。同时，军队装备技术迅猛发展，海军新型舰艇大批下水服役，武器装备技术日新月异，特别是海军部队联合训练演习、执行多样化军事任务和对外交流日益增多，这些客观条件和需求都要求对《海军军事与科技英语》教材的体系框架和具体内容做出全面更新完善，以适应当前军事科技发展和海军部队实际。

鉴于此，本书对第一版20个单元的主题进行了整合和更新，增加航空母舰、导弹工程、无人机、电磁发射、国际海上避碰规则等近年来新出现的装备、军事改革和国际海洋法规内容，力求使其能够体现当今军事领域的发展动态，满足不同海军专业岗位人员英语教学或学习的需要，以适应新时代海军转型建设对培养高素质专业化人才的要求。全书以海军编制与使命、海军兵种知识、海军主要装备和技术、联合演习、对外交流、院校教育等16个主题为主要内容，介绍了海军职业英语核心术语、海军兵种、各专业岗位通用术语和常用英语表达方式，旨在培养和提高使用者以英语为工具，在当代海军基本知识、海军指挥与作战、海军科学与技术、海军对外交流等领域获取、处理与交流信息的能力。全书由16个单元组成，每单元包含3篇课文，并配有相应的海军术语、翻译技巧和写作指导课后练习。

本书特别邀请了胡世平教授审阅书稿，胡教授知识渊博，严谨细致，提出了很多宝贵意见，在此表示衷心感谢！由于编者水平有限，疏漏之处在所难免，敬请广大读者批评指正。

《海军军事与科技英语》编写组

2021年10月

# 目 录

**Appendixes** ...........................................................................................313

# Unit 1　Navy

**Bridge-in**

*Answer the following questions in accordance with the microlesson "The Highlights in PLA Navy History".*

1. When and where was the PLA Navy founded?
2. What kind of development path did the PLA Navy go through?
3. What records did the PLA Navy's first voyage around the world set?

## Text A
## China Navy, Organization and Missions

April 23, 2019 marks the 70th anniversary of the founding of the Chinese PLA Navy. In the initial stage of establishment, it was a small unit stationed in Baimamiao—a small town in Taizhou, Jiangsu province, and later grew in strength. In other words, in April, 1949, the Navy of PLA East China Military Command was founded, which led to the establishment of PLA Navy Headquarters in April, 1950. Now, the PLA Navy has become a pillar of China's national defense and is playing a vital role in global efforts to safeguard peace, maintain stability and promote prosperity on seas and oceans.

### Composition and Organization

The PLA Navy is a service subordinate to the Central Military Commission[1]. Its main body consists of the Navy headquarters and three fleets: the North China Sea Fleet, the East China Sea Fleet, and the South China Sea Fleet. The PLA Navy is an important naval force under the absolute leadership of the Communist Party of China.

The Navy is composed of surface forces, submarine forces, naval aviation, marine corps, naval coastal defense forces and logistics forces providing support and supply. Because of the military reforms, the three fleets are also called the ETC[2] Navy, the STC[3] Navy, the NTC[4] Navy respectively. The TC[5] navies exercise control over naval bases, submarine flotillas, surface ship flotillas and naval aviation brigades.

Now, the Navy has eight academies and schools for training line officers, engineering duty officers, political officers, logistical officers and petty officers. They are Naval University of Engineering, Dalian Naval Academy, Naval Command College, Naval Aeronautical University, Naval Logistical Academy, Naval Submarine Academy, Naval Medical University, and Bengbu Naval Petty Officer Academy. In addition, the Navy has some training bases or centers for enlisted personnel.

### Missions and Tasks

The Navy is responsible for the missions of safeguarding China's maritime security and maintaining the sovereignty of its territorial waters, as well as its maritime rights and interests. Its main tasks include performing mobile operations independently or in coordination with other military services to destroy hostile armed forces on the sea; attacking hostile military bases, ports and important shore targets; interdicting or protecting SLOCs[6]; enforcing blockade or anti-blockade warfare at sea; engaging in submarine or anti-submarine warfare and mine or mine countermeasure warfare; participating in landing or counter-landing operations; performing routine combat activities to prevent any surprise attack from the sea and safeguard national ocean resources and maritime activities, etc.

Overseas interests are a crucial part of China's national interests. One of the missions of China's armed forces is to effectively protect the security and legitimate rights and interests of overseas Chinese people, organizations and institutions. The Navy actively promotes international security and military cooperation and refines relevant mechanisms for protecting China's overseas interests.

To address deficiencies in overseas operations and support, the navy has set up far seas forces, developed overseas logistical facilities and enhanced capabilities of accomplishing various military tasks. In August 2017, the Chinese PLA Support Base in Djibouti[7]came into use. Since then, the base has undertaken the missions of providing logistic support for Chinese navy escort task groups and medical service for over 1,000 Chinese and Djiboutian officers and enlisted persons, conducted such joint exercises as MEDEVAC[8], and counter-terrorism and counter-piracy operations with foreign militaries and contingents, and donated over 600

teaching aids to local schools.

The Navy conducts vessel protection operations, maintains the security of strategic SLOCs, and carries out overseas evacuation and maritime rights protection operations.

When the security situation in Yemen[9] deteriorated in March 2015, a PLA Navy escort task group directly sailed to an engagement area in the Gulf of Aden[10], berthed there, and successfully evacuated 621 Chinese citizens and 279 foreign citizens from 15 countries including Pakistan[11], Ethiopia[12], Singapore, Italy, Poland, Germany, Canada, the UK, India and Japan.

Having participated in a lot of operations such as the Gulf-of-Aden escort duty, the search for missing Malaysia Airlines Flight MH370, and the circumnavigation by the 152 Naval Fleet[13], the PLA Navy has become an important force of safeguarding world peace and promoting win-win cooperation.

### History of Development

The PLA Navy was founded on April 23, 1949. From 1949 to 1955 it set up surface forces, coastal defense forces, naval aviation, submarine forces and marine corps, and accomplished the objective of building light sea-air combat forces. From 1955 to 1960 it established the East China Sea Fleet, the South China Sea Fleet and the North China Sea Fleet. From the 1950s to the end of the 1970s the main task of the Navy was to conduct inshore defensive operations. Since the 1980s, the Navy has fulfilled a strategic transition to offshore defensive operations. But until the 1990s, the Navy was mostly a littoral or brown-water force tasked with the protection of China's waterways. Since the beginning of the 21st century, the Navy has steadily developed into a blue-water force that can effectively safeguard China's territorial sovereignty, security and maritime interests. In particular, the navy has undergone historic changes and made historic achievements since the 18th National Congress of the Communist Party of China[14], which was held in 2012. Now the Navy is also an important force able to protect Chinese interests abroad, follow Chinese foreign policy firmly and elevate the international status of the country.

### Force Building

Over the past seven decades, the Navy has developed into a strategic force consisting of five major arms equipped with both nuclear and conventional weapons, playing an important role in safeguarding world peace.

In the 1950s, Mao Zedong gave the important instruction of building up a strong navy — the instruction that laid the foundation for decades of rapid development of the Navy.

The development of the Navy gained new momentum with the initiation of China's reform and opening-up[15]. In 1979, Deng Xiaoping pointed out that strengthening China's maritime defense was a "priority vital to the fate of the country and its people."

In the 1990s, as the Navy strove to enhance its modernization capabilities, its development entered a new phase. In 1995, Jiang Zemin called for great efforts to build the navy and accelerate its modernization.

In 2006, Hu Jintao stressed the building of a strong navy force in accordance with the missions of the PLA in the new century and at the new historical stage.

As socialism with Chinese characteristics entered a new era, Chinese President Xi Jinping laid out plans for the Navy's development, opening a new chapter of building a world-class navy.

During the past 70 years, the Navy has also made great strides in the development of military equipment, for example, the launch of the first home-made aircraft carrier and the mass deliveries of carrier-based J-15 fighter jets.

Moreover, the Navy has completed the mass upgrading of its fighter jets, early warning aircraft, anti-submarine patrol aircraft, as well as the deployment of new missiles and torpedoes.

In line with the strategic requirements of offshore defense and far sea protection, the Navy is speeding up the transition of its tasks from defense on the near seas to protection on the far seas, and improving its capabilities for strategic deterrence and counterattack, maritime maneuvering operations, maritime joint operations, comprehensive defense, and integrated support, so as to build a strong and modernized naval force.

*(1177 words)*

## Sources:

1. Extracted from and edited based on *China's National Defense in the New Era* issued by the State Council Information Office of the People's Republic of China, July 2019.

2. Xinhua, April 23, 2019, China.org.cn

3. www.mod.gov.cn

1. Central Military Commission: the highest military leading body of the Party under the leadership of the Communist Party of China's (CPC) Central Committee. The Central Military Commission is the supreme leading organ of the armed forces of the People's Republic of China. It directs and commands the national armed forces. 中央军事委员会

2. ETC Navy: Eastern Theater Command Navy 东部战区海军

3. STC Navy: Southern Theater Command Navy 南部战区海军

4. NTC Navy: Northern Theater Command Navy 北部战区海军

5. TC navies: Theater Command navies 战区海军

6. SLOCs: an abbreviation for Sea Lines of Communication 海上交通线

7. PLA Support Base in Djibouti: PLAN's first overseas support base. Djibouti is next to the Babel-Mandab Strait that links the Red Sea and the Gulf of Aden. 吉布提保障基地

8. MEDEVAC: the evacuation of casualties from forward areas to the nearest hospital or base 医疗后送

9. Yemen: a country on the Arabian Peninsula, in Southwest Asia, on the Red Sea 也门

10. Gulf of Aden: arm of the Indian Ocean at the entrance to the Red Sea 亚丁湾

11. Pakistan: a Muslim republic that occupies the heartland of ancient south Asian civilization in the Indus River valley 巴基斯坦

12. Ethiopia: a republic in northeastern Africa on the Red Sea 埃塞俄比亚

13. 152 Naval Fleet: a naval fleet comprised of destroyer Jinan, frigate Yiyang and supply ship Qiandaohu 中国海军152舰艇编队

14. National Congress of the Communist Party of China: a party congress that is held every five years. The National Congress is the highest body within the Communist Party of China. 中国共产党全国代表大会

15. reform and opening-up: an economic policy of reformulating the principal contradiction in Chinese society during 1978's third plenary session of the eleventh central committee of the CPC 中国改革开放政策

 **Word Bank**

| | |
|---|---|
| subordinate [sə'bɔ:dɪnət] | adj. 从属的；隶属的 |
| fleet [fli:t] | n. 船队，舰队；（一国的）海军 |
| flotilla [fləʊ'tɪlə] | n. 小舰队；小型船队；支队 |
| brigade [brɪ'geɪd] | n. [军] 旅 |
| logistical [lə'dʒɪstɪkl] | adj. 后勤方面的 |
| enlisted [ɪn'lɪstɪd] | adj. [军] 士兵的，应募入伍的 |
| sovereignty ['sɒvrɪntɪ] | n. 主权；最高统治权；独立自主 |
| territorial [ˌterə'tɔ:rɪəl] | adj. 领土的 |
| interdict ['ɪntədɪkt] | v. 阻断，封锁 |
| blockade [blɒ'keɪd] | n. 包围，封锁 |
| countermeasure ['kaʊntəmeʒə(r)] | n. 对策；反措施 |
| legitimate [lɪ'dʒɪtɪmət] | adj. 合法的；正当的 |
| mechanisms ['mekənɪzəmz] | n. 机制 |
| escort ['eskɔ:t] | n. [军] 护航；护航舰 |
| | v. 为……护航；护送 |
| contingent [kən'tɪndʒənt] | n. 分遣队；（代表某一组织或国家的）代表团 |
| evacuation [ɪˌvækjʊ'eɪʃn] | n. 疏散；撤离 |
| deteriorate [dɪ'tɪərɪəreɪt] | v. 恶化 |
| berth [bɜ:θ] | v. （使船）停泊；靠码头 |
| circumnavigation [ˌsɜ:rkəmˌnævɪ'geɪʃn] | n. 环球航行；环球飞行 |
| win-win [ˌwɪn 'wɪn] | adj. 双赢的；互利互惠的 |
| inshore [ˌɪn'ʃɔ:(r)] | adj. 近岸的 |
| offshore [ˌɒf'ʃɔ:(r)] | adj. 离岸的，近海的 |
| littoral ['lɪtərəl] | adj. 沿海的；海滨的 |
| waterway ['wɔ:təweɪ] | n. 航道；水路 |
| status ['steɪtəs] | n. 地位；身份；职位 |
| momentum [mə'mentəm] | n. 势头；动力 |
| initiation [ɪˌnɪʃɪ'eɪʃn] | n. 开始，初始 |
| stride [straɪd] | n. 大步；进展 |
| torpedo [tɔ:'pi:dəʊ] | n. 鱼雷 |

| surface forces | [军] 水面舰艇部队 |
| submarine forces | [军] 潜艇部队 |
| naval aviation | [军] 海军航空兵部队 |
| marine corps | [军] 海军陆战队 |
| naval coastal defense forces | [军] 海防部队 |
| logistics forces | [军] 后勤部队 |
| line officer | [军] 指挥军官 |
| engineering duty officer | [军] 工程技术军官 |
| petty officer | [军]（海军）士官 |
| in coordination with | 与……协调 |
| armed forces | [军] 武装部队 |
| aircraft carrier | [军] 航空母舰 |
| fighter jet | [军] 喷气式战斗机 |
| early warning aircraft | [军] 预警机 |
| anti-submarine patrol aircraft | [军] 反潜巡逻机 |

 **Exercises**

## I. Comprehension

**Part A**  Questions

*Answer the following questions in accordance with the text.*

1. When is the anniversary of the founding of the People's Liberation Army Navy?

2. What is the Navy headquarters subordinate to?

3. What are the missions and tasks of PLAN?

4. What marked the progress in the development of the Navy's military equipment during the past seven decades?

5. What are the most recent strategic requirements of PLAN?

**Part B**  Multiple Choices

*Choose the most appropriate answer from the given choices below each question according to the text.*

1. Which of the following is NOT included as PLA Navy fleets?

   A. The North China Sea Fleet.

B. The East China Sea Fleet.

C. The South China Sea Fleet.

D. The West China Sea Fleet.

2. Which of the following descriptions of overseas interests is NOT true?

A. Overseas interests are a minor part of China's national interests.

B. The protection of the security, legitimate rights and interests of overseas Chinese is among the missions of China's armed force.

C. To protect China's overseas interests, the Navy actively promotes international security and military cooperation and refines relevant mechanisms.

D. To address deficiencies in overseas operations and support, the Navy builds the far sea forces, develops overseas logistical facilities, and enhances capabilities of accomplishing diversified military tasks.

3. Which of the following descriptions of Djibouti Support Base is true?

A. It entered service in 2018.

B. It has offered medical services for over 1,000 Djiboutian officers.

C. It has never conducted joint medical exercises with foreign militaries.

D. It donated over 600 teaching aids to local schools.

4. When did the PLAN steadily develop into a blue-water force?

A. From 1949.

B. From 1955.

C. Until the 1990s.

D. Since the beginning of the 21st century.

5. What did Deng Xiaoping say about China's maritime defense in 1979?

A. To build a strong China's maritime defense step-by-step.

B. To strengthen China's maritime defense was a priority vital to the fate of the country and its people.

C. To build the Navy and accelerate its modernization drive with great efforts.

D. To build a strong navy force in accordance with the missions of the PLA in the new century.

## II. Translation

**Part A**   **Terms & Phrases**

*Translate the following terms or phrases from Chinese into English and vice versa.*

1. 潜艇                                              2. 水面舰艇

3. 航空兵                                            4. 海防部队

5. 东海舰队                                          6. 南海舰队

7. 北海舰队                                          8. 海军陆战队

9. 近海防御                                          10. 远海防卫

11. 战略威慑与反击                                  12. 海上机动行动

13. 海上联合作战                                    14. 综合防御作战

15. People's Liberation Army Navy          16. Central Military Commission

17. ETC                                              18. STC

19. NTC                                              20. SLOCs

21. Djibouti Support Base                    22. Gulf of Aden

23. National Congress of the Communist Party of China

24. China's reform and opening-up        25. J-15 fighter jets

26. anti-submarine patrol aircraft         27. petty officer

**Part B**   **Paragraph**

*Translate the following paragraph from English into Chinese.*

In line with the strategic requirements of offshore defense and far sea protection, the Navy is speeding up the transition of its tasks from defense on the near seas to protection on the far seas, and improving its capabilities for strategic deterrence and counterattack, maritime maneuvering operations, maritime joint operations, comprehensive defense, and integrated support, so as to build a strong and modernized naval force.

## III. Reading Report

Have you got a better understanding of PLAN, its organization, and missions after reading? Now write your reading report in not more than 150 words for summing-up.

# Text B
# United States Navy

On, above and below the water, the United States Navy (USN) is a maritime military force, a branch of the United States armed forces that is responsible for naval operations. It is also an America's forward-deployed force. The US Navy is the largest in the world; its battle fleet tonnage is greater than that of the next 13 largest navies combined. The US Navy was founded on 13 October, 1775, and the Department of the Navy was established on 30 April, 1798. The history of the USN is divided into two major phases: the "Old Navy", a small but respectable force of sailing ships that was traced back to the continental Navy and notable for innovation in the use of ironclads during the American Civil War, and the "New Navy", the result of a modernization effort that began in the 1880s and eventually made the US Navy the most powerful in the world.

US Navy is administratively managed by the Department of the Navy, which is headed by the civilian Secretary of the Navy[1], who is appointed by the President and approved by the Senate. The most senior naval officer is the Chief of Naval Operations (CNO)[2], who is a four-star admiral directly under the Secretary of the Navy. The top uniformed member of the Marine Corps[3] is the Commandant of the Marine Corps (CMC)[4] who reports to the Secretary of the Navy. Both are members of the Joint Chiefs of Staff[5], which is the second-highest deliberative body[6] of the armed forces after the National Security Council[7].

US Navy has a dual chain of command to the operating forces — one chain for operational control which carries out specific missions such as operations and exercises, and the other chain for administrative control which takes care of personnel, education, training, maintenance, supply and military readiness. The administrative structure originates with the Secretary of Defense[8], Secretary of the Navy, the Chief of Naval Operations, and the Commandant of the Marine Corps. Below this level the fleet commanders issue orders that are passed to all naval units. The operational structure originates with the President, the Secretary of Defense, the Chairman of the Joint Chiefs of Staff, and the Unified Commanders-in-Chief[9].

US Navy performs four critical military functions for the United States:
- controlling the seas;
- using that control to project American power abroad;
- transporting troops, supplies, and equipment by sea, a process known as sealift;
- operating naval craft armed with nuclear weapons to conduct deterrence and guard

against a nuclear attack on the United States.

US Navy personnel expertly operate virtually every type of military equipment in US **arsenal**, everything from **HumVees** to aircraft carriers. The Navy has the following main components, all of which ensure the Navy is capable of taking on the enemy anywhere in the world:

**The Surface Fleet** — It consists of vessels of all sizes. Whether providing delivery or cover for special operations on inland rivers[10] or battling modern day pirates on the high seas[11], the Navy has different surface ships applicable for various **waterborne** military missions.

**The Submarine Fleet** — Known as the "Silent Service", submarines have played a number of roles in a hundred years of both war and peace: attack, **surveillance**, **commando** penetration, research, and nuclear **deterrent**. Submarines give the Navy the ability to arrive at the scene before the enemy is aware they're on the way.

**The Naval Aviation Wing** — In addition to the surface and submarine warfare capabilities, the Navy can provide firepower and support from the air as well. The Navy's aviation contingent is armed with helicopters, fighter/attack jets, surveillance, transport and **cargo** aircraft and unmanned aerial vehicles (UAV)[12], or drones.

**The Shore "Support" Establishment** — The shore establishment provides support to the operating forces (known as "the fleet") in the form of: facilities for the repair of machinery and electronics; communications centers; training areas and **simulators**; ship and aircraft repair; construction, **intelligence** and **meteorological** support; storage areas for repair parts, fuel, and **munitions**; medical and dental facilities; and air bases.

Since the beginning of 2019, the US Navy has been maintaining its military posture by deploying and engaging ships and aircraft around the world. The Navy has carried out the Asia-Pacific rebalancing strategy, while maintaining its significant forces in the Middle East. But the service also has increased its military presence in the Mediterranean, Baltic[13], Black Seas and the North Atlantic, and has deployed a carrier strike group[14] north of the Arctic Circle[15] for the first time in two decades. The number of Navy's fleets has been increased to seven since the establishment of the US 2nd Fleet on Aug. 24. Now, the fleet is operating in the North Atlantic in response to increased Russian naval activity. The US 2nd, 3rd, 4th, 5th, 6th,7th and 10th Fleets[16] provide the maritime components for US joint and allied operations in the global areas. The ships, aircraft and personnel of these fleets are administered and supported by the major regional and theater naval component commands.

As of Dec. 11, 2018, the Navy had 329,867 **active-duty**, 100,344 Ready Reserve[17] personnel, and 274,300 civilians. The ship combat forces included 287 ships and submarines. The naval aviation possessed about 3,700 aircraft. The goal of the Navy is to build up a sea power of 355 ships, according to the 2019 National Defense Authorization Act[18]. Also as of Dec. 11, 71 ships were deployed overseas, of which 42 were engaged in maritime tasks. Additionally, 29 ships were underway for local operations or training. In 2018, two Virginia-class attack submarines[19], two Arleigh Burke-class guided-missile destroyers (DDGs)[20] and three littoral combat ships (LCSs)[21] were in commission.

In 2018, the US naval aviation underwent a great transition. It owned its first operational F-35C squadron, Strike Fighter Squadron 147. The Navy selected Boeing to build the MQ-25 carrier-based air-refueling UAV. The transition to the P-8A Poseidon maritime patrol aircraft[22] from the P-3C was up to three fourths by the end of the year. And the P-8A has the capability of air refueling.

The United States Navy is unparalleled. Although its size has been reduced considerably since the collapse of the Soviet Union in 1991, the US Navy remains by far the most powerful navy in the world. In addition to the unmatched capabilities of its principal surface combatants, the US naval forces enjoy advantages in technology, training and readiness.

Throughout its history, the United States has depended upon the world's oceans for its security and economic well-being. Businesses use the oceans to transport goods between American cities and to carry imports and exports overseas. The size of the oceans has also become a strategic buffer, which makes it difficult for potential enemies to launch attacks on the United States. For more than 200 years, the dependence on the oceans by the US Navy has helped it realize its basic objectives. The Navy protects American shores from foreign attack, preserves the freedom of commerce at sea, maintains American interests overseas, supports US allies and serves as an instrument of US foreign policy.

*(1170 words)*

**Sources:**

https://www.military.com/join-armed-forces/us-navy-overview.html

## Notes

1. Secretary of the Navy: officer whose duties are to execute all the orders he receives from the president and to conduct all of the affairs of the Department of the Navy, including the

procurement of naval stores and materials, and the construction, armament, equipment and employment of warships as well as all other matters related to the naval establishment of the United States 海军部长

2. CNO: Chief of Naval Operations 海军作战部长

3. Marine Corps: a branch of the US armed forces composed chiefly of amphibious troops under the authority of the Secretary of the Navy 美国海军陆战队

4. CMC: Commandant of the Marine Corps 海军陆战队司令

5. Joint Chiefs of Staff: the principal military advisory group to the President of the United States, composed of the chiefs of the Army, Navy, and Air Force and the commandant of the Marine Corps 参谋长联席会议

6. deliberative body: the branch of government having the power to make laws, as distinguished from the executive and judicial branches of government 审议机构

7. National Security Council: a governmental body specifically designed to assist the President in integrating all spheres of national security policy 国家安全委员会

8. Secretary of Defense: the position of the head of the Department of Defense 国防部长

9. Unified Commanders-in-Chief: a commander in charge of all the armed forces of United States 统一指挥官

10. inland rivers: rivers within the territory of a state as contrasted with the open seas or marginal waters bordering another state subject to various sovereign rights of the bordering state — usually used in plural. 内陆河

11. high seas: the open seas of the world outside the territorial waters of any nation 公海

12. UAV: unmanned aerial vehicles 无人飞行器

13. Baltic: the sea in northern Europe; stronghold of the Russian Navy 波罗的海

14. carrier strike group: a military unit of the US Navy, including about 7,500 military personnel, one aircraft carrier, accompanied by at least one cruiser, and one destroyer (at least two destroyers or frigates) for escort as well as one carrier-based flight wing (approximately 65 to 70 fixed-wing aircraft and helicopters) 航空母舰打击群

15. Arctic Circle: an imaginary line drawn around the northern part of the world at approximately 66° North 北极圈

16. The US 2nd, 3rd, 4th, 5th, 6th,7th and 10th Fleets: the headquarters of these fleets respectively are Norfolk in Virginia, Ford Island in Pearl Harbor, Mayport in Florida, Manama in Bahrain，Naples in Italy, Yokosuka in Japan, and Fort Meade in Maryland 美军第二、三、四、五、六、七、十舰队

17. Ready Reserve: the category of reservists most often called to active duty, consisting of three subcategories, Selected Reserve, Individual Ready Reserve and Inactive National Guard 预备役

18. 2019 National Defense Authorization Act: the bill which authorizes FY2019 appropriations and sets forth policies regarding the military activities of the Department of Defense (DOD), military construction, and the national security programs of the Department of Energy (DOE) 2019年国防授权法案

19. Virginia-class attack submarines: the US Navy's newest undersea warfare platform, which incorporates the latest features of stealth, intelligence gathering and weapons systems technology 维吉尼亚级攻击潜艇

20. DDGs : guided-missile destroyers 导弹驱逐舰

21. LCSs: littoral combat ships 濒海战斗舰

22. maritime patrol aircraft: patrol aircraft, maritime reconnaissance aircraft, or a fixed-wing aircraft designed to patrol for long durations over water and play particular roles in the anti-submarine and anti-ship warfare, and search and rescue 海上巡逻机

## Word Bank

| | |
|---|---|
| maritime [ˈmærɪtaɪm] | adj. 海上的；海事的；海运的 |
| deploy [dɪˈplɔɪ] | v. 部署；展开 |
| tonnage [ˈtʌnɪdʒ] | n. 吨位，载重量；船舶总吨数，排水量 |
| ironclad [ˈaɪənklæd] | n. [军] 装甲舰 |
| civilian [səˈvɪlɪən] | n. 平民，百姓；[军] 文职 |
| admiral [ˈædmərəl] | n. [军] 海军将军，海军上将；舰队司令 |
| operation [ˌɒpəˈreɪʃn] | n. [军] 军事行动 |
| exercises [ˈeksəsaɪzɪz] | n. [军] 军事演习 |
| readiness [ˈredɪnəs] | n. [军] 战备状态 |
| project [ˈprɒdʒekt] | v. 扩及远处；投射；设计 |
| sealift [ˈsiːlɪft] | n. 海上运输，海上补给 |
| deterrence [dɪˈtɜːrəns] | n. 威慑 |
| arsenal [ˈɑːsənl] | n. [军] 兵工厂；军械库；武器；军火库 |
| waterborne [ˈwɔːtəbɔːn] | adj. 水运的；（浮于）水上的 |
| surveillance [sɜːˈveɪləns] | n. 监督；监视 |

| | |
|---|---|
| commando [kəˈmɑːndəʊ] | *n.* 突击队，突击队员 |
| deterrent [dɪˈterənt] | *n.* 威慑；妨碍物 |
| cargo [ˈkɑːgəʊ] | *n.* 货物，船货 |
| simulator [ˈsɪmjʊleɪtə(r)] | *n.* 模拟器 |
| intelligence [ɪnˈtelɪdʒəns] | *n.* [军] 情报，情报工作 |
| meteorological [ˌmiːtɪərəˈlɒdʒɪkl] | *adj.* 气象的；气象学的 |
| munitions [mjuːˈnɪʃnz] | *n.* 军需品，军火（munition的复数） |
| active-duty [ˈæktɪvˈdjuːtɪ] | *adj.* 现役的 |
| underway [ˌʌndəˈweɪ] | *adj.* 在进行中的；（船、火车等）在行进中的 |
| squadron [ˈskwɒdrən] | *n.* [军] 空军中队 |
| buffer [ˈbʌfə(r)] | *n.* 缓冲区；缓冲器 |
| HumVee [ˈhʌmviː] | *n.* 悍马牌军车；多用途轮式车辆，输送车 |

## *Exercises*

### I. True or False

*Decide whether the following sentences are true or false in accordance with the text.*

1. United States Navy is one of America's forward-deployed forces.

2. The most senior naval officer is the civilian Secretary of the Navy, who is appointed by the President and approved by the Senate.

3. The National Security Council is the second highest deliberative body of the armed forces after Joint Chiefs of Staff.

4. To conduct deterrence and guard against a nuclear attack on the United States is not included as one of the military functions of US Navy.

5. The US Navy has the following main components: the Surface Fleet, the Submarine Fleet, the Naval Aviation Wing and the Shore Support Establishment.

6. It is the first time in the latest 20 years for the US Navy to deploy a carrier strike group north of the Antarctic Circles.

7. As of Dec. 11, 2018, the Navy had approximately six hundred thousand personnel, including active-duty, Ready Reserve personnel, and civilians.

8. With its unmatched capabilities of principal surface combatants, and its advantages in technology, training and readiness, US Navy is by far the most capable navy in the world.

## II. Word Match

*Match the words/terms/phrases in the left column with its appropriate correspondents in the right column.*

1. forward-deployed                          A. 驱逐舰

2. UAV                                        B. 预备役

3. Ready Reserve                             C. 海军陆战队

4. Mediterranean                             D. 潜水艇

5. battle fleet                              E. 公海

6. Marine Corps                              F. 地中海

7. National Security Council                 G. 无人飞行器

8. high seas                                 H. 国家安全委员会

9. submarine                                 I. 作战舰队

10. destroyer                                J. 前沿部署的

### Text C
## The Influence of Sea Power upon History

In 1890, Mahan[1] published one of the most important books of the age, *The Influence of Sea Power Upon History, 1660—1783*[2]. Despite its dry-sounding title, Mahan's book instantly became a best seller in the United States. It was reviewed and discussed in every major journal of commentary, news magazine, and newspaper of the time. His book struck the highest levels of the ruling classes like a bolt of lightning and created a tempest of intellectual upheaval not just within the US Navy, but throughout the broader American (and overseas) political, economic, and industrial system. He had written a book about 200 years of naval history and about what that naval history meant to the rise and relationships of state power in the world.

### Alfred Thayer Mahan: The End of the Inner Frontier

In another way of viewing things, the inner frontier of the United States was coming to a distinct end. Mahan's book came at just the right time in history for the nation midwifed into existence by George Washington, who had cautioned against "foreign entanglements," to begin to revise and form new policy and strategy concerning matters far beyond its shores.

This is the root concept of modern US political policy and strategic doctrine of power projection abroad. It is no accident that only eight years after the publication of Mahan's book, the United States embarked on a war with Spain that staked a claim for US military power and political-economic interests on the far side of the planet.

Among other eager readers of Mahan in the early 1890s was a relatively young, but ambitious and up-and-coming, New Yorker named Theodore Roosevelt[3], who absorbed the book (as did another man named Roosevelt, many years later). The older Roosevelt and Mahan became close acquaintances and would correspond extensively over the years.

Mahan's book rapidly circled the globe. Within a year of publication, it was translated into French, German, Spanish, Italian, Russian, and Japanese, among other languages. The First Lord of the British Admiralty[4] read Mahan's book and gave a copy to the king of England, who read it and in turn ordered every officer in the Royal Navy[5] to read it as well.

Kaiser Wilhelm II[6] of Germany "devoured" the work, as he later recalled, and ordered a copy to be placed in every wardroom of every ship in the German fleet. Further to the east, the tsar of Russia read Mahan's work and sent copies to every admiral and captain in his Imperial Navy.

Mahan's book was read and studied in the wardrooms and war colleges and in the chancelleries and foreign ministries of France, Italy, Austro-Hungary[7], Sweden, Greece, Turkey, and many other nations.

What was this magic elixir of sea power that Mahan described? In essence, Mahan mixed salt water with the concepts of Clausewitz[8] and Jomini[9], applying their land-based theories of fighting to waging war at sea. Using a concept central to Clausewitz, Mahan viewed the sea as a "center of gravity," a vital strategic interest of the United States. Any limitation of, or challenge to, US military power, particularly if it came from the sea, would constrain the nation and harm its national interests. Any victory of US arms upon the sea would give the nation the luxury of independent action in pursuing its interests.

Mahan prompted deep, critical thinking about the ability of any given nation to protect itself from attack from the sea and about how to fight upon and command the oceans, when necessary, distant from home shores. Mahan reviewed and examined the 200-year history of construction and employment of naval vessels by Britain, Holland, France, Spain, and Portugal[10].

He discussed the rivalries at sea of these nations and their respective quests over two centuries for dominion over far-distant waves and shores. Not surprisingly, much of Mahan's narrative concerns the respective rivalries of the European states to establish their interests in the New World[11], with extensive coverage devoted to the Seven Years' War and to the War for American Independence.

### Alfred Thayer Mahan: Big Ships with Big Guns

From a purely military standpoint, Mahan set forth a workable, if not workmanlike, theory of naval war fighting. Mahan's theory called for nations to construct and maintain large fleets, composed of big ships armed with big guns. Mahan's theories further called for concentrating fleets into powerful, oceangoing combat forces.

Thus armed and ready, a concentrated fleet would be in a position to project a nation's combat power and seize control of the oceans from an adversary where and when necessary, in furtherance of a nation's international political interests and military goals. The doctrine calls for a fleet to move forward to meet the opponent and, when circumstances dictate, to use defensive naval operations as the basis for offense.

But if Mahan had merely presented a better way for naval fleets to fight it out with other naval fleets, to blast away at each other and wage violent battles upon the water for absolute

sea control, his book would not have had the monumental success that it did. Mahan offered something else to his worldwide readership.

By placing the need for a powerful Navy at the center of national interest, Mahan merged naval operations and political and economic destiny. That is, Mahan does not simply set forth a theory of naval warfare, but uses a nation's distinctive and circumstantial requirement for naval power to lay out the plan for what we might call today a national industrial policy.

According to Mahan, sea power goes hand in hand with commerce and trade.

- Commerce and trade should provide, and must support, a nation and its economy with the ability to produce goods and to make things that others in the world want to obtain.

- With the ability to produce goods for trade comes the need and the ability to produce the vessels necessary to carry that trade.

- Finally comes the national ability to create naval sea power to protect that trade and export a nation's influence to the far corners of the world.

But Mahan also provides a cautionary note: "Where the revenues and industries of a country can be concentrated into a few treasure ships, like the flota of Spanish galleons, the sinew of war may perhaps be cut at a stroke; but when its wealth is scattered in thousands of going and coming ships, when the roots of the system spread wide and far, and strike deep, it can stand many a cruel shock and lose many a goodly bough without the life being touched."

Here, then, is the essence of what drew presidents, prime ministers and kings to the famous book by then-Capt. Mahan. In the course of writing about naval history and its related military affairs, of sea battles long ago, with broadsides blazing and cannonballs whistling between wind-powered man of war, the American naval officer had articulated a political and economic theory for the modern age.

*(1152 words)*

**Sources:** ------------------------------------------------------------------------

Extracted from and edited based on an article in **The Daily Reckoning** *Alfred Thayer Mahan: The Influence of Alfred Thayer Mahan* by Byron W. King, May 12, 2005.

1. Mahan: Alfred Thayer Mahan (1840—1914), American naval officer and historian who was a highly influential exponent of sea power in the late 19th and early 20th centuries. His

notable works include *The Influence of Sea Power upon History, 1660—1783*; *The Influence of Sea Power upon the French Revolution and Empire, 1793—1812*; *The Interest of America in Sea Power, Present and Future.* 马汉（美国著名军事理论家）

2. *The Influence of Sea Power Upon History, 1660—1783*: In this book Mahan argued for the paramount importance of sea power in national historical supremacy. 《海权对历史的影响1660—1783》

3. Theodore Roosevelt: the 26th president of the United States (1901—1908) and hero of the Spanish-American War 西奥多·罗斯福（美国第二十六届总统）

4. British Admiralty: the authority in the Kingdom of England, and later in Great Britain and until 1964 in the United Kingdom, responsible for the command of the Royal Navy 英国海军部

5. Royal Navy: the Navy of the United Kingdom. It is the oldest part of the British fighting forces. Because it is the oldest, it is called the "Senior Service". From the 18th century until World War II, it was the largest and strongest navy in the world. 英国皇家海军

6. Kaiser Wilhelm II: Friedrich Wilhelm Viktor Albert (1859—1941), German Emperor (Kaiser) and King of Prussia from 1888 to the end of World War I in 1918, known for his frequently militaristic manner as well as for his vacillating policies 德皇威廉二世

7. Austro-Hungary: Austria-Hungary, often referred to as the Austro-Hungarian Empire or the Dual Monarchy, was a constitutional monarchy and great power in Central Europe between 1867 and 1918. It was dissolved following its defeat in the First World War. 奥匈帝国

8. Clausewitz: Carl von Clausewitz (1780—1831)，Prussian general and military thinker, is widely acknowledged as the most important of the classical strategic thinkers. 克劳斯威茨（德国著名军事学家）

9. Jomini: Antoine-Henri, baron de Jomini (1779—1869), French general, military critic, and historian, whose systematic attempt to define the principles of warfare made him one of the founders of modern military thought 约米尼（法国军事理论家）

10. Portugal: a republic in southwestern Europe on the Iberian Peninsula 葡萄牙

11. New World: North, Central, and South America, as they were considered by the Europeans after Christopher Columbus traveled there. 美洲新大陆

 **Word Bank**

| | |
|---|---|
| commentary [ˈkɒməntrɪ] | n. 评论 |
| tempest [ˈtempɪst] | n. 骚动；动乱 |
| upheaval [ʌpˈhiːvl] | n. 剧变；隆起 |
| midwife [ˈmɪdwaɪf] | v. 促成；助胎儿出生 |
| entanglement [ɪnˈtæŋɡlmənt] | n. 纠缠；牵连 |
| doctrine [ˈdɒktrɪn] | n. 主义；学说；教义 |
| projection [prəˈdʒekʃn] | n. 规划；投射 |
| devour [dɪˈvaʊə(r)] | v. 急切地读；吞食 |
| tsar [zɑː(r)] | n. 沙皇 |
| chancellery [ˈtʃɑːnsələrɪ] | n. 大臣；总理 |
| elixir [ɪˈlɪksə(r)] | n. 灵丹妙药 |
| wage [weɪdʒ] | v. 进行，发动（运动、战争等）；开展 |
| constrain [kənˈstreɪn] | v. 强迫；束缚 |
| rivalry [ˈraɪvlrɪ] | n. 竞争；对抗；竞赛 |
| workmanlike [ˈwɜːkmənlaɪk] | adj. 技术熟练的；精工细作的 |
| adversary [ˈædvəsərɪ] | n. 对手；敌手 |
| monumental [ˌmɒnjʊˈmentl] | adj. 意义深远的；不朽的 |
| flota [fləʊtə] | n. （西）船队，舰队 |
| galleon [ˈɡælɪən] | n. 15、16世纪西班牙大型帆船 |
| sinew [ˈsɪnjuː] | n. 精力；筋；肌腱 |
| goodly [ˈɡʊdlɪ] | adj. 漂亮的；优秀的；相当多的 |
| bough [baʊ] | n. 大树枝 |
| broadside [ˈbrɔːdsaɪd] | n. 舰舷 |
| cannonball [ˈkænənbɔːl] | n. 炮弹 |
| articulate [ɑːˈtɪkjʊleɪt] | v. 清晰地发（音）；明确有力地表达 |
| a bolt of | 一道…… |
| stake a claim | 提出所有权要求 |
| blast away | 炸开 |
| man of war | 军舰 |

## *Exercises*

Based on what you have acquired after reading, you are supposed to make a further study of the relevant sphere. Write a report in no less than 200 words based on the study. In addition, any complementary image, audio, video, or other first-hand material will be preferred when you present your report in class.

# Unit 2  Surface Ships

**Bridge-in**

*Answer the following questions in accordance with the microlesson "The Super Destroyer in PLAN".*

1. What is the significance of the commission of the 055-type destroyer in PLAN?

2. What are its basic parameters?

3. What are the advantages of the 055-type destroyers compared with other destroyers?

## Text A
## Chinese Destroyers

A **Destroyer** is a versatile warship, from the 1890s to the 2000s. Modern destroyers are equipped with air defense, anti-submarine, sea and other weapons. They can not only carry out offensive air defense and anti-submarine escort missions, but also engage in landing and **anti-landing** operations, and perform missions such as support, **patrol**, escort, **reconnaissance**, naval blockade and rescue at sea and ship-based helicopters' take-off and landing. Of all the modern naval vessels the destroyer is the most versatile due to its extensive combat functions.

In 1954, the first destroyer unit of the People's Liberation Army Navy was established with four Gordy-class Soviet destroyers[1] imported from the Soviet Union. They were respectively named "Anshan", "Fushun", "Changchun", and "Taiyuan". At that time, they were the most powerful surface ships of the PLAN.

The 051-type guided missile destroyer is a product based on the former Soviet Union's Kotlin-class destroyer[2]. This type of ships has served in PLA naval fleets since the late 1960s. It is the first time that China has not relied on or imported foreign technical equipment. And what's more, building the 051-type satisfied the Navy's urgent need for large ships, and the accumulated expertise and technical experience have laid the solid foundation for the future research and development of new destroyers.

The 052-type multi-purpose guided missile destroyer was a missile destroyer. Only 112 and 113 ships were in service in the early 1990s. This class of ship was of great significance to the attempt on new weapon systems. For the first time, it was equipped with the air defense missile system and fully-computerized automatic command and control system. And the advanced gas turbines were also used in the full-enclosed hull. The 052-type destroyer is a milestone in the independent design and construction of ships.

The overall design of the 051B type with a displacement of 6000tons is based on the design of the 052-type destroyer. It is characterized by simple and clear hull and superstructure and reasonable weapons layout. Because of this advantages, the updated 051B type provides the basis of developing the 051C type. Compared with the 052 type, the 051B type has reached a high level in terms of design and construction. It has the shipboard phased array, long-range air defense missile system and automatic air defense system.

The 956-type destroyer purchased from Russia at the end of the 20th century has excellent anti-ship capability. At present, China Navy has four such ships numbered 136, 137, 138 and 139. For ships 138 and 139, a 130mm main gun has been replaced with anti-aircraft missile-launcher on the stern. The then introduction of them enhanced the strength of PLAN greatly, to say the least.

The 052B-type destroyer is also known as the Guangzhou-class destroyer, which is a multi-purpose destroyer capable of performing different operational tasks. In the past two 052B-type destroyers were built. One was named "Guangzhou" (ship number 168) and the other named "Wuhan" (ship number 169). "Guangzhou", or ship 168, which is the first one of 052B-type destroyers, is an ocean-going warship with air-defense, anti-submarine and anti-ship capability.

The 051C-type guided missile destroyer is one of China's latest air defense missile destroyers. The first ship "Shenyang" numbered 115 of this type was launched in 2004 and completed in late 2005. At the end of 2006, it joined the North China Sea Fleet. The second ship "Shijiazhuang" (No.116) was launched in early 2006 and joined the North China Sea Fleet[3] at the end of 2008.

The 052C-type destroyers belonging to the Lanzhou class are the new generation of air defense destroyers of the PLAN. The first ship "Lanzhou" (ship number 170) was equipped with a four-sided active phased-array radar and a shipborne vertical launch system using

air defense missiles called "Chinese Aegis[4]". Another ship named "Haikou" (ship number 171) is at the same level. On December 26, 2008, the destroyer "Haikou", the destroyer "Wuhan" and the integrated supply ship "Weishanhu" were sent to operate in Gulf of Aden to provide an armed escort for China's and other countries' merchant vessels, or protect them from Somali pirates.

The 052D type air defense missile destroyer is a multi-purpose one like the 052C-type. The ship is equipped with a new 64-unit missile vertical launch system, a new 130 mm caliber single-tube stealth naval gun, a new integrated command and combat system, a new Hongqi-9[5] anti-missile air defense missile system, an anti-surface cruise missile system, a new long-range anti-ship missile system, and a new-type active phased-array radar system. Compared with the 052C-type air defense missile destroyer, the 052D-type has great improvement in the overall ship design including the performance of its shipborne phased-array radar, its power plant, etc. Its full-load displacement exceeds 7,000 tons. The first ship was the "Kunming" missile destroyer. It was commissioned on March 21, 2014 and officially joined the PLA Navy battle sequence, numbered 172.

The 055-type is China's newest generation of guided-missile destroyers, or rather guided missile cruiser. The 180-meter-long, 20-meter-wide destroyer is equipped with 112 vertical launch missile cells capable of launching a combination of surface-to-air missiles, anti-ship cruise missiles, land-attack cruise missiles and anti-submarine missiles. It has a displacement greater than 13,000 tons and can fire various kinds of missiles, including China's long-range land-attack cruise missile. Its firepower is thought to be twice that of the 052D-type, the largest and most powerful surface combatant commissioned in the PLA Navy. The emergence of the 055-type missile destroyer is a historic turning point for the Chinese navy moving far into the sea. According to the "White Paper on Military Strategy[6]", the strategic positioning of the Chinese navy is the two main lines of coastal defense and distant guard. The mission of far-sea guarding includes not only the protection of the shipping in the Gulf of Aden, but also the protection and control of China's overseas investment, and overseas Chinese important interests.

With new warships coming into being, China Navy will become much powerful and further the capability of safeguarding China's sovereignty and overseas interests.

*(1075 words)*

*Sources:*

http://www.globalsecurity.org/

**Notes**

1. Gordy-class Soviet destroyers: destroyers designed and developed by Soviet Union in the 1930s 自豪级苏联驱逐舰

2. Kotlin-class destroyer: destroyers designed and developed by Soviet Union in World War II 科特林级驱逐舰

3. North China Sea Fleet: Its headquarters (HQ) is in Qingdao, on the southern coast of the Shandong Peninsula, and was formally established by the Ministry of National Defense in May 1960. The flagship of the fleet is the DDG 112 Harbin. The Fleet's AOR extends from the Korean border to roughly 35°10' N. This generally covers the Shenyang, Beijing, and Jinan military regions. 北海舰队

4. Aegis: referring to the Aegis destroyer, a type of multi-mission guided missile destroyer designed to perform anti-submarine warfare, anti-air warfare, and anti-surface warfare missions in support of US naval operations 宙斯盾导弹驱逐舰

5. Hongqi-9: a kind of air defense missile which is the first medium and long-range air defense missile developed by China 红旗-9

6. White Paper on Military Strategy: It was issued on May 26, 2015 by China, which stressed active defense and pledged closer international security cooperation. It outlined a strategy unifying strategic defense and operational and tactical offense, also underscored the principles of defense, self-defense and post-emptive strikes. 《中国的军事战略》白皮书

**Word Bank**

| | |
|---|---|
| destroyer [dɪˈstrɒɪə(r)] | n. 驱逐舰 |
| anti-landing [ˈæntɪˈlændɪŋ] | n. 抗登陆；反登陆 |
| patrol [pəˈtrəʊl] | n. 巡逻；巡查；巡逻队 |
| reconnaissance [rɪˈkɒnɪsns] | n. 侦察 |
| turbine [ˈtɜːbaɪn] | n. 涡轮 |
| stern [stɜːn] | n. 舰尾；船尾 |
| stealth [stelθ] | n. 隐形 |

| cruise [kruːz] | *n.* 巡航 |
| displacement [dɪsˈpleɪsmənt] | *n.* 排水量 |
| combatant [ˈkɒmbətənt] | *n.* [军] 参战者；战斗人员；战士 |
| commission [kəˈmɪʃn] | *v.* 任命；委任；服役 |
| command and control system | [军] 指挥和控制系统 |
| missile-launcher | [军] 导弹发射器；导弹发射装置 |
| phased-array radar | [军] 相控阵雷达 |
| vertical launch system | [军] 垂直发射系统 |
| battle sequence | [军] 战斗序列，作战序列 |

## I. Comprehension

**Part A**　**Questions**

*Answer the following questions in accordance with the text.*

1. What kind of missions can a destroyer perform?

2. What is the significance of the production of the 051-type guided missile destroyer?

3. What is the significance of building the 052-type multi-purpose guided missile destroyer?

4. What kind of capabilities does the 052B-type destroyer possess?

5. What kind of missile launch system is the 052D-type air defense missile destroyer equipped with?

**Part B**　**Multiple Choices**

*Choose the most appropriate answer from the given choices below each question in accordance with the text.*

1. Which of the following is NOT true about destroyers?

   A. A Destroyer is a versatile warship, from the 1890s to the 2000s.

   B. They can also serve as landing and anti-landing operations.

   C. They can also carry out naval blockade and rescue missions at sea and provide manned carrier aircraft's take-off and landing.

   D. The 055-type is China's newest generation of guided-missile destroyers, or rather guided missile cruiser.

2. Which of the following descriptions of the overall design of the 051B-type is NOT true?

    A. The hull and superstructure are simple and clear.

    B. The weapon layout is very reasonable.

    C. The overall design of the 051B-type is based on the design of the 052-type destroyer.

    D. It has a displacement of 8,000 tons.

3. Which of the following descriptions of the 052C-type destroyer is NOT true?

    A. The 052C-type destroyers are the new generation of air defense destroyers of the PLAN.

    B. It is also known as the Kunming -class destroyer.

    C. The first ship of this type is equipped with an active phased-array radar and a shipborne vertical launch system.

    D. In 2008, ships of this type performed escort missions in the Gulf of Aden.

4. Which of the following descriptions of type 055 destroyer is NOT true?

    A. The 055-type is China's newest generation of guided-missile destroyers, or rather, guided missile cruiser.

    B. It is equipped with 112 vertical launch missile cells capable of launching a combination of missiles.

    C. It has a displacement greater than 17,000 tons and can fire various kinds of missiles.

    D. The emergence of the 055-type missile destroyer is a historic turning point for the Chinese navy moving far into the sea.

5. What is the mission of PLAN's far-sea guarding?

    A. The protection of the shipping in the Gulf of Aden.

    B. The protection and control of China's overseas investment.

    C. The protection of overseas Chinese important interests.

    D. All of the above.

## II. Translation

**Part A**　Terms & Phrases

*Translate the following terms or phrases from Chinese into English and vice versa.*

1. 防空　　　　　　　　　　2. 救援任务

3. 指挥控制系统　　　　　　4. 相控阵

5. 巡航导弹　　　　　　　　6. 战斗序列

7. 反舰巡航导弹　　　　　　8. 反潜导弹

9. 战略定位　　　　　　　　10. 战略利益

| | |
|---|---|
| 11. escort mission | 12. guided missile |
| 13. full load | 14. vertical launch system |
| 15. power plant | 16. surface-to-air missile |
| 17. land-attack cruise missile | 18. White Paper on Military Strategy |
| 19. coastal defense | 20. overseas interests |

**Part B**   **Paragraph**

*Translate the following paragraph from English into Chinese.*

The 055-type is China's newest generation of guided-missile destroyers, or rather, guided missile cruiser. The 180-meter-long, 20-meter-wide destroyer is equipped with 112 vertical launch missile cells capable of launching a combination of surface-to-air missiles, anti-ship cruise missiles, land-attack cruise missiles and anti-submarine missiles. It has a displacement greater than 13,000 tons and can fire various kinds of missiles, including China's long-range land-attack cruise missile.

## III. Reading Report

What have you learned after reading the text? Have you got a better understanding of Chinese destroyers? Write a reading report in about 150 words to generalize your achievement from the text study.

# Text B
## USN's New Littoral Combat Ships (LCS)

The LCS is defined as a ship with the ability to carry out littoral or coastal operational missions. It provides a basic platform for **mission packages** (MPs) applicable to specific types of warfare. The first three MPs under development are to be used for anti-mine, anti-submarine and anti-surface warfare. Future development may include homeland security and maritime **interdiction modules**.

The ships are intended to fight in enclosed or coastal contested waters, with their abilities **optimized** by networked, **off-board** sensors and weapons. They feature an advanced networking capability to share tactical information with other Navy aircraft, ships, submarines and joint units. MPs consist of mission modules—sensors, weapons, and manned and unmanned vehicles used above, on and below the surface—operated by special personnel **detachments**.

The LCS will perform self-defense, high-speed transit, maritime interdiction operations, intelligence, surveillance, reconnaissance(ISR) and anti-terrorism/force-protection missions, and support special operations forces and homeland defense.

### Introduction

Two types of LCS were developed by teams headed by Lockheed Martin[1] and General Dynamics from existing commercial designs. The Lockheed Martine *Freedom*[2] (LCS-1) variant features a steel, semi-planning **mono-hull** based on the hull form of the Italian motor yacht *Destriero*, which gained the record for the fastest crossing of the Atlantic in 1992.

Some weight is reduced by use of an aluminium superstructure, but the LCS-1 type's displacement of about 3,500 tones indicates that the ships are relatively heavy. **Propulsion** is provided by a combined **diesel** and gas (CODAG[3]) plant, which includes two Rolls-Royce MT-30[4] gas turbines. A maximum speed in excess of 45 knots is provided by four KaMeWa[5] **waterjets**.

The General Dynamics-developed *Independence*[6] (LCS-2) variant adopts a very different approach, or an all-aluminium **trimaran** design, derived from the high-speed ferry *Benchijigua Express*[7]. This provides greater volume and deck space than a conventional hull of similar size, and uses less power to reach similar speeds. The 3,200-ton *Independence* is larger than

*Freedom*, though its displacement is a little lower. In addition, it can still sprint at over 45 knots, despite the fact that its CODAG propulsion system provides around a third less power.

Both LCS variants have relatively light core armaments, including MK-110 57mm guns and surface-to-air RIM-116 rolling airframe missiles[8]. Both types can also embark MH-60[9] series Seahawk helicopters and Fire Scout[10] unmanned aerial vehicles.

However, the LCS real operational capacity lies in its three different modularized mission packages, which contain a wide range of equipment and are used for anti-submarine and mine countermeasures and surface warfare operations. For example, the anti-submarine package includes a variable depth sonar integrated with a multifunction towed array and a lightweight torpedo defense module.

**US NAVY LITTORAL COMBAT SHIPS**

|  | LCS-1 FREEDOM VARIANT | LCS-2 INDEPENDENCE VARIANT |
|---|---|---|
| **DISPLACEMENT** | c.3,500 tons full load | c.3,200 tons full load |
| **DIMENSIONS** | 118m × 18m × 4m | 128m × 32m × 5m |
| **ARMANMENT** | 1 × MK-110 57mm main gun; machine guns<br>1×MK-49 RAM launcher for RIM-116 missiles<br>flight deck and hangar for helicopter and UAVs<br>mission modules dependent on assigned role | 1×MK-110 57mm main gun; machine guns<br>1×Sea RAM launcher[11] for RIM-116 missiles<br>flight deck and hangar for helicopter and UAVs<br>mission modules dependent on assigned role |
| **PROPULSION** | CODAG & waterjets, 85MW output, 45+ knots, 3,500nm range at 18 knots | CODAG & waterjets, 62MW output, 45+ knots, 4,300nm range at 18 knots |
| **COMPLEMENT** | c. 50 core crew plus mission specialists | c. 50 core crew plus mission specialists |
| **BUILDERS** | Marinette Marine, Marinette Wisconsin | Austal USA, Mobile Alabama |
| **CLASS** | 8 ships delivered, 8 under construction or on order | 9 ships delivered, 10 under construction or on order |

**Recent Developments**

Now the LCS program has resulted in a number of developments. One of these has been an attempt to increase the LCS fighting potential through upgrading its armaments, especially through adding long-range anti-surface missiles. In May 2018, it was announced that Kongsberg's Naval Strike Missile[12] would be fitted onto the LCS, which could significantly increase the ability of LCS to attack larger surface targets.

A more surprising change has been caused by the adoption of a new operating concept for the LCS that will give up some of the flexibility provided by the modular design. Announced towards the end of 2016, specific ships assigned to divisions took on just one of the three littoral missions **envisaged** for the design. It is also foreseeable that all the operational LCS-1 variant ships will be deployed on the US Atlantic Coast, and the LCS-2 variant on the Pacific Coast.

In September 2016, the Navy announced several significant changes to the LCS program based on operational experience. The original 3∶2∶1 crew concept — three crews, two ships, one deployed — was changed to a Blue/Gold concept similar to that used by the SSBN[13] force, with two crews dedicated to each LCS. The mission package detachments will merge with the LCS crews. Four ships will be organized into a division specializing in a single warfare specialty, with three ships deployed off-shore and the fourth as a training ship that will remain in local waters to train and certify the crews. The first four LCSs will be used for RDT&E[14] and, like the training ships, will be single-crewed, but can be deployed as fleet assets if needed on a limited basis.

The new plan has some obvious benefits. Grouping the same type of LCS, at common bases will make support and maintenance easier. Equally, crew training and efficiency should be improved by assigning specific ships to specific tasks.

This changed approach is also demonstrated by the decision to **truncate** production of the LCS type in favor of a return to more traditional frigate construction for the US Navy. The new strategy has itself undergone a lot of **modification**, but is now anticipated to make the transition take place in the coming FY2020[15]. A number of firms have already been granted contracts to improve the existing designs to meet the requirements of the new small surface combatant known as FFG (X)[16].

### Future

In spite of the decision to end future LCS production, the fact that large numbers of littoral combat ships have already been ordered is that the design will remain very useful for the US Navy's surface fleet for many decades. Indeed, with fewer than half the 35 vessels contracted currently, the LCS is set to expand its military presence across the world's seas in years to come.

SIOUX CITY FREEDOM CLASS

SEAPOWER, January 2019, www. Navyleague.org

CORONADO INDEPENCE CLASS WITH MH-60 SEAHAWK

SEAPOWER, January 2019, www. Navyleague.org

*(1098 words)*

**Sources:**

1. Extracted and edited from SEAPOWER, January 2019, www. Navyleague.org

2. US NAVY SPOTLIGHT, July 2019, www. shipsmonthly.com

 **Notes**

1. Lockheed Martin: Lockheed Martin Corporation, which mainly makes aerospace products, such as aircraft, space launchers and satellites, and also produces defense systems as well as other advanced-technology systems and services 洛克希德马丁公司

2. Freedom: Free-class littoral combatant ship developed by Lockheed Martin company. The first ship was built on June 2, 2005 at the shipyard of Marinette Marine, Marinette Wisconsin. It was launched on September 23, 2006 and commissioned on November 8, 2008. By 2017, 8 ships had been built, of which 4 have since been in service. 自由级濒海战斗舰

3. CODAG: combined diesel and gas 联合柴油机和燃气涡轮

4. Rolls-Royce MT-30: The Rolls-Royce MT-30 (Marine Turbine) is a marine gas turbine engine based on Rolls-Royce Trent 800 aero engine. Rolls-Royce announced the MT-30 programming on September 11, 2001. The first run of the engine was on September 6, 2002. In early 2003 the MT-30 was selected to power the Royal Navy future aircraft carriers (CVFs) and the demonstrator of the US Navy's DD (X) multimillion destroyer. In June 2004 Lockheed Martin granted the MT-30 contract to Rolls-Royce to meet its LCS design. 劳斯莱斯公司MT30燃气轮机

5. KaMeWa: a Swedish company which is an international manufacturer of rotary propeller propulsion system 卡米瓦公司（瑞典）

6. Independence: Independence-class littoral combatant ship developed by General Dynamics company. The first ship was built on January 19, 2006 at the shipyard of Austal USA, Mobile Alabama. It was launched on April 26, 2008 and commissioned on January 16, 2010. By 2018, 13 ships had been built, of which 7 have since been in service. 独立级濒海战斗舰

7. Benchijigua Express: Benchijigua express, the 127-meter-long trimaran ferry was designed and built by Austal in 2005 for the Spanish shipping company Fred Olsen. It was the first trimaran ferry and the longest in the world at that time. It is a milestone not only for Austal, but also in the development of international shipbuilding industry. 三体车客渡船

8. RIM-116 rolling airframe missile: The RIM-116 Rolling Airframe Missile (RAM) is a small, lightweight, and infrared homing surface-to-air missile used by the United States Navy. It is intended originally and primarily as a point-defense weapon against anti-ship cruise missiles. The missile is named because it rolls around its longitudinal axis during its flight to stabilize its flight path. RIM-116 滚转弹体导弹；滚体导弹

9. MH-60: MH-60 helicopter used for special purposes. It has the functions of transportation and attack, and is generally equipped with machine guns and missiles. MH-60 直升机

10. Fire Scout: Fire Scout is a kind of vertical take-off and landing UAV developed by Norge company which can be used for Intelligence, reconnaissance and surveillance (ISR) missios. "火力侦察兵" 无人机

11. Sea RAM launcher: It is a short-range air defense missile launcher usually for RIM-116 missiles. "海拉姆"导弹发射器

12. Kongsberg's Naval Strike Missile: The Naval Strike Missile (NSM) is a littoral/open sea anti-ship and land-attack cruise missile developed by the Norwegian company Kongsberg Defence & Aerospace (KDA). 康斯伯格海军打击导弹

13. SSBN: Ballistic Missile Submarine (nuclear) （核）弹道导弹潜艇

14. RDT&E: Research, Development, Test and Evaluation 研究、开发、测试与评估

15. FY2020: Fiscal Year 2020, a one-year period that companies and governments use for financial reporting and budgeting 2020财政年度（财年）

16. FFG(X): Guided Missile Frigate (Experimental) 导弹护卫舰（实验）

### Word Bank

| | |
|---|---|
| interdiction [ˌɪntəˈdɪkʃn] | n.（强制）禁运，封锁，阻断 |
| module [ˈmɒdjuːl] | n. 模块，功能块 |
| optimize [ˈɒptɪmaɪz] | v. 使最优化 |
| off-board [ɒf bɔːd] | n. 舷外；非舰载 |
| detachment [dɪˈtætʃmənt] | n. [军] 支队，分遣队 |
| mono-hull [ˈmɒnəʊ hʌl] | n. 单体船 |
| propulsion [prəˈpʌlʃn] | n. 推动力；推进 |
| diesel [ˈdiːzəl] | n. 柴油机 |
| waterjet [ˈwɔːtədʒet] | n. 喷水推进器；水射流；喷水 |
| trimaran [ˈtraɪməræn] | n. 三体船 |
| sprint [sprɪnt] | v. 短距离快速奔跑（或游泳）；冲刺 |
| armament [ˈɑːməmənt] | n. [军] 军备；军火，武器（尤指坦克、飞机等配备的大炮） |
| airframe [ˈeəfreɪm] | n. 飞机机架；导弹弹体 |
| envisage [ɪnˈvɪzɪdʒ] | v. 想象，设想；展望 |
| truncate [trʌŋˈkeɪt] | v. 将（某物）截短；缩短；删节 |
| modification [ˌmɒdɪfɪˈkeɪʃ(ə)n] | n. 修改 |
| mission packages | 任务包 |
| unmanned aerial vehicles (UAV) | 无人机，无人飞行器 |
| towed array | [军] 拖曳阵 |

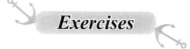

# Exercises

## I. True or False

*Decide whether the following sentences are true or false in accordance with the text.*

1. The LCS provides a basic platform for mission packages used for specific types of warfare.

2. The first three mission packages are used for anti-mine, home security and anti-surface warfare. Future development may include homeland security and maritime interdiction modules.

3. They feature an advanced networking capability to share tactical information with other Navy aircraft, ships, submarines and joint units.

4. The two LCS types were developed by teams headed by Lockheed Martin and General Dynamics from existing warship designs.

5. The propulsion of LCS-1 type is provided by a diesel plant.

6. LCS-2 type uses an all-aluminium trimaran design, which provides greater volume and deck space than a conventional hull of similar size, and needs less power to reach similar speeds.

7. It is foreseeable that all the operational LCS-1 variant ships will be deployed on the US Pacific Coast, and the LCS-2 on the Atlantic Coast according to a new operating concept of the LCS.

8. Grouping the same type of LCSs at different bases will make support and maintenance easier.

## II. Word Match

*Match the words/terms/phrases in the left column with its appropriate correspondents in the right column.*

1. LCS
2. CODAG
3. towed array
4. rolling airframe missile
5. SSBN
6. mission packages

A. 联合柴油机和燃气涡轮
B. 滚体导弹
C. 任务包
D. 情报、监视、侦察
E. 反水雷作战
F. 濒海战斗舰

7. anti-mine warfare

8. ISR

9. unmanned aerial vehicles

10. FFG

G. 无人机

H. （核）弹道导弹潜艇

I. 导弹护卫舰

J. 拖曳阵

# Text C
# The Routines of a Ship

Ships have routine work to do at sea, for example, plan of the day (POD) and shipboard **watches**. The POD is prepared and issued by the **executive officer** and implemented by the OOD[1] and the officers and men of all the departments. Its contents include training, watches, **liberty**, repair and maintenance, and **division bulletin** of the ship. The captain and the executive officer run the ship through departments. The OOD is the man in charge on the bridge. In most cases, he is responsible for the watch and the "**conn**", which means, in nautical terms, that he is in charge of the ship and its direction. Shipboard watches refer to the duty personnel aboard ship on a 24-hour day basis to **man** all stations. Each period of duty is usually four hours.

**Bridge and Deck Watch**

• Command Duty Officer (CDO[2]). The CO[3] normally appoints a CDO whenever the ship is at sea, and this duty is performed by senior officers of departments. The CDO is a line officer eligible for command. On behalf of the CO, he handles routine shipboard operational and watch-related affairs for the entire day.

• Officer of the Watch (OOW[4]). The OOW is an officer on watch on the bridge and responsible for the safe and proper operation of the ship. He reports directly to the CO for the safe navigation and general operation of the ship; and also to the EXO[5] and CDO for carrying out the ship's routines.

• Junior Officer of the Watch (JOOW[6]). The JOOW is the principal assistant of the OOW and assists him in carrying out the duties of the watch. Normally, he answers the radio telephone and **decodes** messages.

• Boatswain Mate of the Watch (BMW[7]). The BMW who is the principal enlisted assistant of the OOW is responsible for the bridge and deck watch. He conducts a **muster** of the incoming watch personnel and sees to it that they are properly posted and the outgoing watch is properly **relieved**.

• Quartermaster of the Watch (QMW[8]). The QMW is an enlisted man who assists the OOW in **navigational** matters. He keeps the ship's **log** and QM's Notebook and plots the ship's course on the bridge's navigational chart. He keeps the OOW informed of the ship's

position and alerts him to any significant course and speed changes required.

- Helmsman. The helmsman, also called steersman, is an enlisted man who steers wheel the course given him by the OOD, using a compass repeater.

- Lee Helmsman. The lee helmsman or second steersman is an enlisted man who controls the engine-order telegraph. He is responsible for transmitting speed and rpm changes ordered by the OOD to the engine room.

- Telephone Talkers. The telephone talkers are the enlisted personnel who manipulate various SPT[9] circuits and intercoms (MC[10]) to relay all messages between the OOW and other watch stations.

- Lookout Watches. The lookouts are enlisted personnel who are stationed at a location where they can best watch the conditions of the sea and/or sky. They act as the eyes and ears of the ship, in addition to the various detection and tracking devices available on board.

- Messenger of the Watch. The messenger is usually a young enlisted man who stands watch on the bridge responsible for delivering messages and answering telephones or carrying out duties as maybe assigned by the BMW or OOW.

- Lifeboat Watch. A large ship carries lifeboats used to help people in danger in the sea. For this purpose, the lifeboat watch is placed on readiness.

- CIC[11] Watch. The CIC is where the captain will direct the fighting. The Tactical Action Officers (TAO) is the captain's representative in the CIC, just as the OOD is his man on the bridge. The TAO stands his watch in the CIC. He takes notes of things that happen chronologically during the watch.

- Equipment Operator. The equipment operators are enlisted personnel who operate that are assigned to operate radar, sonar, depth sounder, tactical radio net and other electronic devices in the CIC.

- Plotter/Recorder/SPT Talker/Technician. These are enlisted personnel who make various plots, manage the status boards communicate and record messages, and repair faculty devices.

### Communication Watch

- Communication Watch Officer (CWO[12]). CWOs are junior officers or petty officers responsible for the reliable, rapid and secure use of external visual and radio communications, other than tactical voice radio, and responsible for the expeditious and efficient message traffic.

- Radio Watch/Signal Bridge Watch. The personnel on duty are the most senior enlisted assistant of the CWO. The radio watch means monitoring the frequencies in use, inspecting the message traffic and logs to detect errors, and taking immediate action in the event of any equipment failure. The signal bridge watch means aiding the CWO in informing the signalmen of the location of ships through the message traffic.

● Radioman. A radioman is on duty at the radio central. His job is to operate the radio telegraph and radio teletype communications equipment, transmit and receive messages in accordance with the standard **phraseology,** and process all types of messages.

● Signalman. A signalman is on duty at the signal bridge, transmitting and receiving tactical signals through flashing light, flaghoist and **semaphore** signaling.

### Engineering Watch

● Engineering Officer of the Watch (EOOW[13]). The EOOW is a commissioned officer who takes charge of the engineering watch under way. His job is to make sure that the ship's main and auxiliary propulsion systems operate safely and properly..

● Engineering Petty Officer of the Watch (EPOW[14]). The EPOW is a principal enlisted assistant of the EOOW and assists him in the proper operation of the ship's power plant.

● Main Engine Watches (MEW[15]). These are the enlisted personnel who operate the main propulsion system and other engine controls and ensure their normal and efficient operation.

● Auxiliary Engine Watches (AEW[16]). These are the enlisted personnel who operate or control the auxiliary engines, generators and **switchboards**, pumps and motors, refrigeration and air-conditioning systems, and other auxiliary machinery.

● Sounding and Security Watch or Patrol. The job is done by the enlisted personnel, including checking the watertight integrity and maintaining the material conditions of readiness throughout the ship.

● **Aft** Steering Watch. It is up to the enlisted personnel to monitor the ship's aft steering, and in case of steering malfunction, they will take over the steering control from the bridge helmsman directions given by the OOW.

A ship is virtually a self-contained and self-sufficient community. Almost any service or function normally found in a city, town, or community ashore is found in varying degrees on a ship. Only when the whole parts of the ship work normally, can the ship sail smoothly.

*(1098 words)*

**Sources:** ----------------------------------------------------------------

http://wk.ixueshu.com/file/80d4a88cf4f0f377.html（2020年6月1日访问）

## Notes

1. OOD: Officer of the Deck 舰值日官；舰上总值班官

2. CDO: Command Duty Officer 指挥值班军官

3. CO: Commanding Officer 舰长；指挥官

4. OOW: Officer of the Watch 舰上值班军官

5. EXO: Executive Officer 副舰长；执行官；办公室主任；主任参谋

6. JOOW: Junior Officer of the Watch 副值班官

7. BMW: Boatswain Mate of the Watch 值班帆缆军士；舰上值日官的助手（由士兵担任）

8. QMW: Quartermaster of the Watch 值班操舵兵

9. SPT: Sound Powered Telephone；a light telephone operated by current generated by the speaker's voice 声能电话，声力电话

10. MC: Main Channel 主用波道；主信道；主通路

11. CIC: Combat Information Center 战斗情报中心

12. CWO: Communication Watch Officer 值班通信军官

13. EOOW: Engineering Officer of the Watch 值班轮机官，机舱值更官

14. EPOW: Engineering Petty Officer of the Watch 值班轮机军士

15. MEW: Main Engine Watches 主机值班员

16. AEW: Auxiliary Engine Watches 辅机值班员

## Word Bank

| | |
|---|---|
| watch [wɒtʃ] | *n.* 值班人员（分队）；（值）班 |
| liberty [ˈlɪbətɪ] | *n.* 短假，短假外出——一般不超过48小时（海军）或72小时（空军） |
| division [dɪˈvɪʒn] | *n.* [军] 师；分队；处或科 |
| bulletin [ˈbʊlətɪn] | *n.* 公报；通报 |
| conn [kɒn] | *n.* 指挥操舵，指挥船只（行动）；驾驶（船） |
| man [mæn] | *v.* 给……配备人员；（炮手）就位 |
| bridge [brɪdʒ] | *n.* 驾驶台；舰桥；桥 |
| decode [ˌdiːˈkəʊd] | *v.* 破译；译码；翻译电码；解密；解码 |
| muster [ˈmʌstə(r)] | *n.* [军] 集合点验；集合 |

| relieve [rɪˈliːv] | v. 接防；接班；解除职务 |
| navigational [ˌnævɪˈgeɪʃənl] | adj. 航行的；导航的 |
| log [lɒg] | n. 日志；（尤指）航海日志；飞行日志 |
| helmsman [ˈhelmzmən] | n. 舵手 |
| steersman [ˈstɪəzmən] | n. 司机或舵手；操舵员 |
| lookout [ˈlʊkaʊt] | n. 观察所；瞭望台；监视哨；观察员；瞭望员 |
| messenger [ˈmesɪndʒə(r)] | n. [军] 通信部队；通信员；通信兵；传令兵 |
| plotter [ˈplɒtə(r)] | n. 标图员；标图器，绘图仪 |
| phraseology [ˌfreɪzɪˈɒlədʒɪ] | n. 用语；措辞；遣词造句 |
| semaphore [ˈseməfɔː(r)] | n. 旗语通信，手旗通信 |
| switchboard [ˈswɪtʃbɔːd] | n. 总机；交换机；配电盘 |
| aft [ɑːft] | adj. 在舰（机）尾的；近舰（机）尾的 |
| executive officer | 副舰长；主任参谋；执行官 |
| lee helmsman | 操舵兵副手；预备舵手 |
| depth sounder | 测深仪 |

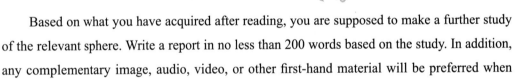

## Exercises

Based on what you have acquired after reading, you are supposed to make a further study of the relevant sphere. Write a report in no less than 200 words based on the study. In addition, any complementary image, audio, video, or other first-hand material will be preferred when you present your report in class.

# Unit 3  Submarine

**Bridge-in**

*Answer the following questions in accordance with the microlesson "Brief Introduction on Development of American Nuclear Submarines".*

1. What's the name of the first nuclear submarine in the world?
2. Who is "the father of nuclear submarine"?
3. Can you list some major types of nuclear submarines in the US?

## Text A
## A Glimpse of American Strikers Beneath the Sea

Submarines, as powerful strikers beneath the sea, have been playing a significant role in the enhancement of a nation's naval power. The US Navy now has three major types of submarines: ballistic missile submarines (SSBN[1]), guided-missile submarines (SSGN[2]) and attack submarines (SSN[3]) . In the US Navy, all combatant submarines are nuclear-powered. Ballistic submarines, carrying long-range, solid-fueled missiles that can be launched, undertake a single strategic deterrence. Attack submarines carry out several tactical missions, for example, launching torpedoes and cruise missiles to destroy hostile ships and submarines and using sensitive underwater sound receivers and transmitters (sonar) to gather intelligence.

### Ballistic-Missile Submarines (SSBN)

The 18 Ohio-class[4] SSBNs are the US's sole sea-based strategic deterrent force. The last one was commissioned in September 1997. The first eight boats of the class initially carried the UGM-96 Trident I C4 missile[5]. In March 1990, the ninth boat, Tennessee, was the first equipped with the advanced UGM-133A Trident II D5 missile[6]. All the boats built later carried

D5 beginning in 2003. The first four C4 boats were converted to guided-missile submarines (SSGNs), while the other four were retrofitted for D5 missiles.

The crew of each SSBN are divided into two groups, Blue and Gold, which alternate their duties on patrol. This can maximize the strategic availability: reducing the number of submarines required to meet strategic requirements and allowing for proper crew training, readiness and morale. Normally, five SSBNs are at sea at any given time.

The Ohio-class SSBNs will be out of commission in 2027, when the new Columbia-class submarines will begin to enter service. General Dynamics Electric Boat[7] was granted a $5.1 billion contract in September 2017 to complete the design of the first boat, SSBN 826. Including Columbia, SSBNs No.826 to No.837 will be raised to the new Columbia class, which was once known as the Ohio-class Replacement Program[8].

The new design includes a new reactor which can enhance the undersea capabilities of the submarines and prolong its service life. The Columbia-class[9] also will feature an X-stern with a water-jet propulsor, electric drive, sail planes, a six-mast sail and a large-aperture bow sonar.

The Columbia class will retain the Trident D5LE missile system. Its construction is planned to begin in 2021. It is expected to be launched in 2026 and make its first patrol in 2031. The Columbia-class will completely have replaced the Ohio class by 2039.

### Guided-Missile Submarines (SSGN)

The first four Ohio-class submarines were converted in the mid-2000s to the SSGNs carrying cruise missiles for strikes and special operations. Most of the former Trident missile tubes now are fitted with Multiple All-Up-Round Canisters (MACs[10]), each of which can accommodate seven Tomahawk land-attack cruise missiles,with a total number up to 154 missiles. The MACs can be removed and replaced with stowage canisters to accommodate equipment for 66 Special Operations Forces (SOF[11]) members who can embark aboard each SSGN. The missile tubes also provide additional capability to host future payloads, such as new types of missiles and other weapons, UAVs[12] and unmanned underwater vehicles.

To help facilitate SOF operations, the two forward-most missile tubes have been converted into lock-in/lock-out chambers that double as docking stations for Dry-Deck Shelters (DDSs). The SSGNs can carry two DDSs or two future Dry Combat Submersibles.

SSGNs also contain the Common Submarine Radio Room, two high-data-rate antennas and the battle management center, thereby improving the ships' command-and-control

capabilities.

Following conversion, the Ohio-class submarines returned to service on February 7, 2006 and were deployed in October 2007. Florida class was redelivered in April 2006. Michigan class and Georgia class returned to service in 2007 and 2008, respectively. The crew of each SSGN are divided into Blue and Gold groups that man the submarine by turns and thus maximized its strategic availability.

Florida became the first of its class to participate in combat operations. It launched more than 90 Tomahawk missiles against targets in Libya during Operation Odyssey Dawn in March 2011.

### Attack Submarines (SSN)

Submarines of the Los Angeles class[13] entered service in 1976, but a number of earlier boats are already out of commision. The last submarine in the class, Cheyenne, was commissioned in September 1996. The improved Los Angeles-class boats, beginning with San Juan, are quieter and originally featured improved combat systems. However, the transition of submarines equipment to common, open-architecture and commercial, off-the-shelf (COTS[14]) Submarine Warfare Federated Tactical Systems[15]provides all classes with the same baseline systems that can be easily upgraded with improved hardware and software.

Three Los Angeles-class boats were not in service in 2016. La Jolla was converted into a moored training ship; San Francisco was out of commission in 2017. The Navy planned to inactivate eight more Los Angeles-class boats through 2019. Dallas stopped operating on June 15, 2017 and was decommissioned on April 4, 2018. Buffalo ended its service on September 30, 2018, Jacksonville on May 1, 2018, and Bremerton[16] on July 9, 2018.

Now there are three Seawolf-class[17] submarines engaged in multiple operational missions, including mine warfare, antisubmarine warfare, anti-ship attack and littoral special operations. The third boat of the class, Jimmy Carter, was commissioned on February 19, 2005. As a result of research and development, the enhanced payload allows Jimmy Carter to conduct special missions. This will provide the basis for improvement in submarine technology and capability.

The introduction of the Virginia-class[18] in 2004 provided the fleet with advanced stealth submarines with the enhanced ability to gain access and remain undetected. Virginia-class submarines are configured to carry a DDS. They also incorporate significant habitability upgrades to eliminate "hot bunking" by the one-for-one bunk-to-sailor ratio.

The Virginia boats use non-hull-penetrating photonics masts instead of traditional

**periscopes**. Considering the arrangement of the control room and the location of the sail no longer determined by the boat's optical system, designers moved the sail forward for improved **hydrodynamics** and positioned the command-and-control room further aft and down one deck, making it larger and more adaptable. The boat's wide-aperture array sonar is optimized for littoral and blue-water operations. And it has improved mine-detection and avoidance capabilities and raised search speed. Virginia-class boats also have a fly-by-wire ship-control system for the precise handling and increase of depth control while operating in shallower waters.

The SSN(X), if the Navy proceeds with a new class, will follow production of 48 Virginia-class SSNs, the last one of which is scheduled to be delivered in 2034. The Navy plans to make alternatives in 2024 and expects the construction of the first SSN(X) in 2034. Affordability will be a key point in the design, which needs to improve the existing technology.

*(1079 words)*

### Sources:

1. Extracted and edited from "The Submarine in the U.S Navy" in *Sea Power* issued by US Navy league, volume 62, number 1, January 2019.
2. www. navyleague. Org.

### Notes

1. SSBN: Ballistic Missile Submarines 弹道导弹核潜艇
2. SSGN: Guided-missile Submarines 巡航导弹核潜艇
3. SSN: Nuclear-powered Attack Submarines 攻击型核潜艇
4. Ohio-class: Ohio-class is a class of nuclear-powered submarine built by the US Navy in 1976. A total of 18 Ohio-class submarines are in service in the US Navy. 俄亥俄级是美国海军1976年建造核潜艇的一个类型，目前美国海军有18艘俄亥俄级的核潜艇正在服役。
5. UGM-96 Trident I C4 missile: The missile has a maximum range of 7400 km and a hit accuracy of 230-500ms by using a high-efficiency propulsion system, an additional third propulsion rocket and more advanced guidance technology . "三叉戟I"型C-4导弹，编号UGM-96A
6. UGM-133A Trident II D5 missile: a new type of submarine launched ballistic missile with

larger diameter UGM-133A 一种新型弹道导弹

7. General Dynamics Electric Boat: A division of general dynamics which has been the main builder of US Navy submarines for more than 100 years 通用动力电船公司

8. Ohio-class Replacement Program: 俄亥俄级核潜艇置换计划

9. Columbia class: The Columbia-class strategic nuclear submarine will be the largest submarine ever built by the US Navy, with a length of 171 meters, a width of 13 meters and a submergence displacement of 20,810 tons. 哥伦比亚级战略核潜艇是美国海军建造的最大的潜艇，长171米，宽13米，水下排水量20 810吨。

10. MAC: Multiple All-Up-Round Canisters 多个满载的圆形导弹装运箱

11. SOF: Special Operations Forces 特种作战部队

12. UAV: Unmanned Aerial Vehicle 无人机

13. Los Angeles class: a high-speed multi-purpose nuclear submarine is also the fifth-generation attack submarine of the United States. 洛杉矶级核潜艇是一种高速的多功能核潜艇，也是美国第五代攻击型核潜艇。

14. COTS: commercial, off-the-shelf 商品现货或准军用的

15. Submarine Warfare Federated Tactical Systems: 潜艇战联合战术系统

16. Bremerton: Bremerton naval base, located in the northwest of the Pacific coast of the United State. 布雷默顿军港位于美国太平洋沿岸西北部。

17. Seawolf class: anti-submarine hunting and killing nuclear submarines. 海狼级核潜艇是一种反潜核潜艇。

18. Virginia class: The first US navy nuclear submarine was designed for both ocean and coastal functions. 弗吉尼亚级核潜艇是美国首次设计的兼顾近海和远海作战功能的核潜艇。

## Word Bank

| | |
|---|---|
| striker [ˈstraɪkə(r)] | *n.* 打击者，打手 |
| ballistic [bəˈlɪstɪk] | *adj.* 弹道的 |
| strategic [strəˈtiːdʒɪk] | *adj.* 战略（上）的；有战略意义的；至关重要的 |
| tactical [ˈtæktɪkl] | *adj.* 战术的；策略上的 |
| intelligence [ɪnˈtelɪdʒəns] | *n.* （军）情报 |
| deterrent [dɪˈterənt] | *n.* 制止物；威慑物 |
| commission [kəˈmɪʃn] | *v.* 使服役 |

retrofit [ˈretrəʊfit]　　　　　　　　　v. 给机器设备装配（新部件）；翻新

readiness [ˈredɪnəs]　　　　　　　　n. 战备

morale [məˈrɑːl]　　　　　　　　　n. 士气，斗志

hull [hʌl]　　　　　　　　　　　　n. 船体

stern [stɜːn]　　　　　　　　　　　n. 船尾；末端

propulsor [prəʊˈpʌlsə]　　　　　　n. 推进装置；推进器

aperture [ˈæpətʃə]　　　　　　　　n. 孔；穴；孔径；缝隙

bow [baʊ]　　　　　　　　　　　　n. 船头，舰首

sonar [ˈsəʊnɑː]　　　　　　　　　　n. 声呐；声波定位仪

patrol [pəˈtrəʊl]　　　　　　　　　n. 巡逻；侦察队

canister [ˈkænɪstə]　　　　　　　　n. 导弹装运箱；霰弹筒

stowage [ˈstəʊɪdʒ]　　　　　　　　n. 装载，贮藏，装载物

embark [ɪmˈbɑːk]　　　　　　　　　vi. 上飞机，上船；vt. 使……上船或飞机

payload [ˈpeɪləʊd]　　　　　　　　n. 有效载荷；战斗装药

facilitate [fəˈsɪlɪteɪt]　　　　　　v. 促进，助长；使容易；帮助

forward-most [ˈfɔːwəd-məʊst]　　　最前面的

docking[ˈdɒkɪŋ]　　　　　　　　　n. 入船坞；（航天器在轨道上的）对接

antenna[ænˈtenə]　　　　　　　　n. 天线；触角，触须

redeliver [ˈriːdɪˈlɪvə]　　　　　　v. 再投递，再交付

moor [mʊə]　　　　　　　　　　　v. 停泊，系泊（船只）

littoral [ˈlɪtərəl]　　　　　　　　n. 沿（海）岸地区

stealth [stelθ]　　　　　　　　　　n. 秘密行动；鬼祟；隐形

configure [kənˈfɪgə]　　　　　　　v. 配置；设定；使成形

incorporate [ɪnˈkɔːpəreɪt]　　　　vt. 包含；使混合 vi. 包含；吸收；合并；混合

habitability [hæbɪtəˈbɪlɪtɪ]　　　　n. 适居性；可居住性

photonics [fəʊˈtɒnɪks]　　　　　　n. 光子学

periscope [ˈperɪskəʊp]　　　　　　n. 潜望镜

hydrodynamics [ˈhaɪdrəʊdaɪˈnæmɪks]　　n. 流体力学；流体动力学

high-data-rate antennas　　　　　高数据速率天线

battle management center　　　　作战管理中心

# Exercises

## I. Comprehension

**Part A**  Questions

*Answer the following questions in accordance with the text.*

1. What are the three major types of submarines in the US navy?

2. What is the single strategic mission of the Ballistic submarines?

3. When was the last of 18 Ohio-class boats commissioned?

4. Why are the crew of each SSBN devided into two groups?

5. When did Michigan and Georgia return to service?

**Part B**  Multiple Choices

*Choose the most appropriate answer from the given choices below each question in accordance with the text.*

1. What is not the feature of the X-stern in the Columbia class?

   A. Electric drive.

   B. Sail planes.

   C. A six-mast sail.

   D. A large-aperture stern sonar.

2. Which missile system will be retained in the Columbia subs?

   A. Trident I C4 missile system.

   B. Trident II C4 missile system.

   C. Trident II D5 missile system.

   D. Trident D5LE missile system.

3. Which submarine became the first of its class to participate in combat operations and launched more than 90 Tomahawk missiles against targets in Libya during Operation Odyssey Dawn in March 2011?

   A. Michigan.

   B. Florida.

   C. Georgia.

   D. Tennessee.

4. When did Dallas stop its activities at sea?

    A. On June 15, 2017.

    B. On April 4, 2018.

    C. On September 30, 2018.

    D. On July 9, 2018.

5. Which is not the operational mission of the attack submarine?

    A. Anti-mine operation mission.

    B. Anti-submarine operation mission.

    C. Anti-ship operation mission.

    D. Littoral special operation mission.

## II. Translation

**Part A**  **Terms & Phrases**

*Translate the following terms or phrases from Chinese into English and vice versa.*

| | |
|---|---|
| 1. 弹道导弹 | 2. 作战潜艇 |
| 3. 战略任务 | 4. 收集情报 |
| 5. 核动力的 | 6. 威慑兵力 |
| 7. 三叉戟导弹 | 8. 船号 |
| 9. 水下无人机 | 10. 承受力 |
| 11. 多样化作战任务 | 12. 训练舰 |
| 13. 可居住性 | 14. 避碰能力 |
| 15. SSBN | 16. SSGN |
| 17. SSN | 18. SOF |
| 19. Sea-based strategic deterrent force | 20. command-and-control |
| 21. water-jet propulsor | 22. replacement programme |
| 23. anti-submarine | 24. anti-ship |
| 25. battle management center | 26. blue-water operations |
| 27. submarine warfare | 28. commission |

**Part B**  **Paragraph**

*Translate the following paragraph from English into Chinese.*

    There are three major types of submarines in the United States Navy: ballistic missile submarines (SSBN) , guided-missile submarines (SSGN) and attack submarines (SSN). In

the US Navy, all combatant submarines are nuclear-powered. Ballistic submarines have a single, strategic mission: carrying nuclear submarine-launched ballistic missiles for strategic deterrence. Attack submarines have several tactical missions, including sinking ships and subs, launching cruise missiles, and gathering intelligence.

## III. Reading Report

What have you learned after reading the text? Have you got a better understanding of American submarine force? Now write a reading report in no more than 150 words to generalize what you have learned from text study.

# Text B
## Choke Point[1]: Anti-Submarine Warfare[2] in the Indian Ocean

Pakistan is India's **archenemy**. Especially its expected purchase of a submarine from China has aroused India's worry. On the other hand, in the Gulf of Aden, Saudi Arabia, the United Arab Emirates (UAE) and Egypt are waging a **proxy** war in **Yemen** against Iran, Turkey and Qatar. This has led to an increase of naval bases in Djibouti. With more and more surface vessels operating in littoral waters, the Strait of Hormuz has been turned into a choke point.

These are not the notes for the script of the next "**House of Cards**" — type series taking place in the Indian Ocean, but merely a brief summary of the main **dynamics** playing the series out in the area, which reflects the complexity of **geopolitical** interests at stake. It is through this **prism** that people can perceive one must look at anti-submarine warfare (ASW) in the Indian Ocean.

### ASW—Sub-Surface Response

"Submarines are still a very powerful threat in terms of sea denial, especially for extended **SLOCs**," said Mr. Caris. However, some countries like India and Singapore do not have the financial means to develop a **multilayer** ASW capability to some extent.

Now, the People's Liberation Army Navy aroused the particular concern of nations bordering the Indian Ocean or along the Strait of Malacca[3]. Since the introduction of nuclear-powered submarines (the Type-093 Shang class) and nuclear-powered ballistic missile submarines (the Type-095 Jin class) into the South Sea Fleet in the early 2000s, the PLAN has been able to carry out missions for a long time outside its usual territorial sphere of influence.

India is extremely concerned over China playing a role in the region. According to Mr Caris: "India needs to deal with all the threats present in Indian waters, ranging from Chinese submarines in transit, to littoral submarine threats from Pakistan, which means that it is the most full-**spectrum** ASW navy in the region." To increase its subsurface level of ASW capabilities, India has ordered six Scorpene-class submarines from Naval Group, known in India as the Kalvari class which are equipped with MBDA SM-39 anti-ship missiles. The first of that class, INS Kalvari, was **commissioned** in December 2017. Naval Group said that the Indian Navy (IN) would receive the last one by 2027.

Located along the Strait of Malacca, Indonesia also finds it necessary to protect its SLOCs and monitor Chinese activity. In its 2024 Defense Strategic Plan, the Indonesian government pointed out that the Indonesian Navy would be equipped with ten new submarines by 2024 to complement the two Cakra-class submarines made in Germany and commissioned in 1981. In December 2011, The TNI-AL signed a contract with Daewoo Shipbuilding and Marine Engineering (DSME[4]) for the construction and delivery of three Type-209 Nagapasa-class diesel-electric attack submarines (SSK[5]) . The first one was delivered in August 2017, while the last is scheduled for delivery by 2021. Currently, the TNI-AL is considering different options for the next batch, including the Russian Kilo-class[6] and Naval Group's Scorpene class.

Although it has the same concern as its neighbors Malaysia, whose effort to develop its submarine fleet has been hampered by a constant cut in its military budget. Currently, the RMN operates a fleet of two Perdana Menteri (Scorpene)-class diesel-electric submarines that were procured in 2002 and were delivered in 2009. Over the past decade, negotiations have been ongoing with the government about funding a project to get additional two submarines: one to be gotten between 2031 and 2035 and the other between 2036 and 2040.

Compared to its Malaysian and Indonesian neighbors, Singapore already has a strong submarine fleet, with two Archer-class and four Challenger-class diesel-electric submarines. Nevertheless, Singapore announced in May 2017 that it would acquire another two Type 218SG attack submarines with Thyssen Krupp Marine Systems (TKMS[7]). The two new ships are scheduled to be delivered from 2024 on, while the first two ships, currently at different stages of construction, are set to be delivered to the Singapore Navy in 2021 and 2022.

Australia is also boosting its submarine fleet with six Barracuda-class submarines[8], based on the Scorpene class, ordered from Naval Group in March 2016 under the programme SEA 1000. The first of that class is scheduled to be delivered by 2020, and the second, third and fourth are currently at different stages of construction, and the fifth has been ordered.

"Going West from India, ASW capabilities are much more limited,"added Mr Caris, "as these countries do not have the same multilayered, long-range and close-in approaches." Indeed, at the moment only Pakistan and Iran are operating submarines. Currently, Pakistan possesses three Agosta 90B and two Agosta 70 submarines, the former being adapted by Turkish STM for upgrading their sonar systems, periscope systems, command and control systems, radar and electronic support systems. Turkish STM[9] has released the news that the first submarine is to be delivered in 2020. According to local sources, Pakistan is expected to procure a number of Type 041 Yuan class submarines from China.

Chock-a-Block

"In the coming years, the geopolitical environment in the Indian Ocean is likely to become highly complex with reduced trust between countries that represent 'have' and 'have not' of submarines," notes Captain Khurana. "In functional terms as well, the sub-surface maritime environment in the region is likely to deteriorate, possibly leading to adverse consequences such as unintentional naval encounters and issues of safety of crews resulting from problems of water-space management."

At present, the Strait of Malacca is a choke point, which has brought issues as **highlighted** by Captain Khurana, thereby affecting the eastern and central part of the Indian Ocean. Nevertheless, the increasing of submarine capabilities in the west of the Indian Ocean is imminent, but that is far more limited than in the East due to a wide range of factors. Building naval bases on regional islands and along the coast in Oman, Djibouti and Somalia, is becoming a matter of great concern to turn regional attention to the importance of ASW capabilities. Then, the following issues to be considered by Naval Forces are about the enhancement of surface and air capabilities for ASW in the region, and the increase of naval bases there.

*(1161 words)*

*Sources:*

*Naval forces,* volume 39, number 2, 2018.

### Notes

1. choke point: a place where people or vehicles are stopped and inspected or searched 咽喉要塞

2. anti-submarine warfare: a kind of combat against enemy submarines. It's one of the styles of naval warfare. The purpose is to eliminate or weaken the enemy submarine forces. 反潜战是攻击敌人潜艇的战争，是海战的一种形式，其目的在于消灭或削弱敌人的潜艇兵力。

3. the Strait of Malacca: It is a long strait between the Malay Peninsula and Sumatra island of Indonesia, under the common jurisdiction of Singapore, Malaysia and Indonesia. 马六甲海峡是一段位于马来西亚和印尼之间的海峡，新加坡、马来西亚和印尼共同享有对马六

甲海峡的管辖权。

4. DSME: Daewoo Shipbuilding and Marine Engineering 大宇造船与海洋工程公司

5. SSK: Diesel-electric attack submarines 柴电混合动力攻击潜艇

6. Kilo-class: This type of submarine is the most successful conventional submarine developed in the naval era of the former Soviet Union. It is mainly used for anti-ship and anti-submarine operations in the offshore shallow waters. 基洛级潜艇是苏联海军时代中发展得最成功的常规潜艇，它在近海作战中主要用于反舰和反潜。

7. TKMS: Thyssen Krupp Marine Systems 蒂森克虏伯海洋系统

8. Barracuda-class submarine: Barracuda class nuclear submarine is the next generation of French nuclear powered attack submarine. It is designed by DCN to replace Ruby class nuclear submarine. 梭鱼级核潜艇属于法国下一代潜艇攻击型核潜艇。设计它是为了取代红宝石级核潜艇。

9. STM: A Turkish military company 一家土耳其军工企业

 **Word Bank**

| archenemy [ˈɑːtʃˈenəmɪ] | n. 最大的敌人，首敌 |
|---|---|
| proxy [ˈprɑːksɪ] | n. 代理人；受托人；代表；(测算用的)代替物，指标 |
| dynamics [daɪˈnæmɪks] | n. 动力学；动力 |
| geopolitical [ˌdʒiːəʊpəˈlɪtɪkl] | adj. 地缘政治学的 |
| prism [ˈprɪzəm] | n. 三棱镜 |
| multilayer [ˌmʌltɪˈleɪə] | adj. 多层次的 |
| spectrum [ˈspektrəm] | n. 谱；光谱；声谱；波谱；频谱；范围；各层次；系列；幅度 |
| commission [kəˈmɪʃn] | v. 服役 |
| hamper[ˈhæmpə] | v. 妨碍，束缚，限制 |
| procure [prəˈkjʊə] | v. （设法）获得，取得，得到 |
| highlight [ˈhaɪlaɪt] | v. 突出，强调 |
| Yemen [ˈjemən] | n. 也门共和国 |
| Djibouti [dʒɪˈbuːtɪ] | n. 吉布提 |

| | |
|---|---|
| Somalia [səˈmɑːlɪə] | *n.* 索马里 |
| SLOCs | 海上交通线 |
| House of Cards | 纸牌屋（文中比喻军事力量的较量与博弈） |
| Defense Strategic Plan | 战略防御计划 |

# Exercises

## I. True or False

*Decide whether the following sentences are true or false in accordance with the text.*

1. India's archenemy is Pakistan.

2. Among the three Type-209 Nagapasa-class diesel-electric attack submarines of Indonesia, the first one was delivered in August 2017, while the last is scheduled to be delivered by 2021.

3. The two new Type-218SG attack submarines of Singapore are scheduled to be delivered from 2022 on.

4. Australia is boosting its submarine fleet with the six Barracuda-class submarines.

5. Pakistan is expected to procure an undisclosed number of Agosta 90B submarines from China.

6. At present, the strait of Malacca is a choke point, which has brought the issues as highlighted by Captain Khurana, thereby affecting the Eastern and Central part of the Indian Ocean.

## II. Word Match

*Match the words/terms/phrases in the left column with its appropriate correspondents in the right column.*

| | |
|---|---|
| 1. ASW | A. 战略防御计划 |
| 2. choke point | B. 海上交通线 |
| 3. SLOCs | C. 咽喉要塞 |
| 4. Defence Strategic Plan | D. 反潜战 |
| 5. anti-ship missiles | E. （兵力）博弈较量 |
| 6. Strait of Malacca | F. 海军兵力 |

7. naval forces                        G. 马六甲海峡

8. Djibouti base                       H. 反舰导弹

9. Indonesian Navy                     I. 吉布提基地

10. House of Card                      J. 印尼海军

# Text C
## Submariners Defy Death in the Depths

This is a story about the crew members cited for their well-honed skills and exceptional courage in averting a disaster. For senior captain[1] Wang Hongli and his crew, reacting fast enough in their submarine in the abyss of the ocean is a matter of life and death.

In a recent naval patrol mission, his team had just three minutes to save their Submarine 372[2] from plunging into an underwater trench thousands of meters deep. The vessel had encountered a sudden change in water conditions, which led it to sink uncontrollably fast.

"We couldn't control the boat's depth despite my order to fill the ballast tanks. It fell tens of meters in less than three minutes," Wang said. His crew quickly seized the little time they had, opening all the emergency air flasks within 10 seconds to fill the tanks. They managed to close more than 100 valves and related equipment in less than a minute. In two minutes, all the cabins were sealed.The team's swift, coordinated reaction saved the submarine and the lives of the crew.

"It is not uncommon for a submarine to temporarily lose control of its depth due to the change in seawater density and under-surface current, but most of the time we can fix that by rebalancing or speeding up," Wang, commander of an elite submarine flotilla under the PLA Navy's South Sea Fleet, recently told the reporters at a news conference.

"But this time, the submarine was sailing in deep waters and it was sinking very fast, so if we hadn't moved fast enough, the boat and its whole crew would have been pulled into the abyss in a very short time."

One of the vessel's pipes in the main engine cabin was also damaged by the increased water pressure, resulting in an influx of seawater and the main engine losing its power.

Ma Ze, a staff officer from the PLA Navy headquarters in Beijing who took part in the mission, explained how serious the situation was. "Everyone who has served on a submarine knows that three situations pose the most dangerous threats to a boat—uncontrollable sinking caused by loss of buoyancy, influx of seawater and equipment catching fire. Submarine 372 were subjected to two of them at one time, which truly presented a life-and-death matter for its crew."

Many agreed that the crew's escape from death was a miracle in the navy's history. The tough training, lofty dedication and unwavering faith in teamwork were what Wang's crew

used to save themselves.

### Quick Response

"The submarine's officers and sailors were so well-trained as not to be overcome by panic during the emergency," said Captain Yi Hui of Submarine 372.

Chen Zujun, chief of the electrical division, was on duty in the main engine cabin with two of his **subordinates**, Mao Xuegang and Zhu Zhaowei. After hearing a bang, the three men found seawater flooding the cabin. Dense fog also **blurred** their vision.

Chen immediately ordered them to close the **hatches** and block the leak. He shut down the main engine and other electrical **apparatus** in the section while Mao and Zhu struggled to fix the broken pipes. Lian Shicai, Submarine 372's chief petty officer[3], said the training and exercises have **implanted** ideas of quick response in the crew.

The flotilla has also been encouraging crew members to repair **malfunctioning** or broken parts on their own and will give awards to those who succeed, thereby enhancing submariners' knowledge and capabilities, said the vessel's power chief[4], Xie Baoshu.

"From the beginning of each year, we would make a comprehensive and systematic yearly plan for training and drills. All the crew, including the captain and political commissar[5], must attend and pass theoretical and practical tests for their posts." said Captain Yi.

### Mission Priority

After Submarine 372 surfaced following its emergency, senior officers on board decided not to report the incident to the South Sea Fleet headquarters until the vessel completed its mission.

"At first, I was not sure whether the boat and its crew could carry on the mission because the vessel had been flooded by seawater. A lot of equipment had malfunctioned and all the men were exhausted after nearly three sleepless days of repair," Yi said. "But the officers and sailors persisted in completing the patrol and meanwhile the equipment was gradually being restored. This gave us more confidence to go on with the mission."

Wang also found the submariners facing another major challenge after the emergency— dealing with foreign military ships and aircraft.

"The rivals were coming towards us but our sailors didn't **flinch** ... I was thinking that, since they (foreign navies) were generous enough to give us a combat training opportunity for free, we shouldn't waste it," Wang said.

The submarine successfully broke through several rounds of encirclement and pursuits by foreign navies and continued its patrol in the following days before returning to the base.

### Presidential Awards

Zhi Tianlong, president of the PLA Navy Submarine Academy[6], said Wang and his men's handling of the incident was exemplary.

"They succeeded in defusing such a complicated and grave emergency. Their performance was excellent and it will be written into our textbooks. The navy will introduce their experience into all submarine forces," said Zhi, who has served in the navy's submarine units for more than three decades.

To further recognize the Wang's and crew's courageous acts and great efforts, Senior Captain Wang was awarded a first-class military service citation[7] in September by President Xi Jinping, who is also chairman of the Central Military Commission[8], while the PLA Navy awarded the crew a first-class merit citation[9], which is rare in peacetime.

Admiral Wu Shengli, commander of the PLA navy, said at the award **ceremony** that the Submarine 372 crew's feat will inspire all its servicemen to honor their duties and build a strong navy.

"The flotilla organizes long-distance patrols every year. These operations will continue to expand in distance and duration, and our submarines will continue to explore new depths," Wang said.

"We value precious experience we get from our operations. Crew members are required to review and learn from the performance of their missions and review their progress, so that they can constantly improve their military quality and capability," he said.

Vessel steering chief[10] Zhao Manxing said every submariner in his flotilla aspires to adventure and honor. "Fighting windstorms and billows is what a man should do in his youth, so I joined the submarine fleet," he said.

"We fear no hardship or death."

*(1118 words)*

**Sources:**

http://africa.chinadaily.com.cn/china/2014-12/18/content_19111855.htm

# Notes

1. senior captain: In the current military rank system in China, a senior commander is a rank higher than a colonel but lower than a major general. 在中国当代军衔体系中，大校是低于少将高于上校的一级军衔。

2. Submarine 372: In the afternoon of September 6, 2016, the Central Military Commission awarded the honorary title of "model boat for practicing the goal of building a strong army" for Navy submarines 372. 2016年9月6日，中央军委授予海军372号潜艇"践行强军目标的模范舰"的荣誉称号。

3. chief petty officer: a senior non-commissioned officer in the navy 海军军士长

4. power chief : Officer in charge of power systems in a warship or submarine 机电长

5. political commissar: Leading cadres in charge of party work and political work in the Chinese PLA, units at or above the regimental level 政委

6. PLA Navy Submarine Academy: The Navy Submarine Academy of the Chinese People's Liberation Army (PLA) is a highly specialized technical command academy directly under the PLA Navy, and is the only higher education institution of submarine arms in Asia. 中国人民解放军海军潜艇学院是一所高度专业化的技术指挥类院校，直接隶属海军管辖，是亚洲唯一一所潜艇的兵种类院校。

7. First-class military service citation: one of the PLA medals, often awarded to soldiers who have made outstanding contributions 一等功

8. CMC: abbreviation for the Central Military Commission 中央军事委员会

9. first-class merit citation: one of the PLA's awards, often awarded to organizations or collectives with outstanding contributions 集体一等功

10. vessel steering chief: officer in charge of navigation on a warship or submarine 航海长

# Word Bank

| | |
|---|---|
| exceptional [ɪkˈsepʃənl] | *adj.* 杰出的；优秀的；卓越的；罕见的 |
| avert [əˈvɜːt] | *v.* 防止，避免；转移 |
| abyss [əˈbɪs] | *n.* 深渊 |
| trench [trentʃ] | *n.* 沟；渠；战壕；堑壕；海沟；大洋沟 |
| flask [flæsk] | *n.* 烧瓶 |

valve [vælv]            *n.* 阀；阀门；活门；气门

flotilla [fləʊˈtɪlə]        *n.* 船队；小型舰队；支队

influx [ˈɪnflʌks]          *n.* （人、资金或事物的）涌入，流入

buoyancy [ˈbɔɪənsɪ]       *n.* 浮力；（物体在液体里的）浮性

unwavering [ʌnˈweɪvərɪŋ]    *adj.* 不动摇的，坚定的

subordinate[səˈbɔːdɪnət]     *n.* 部属；部下，下级

blur [blɜː(r)]             *v.* 涂污，弄脏；（使）变模糊，（使）难以区分

hatch [hætʃ]            *n.* （船甲板或飞机底部装货物的）舱口；（飞机
                                     或宇宙飞船的）舱门

apparatus[æpəˈreɪtəs]       *n.* 仪器，器械；机器

implant [ɪmˈplæntɪd]        *v.* 灌输，注入（观念、看法等）

malfunction [ˌmælˈfʌŋkʃn]    *v.* 运转失常；失灵；出现故障

flinch [flɪntʃ]             *v.* 退缩；畏惧

encirclement [ɪnˈsɜːklmənt]    *n.* 环绕

exemplary[ɪgˈzemplərɪ]       *adj.* 典范的；可仿效的

defuse [ˌdiːˈfjuːz]           *v.* 拆除（爆炸物）的引信；减少⋯⋯的危险性；
                                     缓和

duration [djʊˈreɪʃn]         *n.* 持续，持续的时间，续航力

aspire[əsˈpaɪə]             *v.* 渴望，追求

billow [ˈbɪləʊ]            *n.* 巨浪

## *Exercises*

    Based on what you have acquired in this text, you are supposed to conduct an online study to explore further into the relevant sphere. Comb and frame what you have learned with an online study report in no less than 200 words. In addition, any assistant image, audio, video, or other first-hand material will be preferred when you present your report in class.

# Unit 4　Naval Aviation

**Bridge-in**

*Answer the following questions in accordance with the microlesson "National Guardians of the PLAN Aviation".*

1. What exactly happened on 1st April, 2001?

2. What do you think about Zhang Chao's choice at the last moment of his life?

3. What can we infer from those heroic behaviors as a cadet?

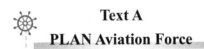

## Text A
## PLAN Aviation Force

The PLA Navy's aviation force is known as Naval Aviation. It has developed into a maritime attack and support force equipped with more than 690 aircraft including shore-based aircraft, ship-based aircraft, carrier aircraft, and seaplanes, and with a total number of about 26,000 personnel. As the second largest naval aviation in the world, it is playing an increasingly important role in safeguarding China's territorial sovereignty and maintaining the maritime rights and interests of the nation. Moreover, military transportation has brought changes to Naval Aviation. Now, it takes on various missions and tasks including maritime patrol, airborne early warning (AEW), anti-submarine warfare (ASW), offensive strikes at land targets and on ships at sea, logistical support, and helicopter support for the PLAN's escort task force in the Gulf of Aden. The fully-expected and far-sighted Chinese aircraft carrier program will bring a brand new dimension to Naval Aviation as it seeks to operate farther offshore, so as to protect Chinese interests abroad.

## A Brief History

Following its founding in April, 1949, the PLAN issued its first three-year plan. The portions pertaining to the creation of Navy Aviation Department included establishing three air divisions and three aviation schools, building two to three Naval Aviation airfields each in strategic combat area, and purchasing 360 aircraft and necessary support equipment from the Soviet Union.

Although the outbreak of the Korean War made it possible for the PLAN to fulfill its goals on schedule, the three-year plan laid the foundation for creating an aviation arm. Based on this plan, the Central Military Commission (CMC) established the PLAN 1st Aviation School on 1 October, 1950 in Qingdao on the Shandong peninsula, which was a starting point of the building-up of Naval Aviation.

On June 27, 1952, the Naval Aviation 1st Division was set up at Shanghai Hongqiao airfield, followed by several Naval Aviation units, schools, and fleet aviation troops. The air division was manned with the first group of graduates of the aviation school in Qingdao.

Naval Aviation celebrates the anniversary of its founding on September 6 every year, because it was on that day in 1952 that the Naval Aviation Department was established in Beijing as one of six separate administrative departments within PLAN Headquarters. And the Naval Aviation Headquarters was set up at Liangxiang Airfield near Beijing.

By the end of 1954, Naval Aviation had five air divisions and one independent regiment. By 1960, the force possessed 500 aircraft, which were organized into nine divisions and three independent regiments.

Nowadays, Naval Aviation has the number of aircraft similar to that of the PLA Air Force, including fighter aircraft, bombers, strike aircraft, reconnaissance aircraft, with electronic warfare aircraft, maritime patrol aircraft, transport aircraft, and multi-purpose helicopters. Since China began building aircraft carriers, Naval Aviation has been optimizing its combat force structure and capabilities.

## Missions and Tasks

The missions and tasks of the PLAN Aviation Force not only include providing fleet air defense for surface ships, submarines, ports and naval installations, maintaining a constant air patrol, and defending China's coastline and territorial waters, but also refer to air fight, air-to-ground attack, air interdiction, anti-ship attack, ASW[1], SAR[2], transportation bombing and tactical support for amphibious operations.

Types of Aircraft in Service

### *Fighters*

The PLAN Aviation Force has different types of fighters, such as J-7E and J-8II. The J-7E is an improved version of the original Soviet MiG-21. With new double delta wings[3] and PL-8 AAM[4], the J-7E is quite an effective dogfighter. The J-8II is an indigenous fighter with a nose-mounted radar[5] and capable of conducting high-altitude interceptions at high speed. Both types of fighters are capable of being in-flight refueled by the Navy's own H-6DU tankers, modified from former navy H-6D missile bombers. The Navy's air defense troops can always be supported by the PLA Aviation Force that operates more advanced combat aircraft including J-10, J-11BH, J-15, and J-16H fighters.

Strikes and anti-ship attacks are carried out by the Q-5, JH-7, Su-30MK2 and H-6. The Q-5 was designed based on the J-6, with a nose radar mounted in the cockpit. It has become the first light nuclear attack aircraft of the China Air Force since the 1970s. China Naval Aviation has more than 40 Q-5s in service. They are variants equipped with search radars. Their main armaments are air-dropped torpedoes and rocket-launched air anti-ship missiles. The JH-7 is an indigenous, supersonic, heavy attack aircraft operated by two pilots. Its general performance and weapons delivery capability are thought to be comparable to early models of Panavia Tornado. The most acquisition by the PLAN Aviation Force is a batch of 24 Su-30MK2. These aircraft are highly advanced and improved variants of the Su-30. The MK2 has a long-range search radar that can detect and attack surface targets with powerful long-range missiles. The H-6 is an improvement on the 1950s' Soviet Tu-16 Badger. As its airframe is of the latest design, it has become a greatly improved model (similar to the upgraded US B52). Chinese Navy's H-6 variants include the H-6D, which is capable of carrying two anti-ship missiles.

### *Helicopters*

Helicopters are an important asset to China's surface force. Over the years, the PLA Naval Aviation has possessed different kinds of helicopters like the Changhe Z-8 , Harbin Z-9 and Russian Ka-28 Helix. The Changhe Z-8 is the largest ship-borne helicopter[6] which has ever been made in China, which is largely similar to the French Super Frelon design. The efficient Z-8 plays a variety of auxiliary roles, such as towing mine clearance devices[7], conducting vertical inflight refueling of smaller ships, and supporting the PLAN submarine force. It is also quite capable of making attacks on submarines using dipping sonar and torpedo[8], and on surface ships using the YJ-82 missile.

The Z-9C and the French AS 565 have become standard helicopters for PLAN surface ships. The Z-9C is an indigenous version of the AS 565, which is a multi-purpose medium-sized helicopter capable of ASW, SAR and striking surface targets. In addition to the purchase of Russian Sovremenny-class destroyers, the Ka-28 Helix was imported. It is vastly superior to the Z-9C and Z-8 in performance, and it is a new standard type for Chinese destroyers and frigates.

### Future

China's annual recruitment of naval pilots is currently underway. More than 4,500 candidates from 22 provinces, municipalities and autonomous regions across the country have passed the initial selection, doubling the number from last year on. Considering demand for new aircraft and more carrier pilots, the PLAN is intensifying its pilot recruitment campaign to meet the needs of its aircraft carriers. As China's aircraft carrier fleet expands and grows stronger, the PLAN's carrier-borne fighter force is further developing its combat capability and moving towards gaining full joint-operation capability. With the Liaoning and Shandong carriers going operational and more to follow, the PLAN's long-term goals and operational concept have profoundly changed. The Navy's modernization is speeding up the development of its aviation branch, which has become the center of attention in the military field.

*(1161 words)*

**Sources:**

1. https://news.cgtn.com/news/3d3d414d3341544d34457a6333566d54/index.html
2. http://www.china.org.cn/china/2018-09/17/content_63527323.htm

## Notes

1. ASW: Anti-submarine warfare (ASW) generally refers to the military action or task type of searching, detecting, driving, attacking and destroying submarines with various means and equipment. 反潜战

2. SAR: search and rescue, referring to search and rescue work carried out by a helicopter 搜救

3. double delta wing: (aircraft with) swept-back wings that give it a triangular appearance 三角翼（飞机）

4. AAM: air-to-air missile 空对空导弹

5. a nose-mounted radar: a device or system for determining the presence and location of an

object by measuring the direction and timing of radio waves in front of the aircraft 安装在机头的雷达，机头雷达

6. ship-borne helicopter: aircraft aboard a ship which are capable of hover, vertical flight, and horizontal flight in any direction 舰载直升机

7. towing mine clearance devices: a kind of mine sweeping system of removing all mines from a route or an area towed by ships or minesweeper helicopters 拖曳扫雷系统

8. dipping sonar and torpedo: an underwater sonar and torpedo suspended from the water by a shipboard helicopter. It is used to protect surface ships from being searched and tracked by enemy submarine sonar. 吊放声纳和鱼雷

| | |
|---|---|
| pertain [pəˈteɪn] | v. 关于；有关 |
| interdiction [ˌɪntərˈdɪkʃn] | n. 禁止，制止；封锁 |
| delta [ˈdeltə] | n.（河口的）三角洲 |
| dogfighter [ˈdɒgfaɪtə] | n. 格斗战机；夺取空中优势的战斗机 |
| indigenous [ɪnˈdɪdʒɪnəs] | adj. 土生土长的；本地的；根生土长 |
| interception [ˌɪntərˈsepʃn] | n. 拦截，截住；截断，截取；侦听，窃听 |
| in-flight [ˈɪnflaɪt] | adj. 飞行中发生的；飞行中进行的 |
| tanker [ˈtæŋkə] | n. 油轮；运油飞机；油槽车；坦克手 |
| variant [ˈveərɪənt] | n. 变体；变种；变型 |
| supersonic [sjuːpəˈsɒnɪk] | adj. [物] 超声的；超音速的 |
| batch [bætʃ] | n. 一批；一组；一群 |

## *Exercises*

### I. Comprehension

**Part A**   Questions

*Answer the following questions in accordance with the text.*

1. What is the current strength of the Naval Aviation Force?

2. What are the origins of the Naval Aviation?

3. What are the missions and tasks of the PLA Naval Aviation Force?

4. How many types of fighters are modified based on other nation's design?

5. What's the future trend of the Naval Aviation Force?

**Part B** Multiple Choices

*Choose the most appropriate answer from the given choices below each question in accordance with the text.*

1. When and where was the PLAN's aviation founded?

    A. On 26th April, 1949; in Guangzhou.

    B. On 6th September, 1952; in Beijing.

    C. On 11th November, 1949; in Shanghai.

    D. On 1st August, 1949; in Beijing.

2. Which one is wrong for the primary missions of the Naval Aviation Force?

    A. Providing fleet air defense for PLA surface combatants.

    B. Providing patrol and protection for aircraft carriers.

    C. Air patrols and defense of international waters .

    D. Air defense of the mainland's coastline.

3. What is the characteristic of the J-8 II?

    A. It can conduct high-altitude interceptions.

    B. It can perform vertical inflight refueling.

    C. It can operate amphibious warfare.

    D. It can use a longer range search radar.

4. What are the main helicopters operated by the Naval Aviation Force?

    A. Changhe Z-8.

    B. Harbin Z-9C.

    C. Russian Ka-28 Helix.

    D. All above.

5. What's the name of the largest helicopter built in China?

    A. H-6.

    B. J-15.

    C. Z-8.

    D. Z-9C.

## II. Translation

Part A   **Terms & Phrases**

*Translate the following terms or phrases from Chinese into English and vice versa.*

1. 独立团
2. 战略防御区
3. 垂直空中加油
4. 扫雷系统
5. 高空拦截
6. 防空覆盖
7. 主炮
8. 远程导弹
9. 三角翼
10. 水面战斗
11. Naval Aviation
12. SAR
13. ASW
14. SAM
15. AEM
16. air-to-ground attack
17. anti-ship missile
18. air interdiction
19. maritime patrol
20. weapons delivery capability

Part B   **Paragraph**

*Translate the following paragraph from English into Chinese.*

Following its founding in April 1949, the PLAN issued its first three-year plan. The portions pertaining to the creation of Naval Aviation Department included establishing three air divisions and three aviation schools, building two to three Naval Aviation airfields each in a strategic combat area and purchasing 360 aircraft and necessary support equipment from the Soviet Union.

## III. Reading Report

What have you learned after reading the text? Have you got a better understanding of Naval Aviation, its organization, and missions? Now write your reading report in no more than 150 words to generalize your achievement in text study.

# Text B
## A Glimpse of Aircraft Carrier

An aircraft carrier is a warship designed with a primary mission of launching and recovering aircraft, acting as a seagoing airbase. Aircraft carriers allow a naval force to project air power very far without having to depend on local bases for staging aircraft operations. They have evolved from wooden vessels, used to deploy a balloon into nuclear-powered warships that carry dozens of fixed-wing and rotary-wing aircraft. The carrier's mobility allows aircraft to be deployed ongoing or sudden conflicts. The aircraft battle group is routinely sent to international waters, and the aircraft that travel with the carrier are available to perform a variety of missions ranging from surveillance to strikes.

### Early Stage of Aircraft Carrier

In 1918, HMS Argus became the world's first carrier capable of launching and landing naval aircraft. She was a British aircraft carrier that served in the Royal Navy from 1918–1944. It was the world's first example of what is now the standard pattern of aircraft carrier, with a flush deck[1] enabling aircraft to take off and land. It also had the nickname "Ditty Box[2]" due to its similarity to the article of a sailor's kit.

In the mid-1920s, carrier evolution was well underway. Most early aircraft carriers were conversions of ships that had served as different types: cargo ship, cruiser, battlecruiser, or battleship.

During World War II, those ships became the backbones of the carrier forces of several countries' navies, known as fleet carriers. With the growth of air power as a significant factor in warfare, aircraft carriers were upgraded as carrier-launched aircraft characterized by superior flying range, flexibility and combat efficiency. Following the war, carrier operations continued to increase in size and importance. Supercarriers, the latest aircraft carriers, have become the **pinnacle** of carrier development. Most are powered by nuclear reactors and form the core of a fleet designed to operate far from home. Amphibious assault ships serve the purpose of carrying and landing Marines, and operate a large contingent of helicopters for their purpose. Also known as "commando carriers[3]" or "helicopter carriers", many amphibious assault ships have a secondary capability to operate V/STOL[4] aircraft.

Lacking the firepower of other warships, carriers by themselves are considered vulnerable to attack by other ships, aircraft, submarines, or missiles. Therefore, aircraft carriers are generally accompanied by a number of other ships, to provide protection for the relatively unwieldy carrier, to carry supplies, and to provide additional offensive capabilities. This is often termed a battle group or carrier group, sometimes a carrier battle group.

### Types of Aircraft Carriers

#### *Anti-submarine warfare carrier*

An ASW carrier (Anti-Submarine Warfare carrier) is a type of small aircraft carrier whose primary mission is to hunt and destroy submarines. This type of ship came into existence during the Cold War with the development of escort carriers used in the ASW role in the North Atlantic during World War II. After World War II, confrontation from the Soviet Union posed a serious naval threat to most western nations. By investing heavily in building attack submarines and missile-launching submarines, the Soviets ended the naval competition with triumph over western surface ship superiority. The only country currently building new ASW tough-deck helicopter-only ships is Japan. It terms this kind of vessels helicopter destroyer instead of ASW carrier.

#### *Light aircraft carrier*

A light aircraft carrier is smaller than a standard carrier. Different countries give their own definition of the type of aircraft. Generally a light carrier is only ½ to ⅔ the size of a full-sized or "fleet" carrier. In World War II, the United States Navy produced a number of light carriers by converting cruiser hulls, such as the Independence-class aircraft carriers[5]. Because of their sufficient fast speed, they are able to take part in fleet actions with larger carriers. The British light fleet carrier designed in 1942 was a scaled-down version of their Illustrious-class fleet carrier[6]. Although it was based on merchant standards, the design incorporated better water-tight subdivision[7].

#### *Supercarrier*

Supercarrier is an unofficial descriptive term for the largest type of aircraft carrier. This kind of carrier usually displaces 70,000 tons or more. In comparison, a few countries possess medium carriers, each with a tonnage of about 40,000 tons (such as Charles de Gaulle[8]), whereas a light carrier close to 20,000 tons is more typical. Supercarriers are the largest warships ever built. The first ship described by *The New York Times* as a supercarrier was HMS Ark Royal[9] built in 1938, with a length of 685ft and a displacement of 22,000 tons.

It was designed to carry 72 aircraft. The post-war standard for supercarriers was set by the USS United States and USS Forrestal. Nowadays, the US Gerald R. Ford-class of aircraft carriers will eventually replace the Nimitz-class. The Ford class looks similar in appearance, but it has involved some new technologies, such as EMALS, or **electromagnetic** aircraft launch system.

### *Escort carrier*

The escort aircraft carrier or escort carrier, also called a "jeep carrier[10]" or "baby flattop[11]" in the USN or "Woolworth Carrier" by the Royal Navy, was a small and slow type of aircraft carrier used by several countries in World War II. They were typically half the length and one-third the displacement of the larger fleet carriers. While they were slower, less armed and **armored**, and carried fewer planes, they were less expensive and could be built in less time. They were too slow to keep up with the main forces operating fleet carriers, cruisers and guided missile destroyers.

### Future of the Chinese Aircraft Carrier

In recent years, the US has put its Indo-Pacific strategy into effect and has treated China as a strategic rival, so maritime disputes and even **confrontation** between the two navies are mostly on the upward trend. The PLAN is shifting its focus from "offshore waters" to "high seas," by **implementing** a combined strategy of offshore defense and open-sea protection.

China's aircraft carriers will provide a strong support for "open-sea protection". No one can stop China from developing its sea power and going to the distant oceans. The PLAN aircraft carrier will certainly become a backbone of modern blue-water navy.

*(1011 words)*

### Sources:

1. http://militaryvetshop.com/History/aircraftCarriers.html（2021年3月访问）
2. https://chinapower.csis.org/china-carrier-type-002/#（2021年4月访问）

## Notes

1. flush deck: any continuous, unbroken deck from stem to stern on an aircraft carrier（航母的）平甲板
2. ditty box: a small box with a hinged lid and lock used by a crew member for personal

belongings（水手、渔民等）装针线等零星杂物的提箱

3. commando carrier: an aircraft carrier used to launch attack in a short period of time 突击型航母

4. V/STOL: vertical short takeoff and landing （飞机）短距离或垂直起降

5. Independence-class aircraft carriers: light carriers built for the United States Navy that served during World War II 独立级航母（美军在二战中大量服役的航空母舰）

6. Illustrious-class fleet carrier: aircraft carriers built by Great Britain and used by the Royal Navy during World War II 卓越级航母（英国海军无敌级航空母舰轻型舰中的代表）

7. water-tight subdivision: several watertight compartments partitioned by the bulkheads 水密分舱

8. Charles de Gaulle: the flagship of the French Navy and the largest European aircraft carrier. She is the tenth French aircraft carrier, but the first French nuclear-powered surface vessel. 戴高乐号航母。"戴高乐"号是法国海军第一艘核动力中型航空母舰，也是目前唯一一艘现役的航空母舰。它于1983年5月开工建造，1994年下水，2000年9月正式服役。

9. HMS Ark Royal：It was an aircraft carrier of the Royal Navy that served during the Second World War. 皇家"方舟"号航空母舰

10. jeep carrier: nickname of an antisubmarine escort carrier [美俚]护航反潜航（空）母（舰）

11. baby flattop: nickname of a light aircraft carrier [美俚]（由商船改装的）轻型（护航）航母

## *Word Bank*

| | |
|---|---|
| pinnacle [ˈpɪnəkəl] | *n.* 顶峰；顶点；极点 |
| vulnerable [ˈvʌlnərəbl] | *adj.* 易受伤的；脆弱的；敏感的 |
| unwieldy [ʌnˈwiːldɪ] | *adj.* 笨重的；不灵活的；庞大的 |
| subdivision [sʌbdɪˈvɪʒən] | *n.* 细分；一部 |
| displacement [dɪsˈpleɪsmənt] | *n.* 取代，位移；[船] 排水量 |
| electromagnetic [ɪˌlektrəʊmægˈnetɪk] | *adj.* 电磁的 |
| armor [ˈɑːmər] | *n.* 盔甲；装甲，防弹钢板；装甲部队，装甲车辆 |
| | *v.* 为……装甲；为……提供（感情等的）防御 |
| confrontation [ˌkɒnfrʌnˈteɪʃn] | *n.* 对抗；面对；对峙 |

implement [ˈɪmplɪmənt]　　　　　　*v.* 实施，执行；实现，使生效

　　　　　　　　　　　　　　　　*n.* 工具，器具；手段

## I. True or False

*Decide whether the following sentences are true or false in accordance with the text.*

1. An aircraft carrier is a warship designed with a primary mission of launching and recovering aircraft, acting as a seagoing airbase.

2. The aircraft that travel with the carrier are available to perform only military strikes.

3. HMS Argus was the world's first carrier served in the United States Navy.

4. Aircraft carriers were upgraded as carrier-launched aircraft characterized by superior flying range, flexibility and combat efficiency in World War II.

5. Amphibious assault ships, also known as "commando carriers" or "helicopter carriers", have a secondary capability to operate aircraft.

6. In World War II, the United States Navy produced a number of light carriers by converting merchant hulls.

7. Unlike escort carriers, light aircraft carriers had enough speed to take part in fleet actions with larger carriers.

8. The post-war standard for supercarriers was set by the USS United States.

9. The Ford class looks different in appearance, but it has involved some new technologies, such as EMALS, or electromagnetic aircraft launch system.

10. The PLAN is shifting its focus from "offshore waters" to "high seas," by implementing a combined strategy of offshore defense and open-sea protection.

## II. Word Match

*Match the words/terms/phrases in the left column with its appropriate correspondents in the right column.*

1. recovering aircraft　　　　　　　A. 轻型航母

2. project air power　　　　　　　　B. 近海水域

3. rotary wing aircraft　　　　　　　C. 力量投送

4. stage aircraft operations　　　　　D. 回收飞机

5. launch aircraft

6. nuclear reactor

7. a carrier battle group

8. light carrier

9. offshore waters

10. high seas

E. 公海

F. 核反应器

G. 旋转翼飞机

H. 实施飞机作战行动

I. 发射飞机

J. 航母战斗群

# Text C
## Shipborne Helicopters—The Cos Extended Arm

Helicopter, a fixed-wing aircraft[1] with one or more power-driven horizontal propellers or rotors that enable it to take off and land vertically, to move in any direction, or to remain stationary in the air. It is the most logical form of flight demanding challenge in flying, requiring more sophistication in structure, power, and control than conventional fixed-wing aircraft. So they are widely used to provide operational and logistical support for all kinds of ships.

### US SH-60

The Sikorsky SH-60 "Seahawk" is the navalized derivative of the ubiquitous land-based UH-60 "Black Hawk"-series transport helicopters[2]. The appearance of the UH-60 dates back to the 1970s. The UH-60 began to serve the United States Army in 1979. By comparison, the SH-60 has good over-water flying performance characteristics that are required of maritime aircraft. It involves the folding appendages (tail, horizontal stabilizer[3], collapsible main rotor) for onboard stowage, the strengthened understructures for shipborne landing and the specialized coatings used as protection against the corrosive effects[4] of the salty sea air. Until now, it has been a primary type of helicopter of the United States Navy.

The Navy SH-60 is different from the Army's UH-60 in that it has abandoned the left side sliding access door[5] for cabin entry/exit. Additionally, the SH-60 is fitted with high-power turboshaft engines and an electrically collapsible main rotor blade assembly for a more compact footprint aboard ships. The horizontal stabilizer is designed to fold when the vertical tail[6] unit swings over the portside of the tail wheel. The tail wheel structure serves the function of reducing the surface contact area aboard space-strapped ships and allowing the tail to hinge.

The Seahawk can be applied to undertaking a variety of critical missions, including replenishment at sea, search and rescue of drowned pilots and sailors, humanitarian relief[7], special forces insertion/extraction, MEDEVAC, cargo hauling, submarine/surface warship hunting, and mine warfare.

### US MH-60S

The multi-mission Sikorsky MH-60S Knighthawk helicopter entered service in February 2002. The US Navy possesses a total of 237 helicopters to carry out missions such as vertical replenishment[8], search and rescue, combat support, special warfare support and airborne mine

countermeasures.

It was originally designated CH-60S, as a substitute for the US Navy's Boeing CH-46D Sea Knight heavy-lift helicopters in the vertical replenishment role. The helicopter was redesignated MH-60S as a result of an expansion in mission requirements, including a range of additional combat support capabilities.

The MH-60 uses the baseline structure of the Black Hawk with Seahawk T-700-GE-401C engines, hover-in-flight refueling[9] and fuel dumping. It also has the Seahawk's rotor system and dynamics, including the automatic rotor blade folding system, rapid folding tail pylon, transmission and drive train with improved durability gearbox, rotor brake and automatic flight control computer. It uses the naval cockpit doors and the Seahawk rescue hoist for search and rescue missions.

The MH-60S based on "Black Hawk" airframe provides a larger two-door cabin for cargos and passengers. It retains the Black Hawk's provisions for mounting the external pylons to carry stores and equipment, providing the added capability to carry out a wide range of missions. It has the Black Hawk's 9,000lb external cargo hook, gunner's window, landing gear with tie-downs and wire strike protection, along with hover IR suppresser[10], automatic stabilization equipment and fuel cells.

The helicopter is designed in an air transport configuration that is easily modified with mission kits, for example, mine countermeasures systems[11] and combat search and rescue devices. The main cabin equipped with the air-condition system can accommodate up to 20 armed troops.

### PLAN Z-8

Between 1975 and 1977 the first batch of 12 or 13 French navalized Aerospatiale SA321 Super Frelon helicopters was delivered to China, which were two main variants used for Anti-Submarine Warfare (ASW) and Search and Rescue (SAR) operations. It was the first helicopters in China's inventory that were capable of taking off from and landing on the flight decks of warships. China acquired a production license for the Super Frelon helicopters, which were the locally produced Z-8.

The basic Z-8 is a land-or ship-based ASW or SAR helicopter. The ASW version is fitted with a surface-search radar, French HS-12 dipping sonar and sonobuoys. Also it carried a Whitehead A244S torpedo under the fuselage. It can also be equipped with YJ-81 and YJ-83K anti-ship missiles, as well as external pods with guns or unguided projectiles.

The Z-8 has three engines, two of which are fitted close to each other, while the third one is located behind the main rotor system. This kind of helicopter is powered by Chinese WZ-6 engines modeled on Turbomeca Turmo. Each engine drives a 6-blade main rotor to produce 1511 shaft horsepower (SHP). Additional fuel tank can be installed inside the cabin for extended range.

This helicopter was designed to operate in bad weather conditions. Its fuselage is like a boat, so it can land on water in case of emergency. In addition to carrying around three tons of cargo, it can accommodate up to 27 fully-armed troops or 15 stretchers. Passengers enter and leave the helicopter via sliding side doors or rear **ramp**.

### *PLAN Z-9C*

The Z-9C is a naval helicopter of Chinese origin. It is classified by the PLA Navy as an anti-submarine, anti-ship and SAR helicopter.

A roof-mounted FLIR sensor is of great aid to search and rescue operations and visual reconnaissance. The nose houses the KLC-1 radar, which is an X-band radar used for surface search. If it locates a surface target and transmits the information to a ship, then the ship can attack target with missiles such as YJ-83 beyond the radar horizon. In the anti-submarine role a dipping sonar is used to detect targets for torpedo attack.

The Z-9C is able to carry and launch two lightweight torpedoes, one on each side of the fuselage. As an anti-ship helicopter, the Z-9C, however, does not carry anti-ship missiles.

The Z-9C uses two turboshaft engines to power its main four-blade rotor and the tail rotor. Its maximum speed is over 300 km/h. It is used extensively by the Chinese navy, for example, various frigates and destroyers, because it is able to play an effective role in ASW.

*(1055 words)*

**Sources:**

1. https://www.airuniversity.af.edu/CASI/Display/Article/1400987/pla-naval-aviation-training-and-operations
2. http://www.military-today.com/helicopters/z8.htm
3. https://military.wikia.org/wiki/Harbin_Z-9

## Notes

1. fixed-wing aircraft: a fixed-wing aircraft is an aircraft, such as an aeroplane, which is capable of flight using wings that generate lift caused by the vehicle's forward airspeed and

the shape of the wings 固定翼飞机

2. transport helicopter: a helicopter used for transportation 运输直升机

3. horizontal stabilizer: the horizontal airfoil of an aircraft's tail assembly that is fixed and to which the elevator is hinged 水平安定面

4. corrosive effects: capable of destroying solid materials 腐蚀效应

5. sliding access door: a door opened or closed by a slide 滑动门

6. vertical tail: the vertical airfoil in the tail assembly of an aircraft 垂直尾翼, 直尾

7. humanitarian relief: Humanitarian relief is based on humanitarian to provide material or logistics support to the recipients. The main purpose is to save lives, relieve the unfortunate situation, and maintain human dignity. 人道主义救援

8. vertical replenishment: the use of a helicopter for the transfer of materiel to or from a ship 垂直补给

9. hover-in-flight refueling: helicopter or aircraft with vertical take-off and landing performance, stays above a certain place at a certain altitude for refueling （飞机）悬停空中加油

10. IR suppresser: infrared device, such as a resistor or grid, that is used in an electrical or electronic system to reduce unwanted currents 红外抑制器

11. mine countermeasures systems: systems used for preventing or reducing damage or danger from mines 反水雷系统

  **Word Bank**

| | |
|---|---|
| rotor [ˈrəʊtə] | *n.* [电][机][动力] 转子；水平旋翼；旋转体 |
| stationary [ˈsteɪʃənərɪ] | *adj.* 固定的；静止的；定居的；常备军的 *n.* 不动的人；驻军 |
| logistics [ləˈdʒɪstɪks] | *n.* [军] 后勤；后勤学 |
| logistical [ləˈdʒɪstɪkl] | *adj.* 后勤方面的 |
| ubiquitous [juˈbɪkwɪtəs] | *adj.* 普遍存在的；无所不在的 |
| appendage [əˈpendɪdʒ] | *n.* 附属物 [军] 附具，附件（同武器，船只或连带使用的器具，备用仪器） |
| stowage [ˈstəʊɪdʒ] | *n.* 装载；贮藏；贮藏舱 |
| coating [ˈkəʊtɪŋ] | *n.* 涂层；包覆层；保护层 |

turboshaft [ˈtɜːbəʊʃæft]        *n.* [机] 涡轮轴

hinge [hɪndʒ]                   *n.* 铰链，折叶；关键，转折点；枢要，
                                中枢

                                *v.* 用铰链连接

pylon [ˈpaɪlən]                 *n.* （机身下的）吊架；（机场）标塔；
                                （高压输电线的）桥塔

gearbox [ˈɡɪəbɒks]              *n.* 变速箱；齿轮箱

cockpit [ˈkɒkpɪt]               *n.* 驾驶员座舱；战场

sonobuoy [ˈsɒnəbɔɪ]             *n.* 声纳浮标

fuselage [ˈfjuːzɪlɑːʒ]          *n.* [航] 机身（飞机）

ramp [ræmp]                     *n.* 斜坡，坡道；敲诈

                                *v.* 蔓延；狂跳乱撞；敲诈；使有斜面

 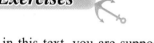

## Exercises

Based on what you have acquired in this text, you are supposed to conduct an online study to explore further into the relevant sphere. Comb and frame what you have found with an online study report in no less than 200 words. In addition, any assistant image, audio, video, or other first-hand material will be preferred when you present your report in class.

# Unit 5  Marine Corps

**Bridge-in**

*Answer the following questions in accordance with the microlesson "PLAN Marine Corps".*

1. Can you define the PLAN Marine Corps?

2. How much do you know about the training of the PLAN Marine Corps?

3. Can you list some of the non-traditional international security missions in which the PLAN Marine Corps is involved?

## Text A
## PLAN Marine Corps

The Marine Corps is the PLA Navy's rapid reaction force for amphibious assault operations and is being converted into a "multidimensional integrated combat force". The Marine Corps is a combined-arms force consisting of infantry, artillery, armour, engineering, communication, chemical defense, and reconnaissance troops. The primary missions or tasks include providing force projection from the sea, delivering combined-arms to seize or defend beachheads for landing operation, and participating in other land operations to support naval campaigns. Its other responsibilities involve training personnel, making plans and regulations, and developing tactics, techniques, and equipment used for amphibious landing forces.

### Brief History of the PLAN Marine Corps

The 1st Marine Regiment of the PLAN was established in 1953 and expanded into the first Marine Division in the following year. The division participated in the Yijiangshan Island campaign[1] and other island campaigns along the Chinese coast during the late 1950s. Because of the military reforms at that time, the marine units were disbanded and their personnel and equipment were transferred to the PLA Army. On May 5, 1980, the 1st Marine Brigade was reorganized in Ding'an County, Hainan, and later its headquarters was relocated in Zhanjiang, Guangdong province.

From then on, it was the Navy's only marine unit. In September 1997, a certain division of the Army, also stationed in the vicinity of Zhanjiang, was incorporated into the PLAN South Sea Fleet and redesignated as a marine brigade. It has contributed to strengthening the power of the Marine Corps.

Because of the military reform, the Marine Corps has been expanded and its combat capability is being further enhanced.

### Organizational Structure

The 2008 Chinese White Paper on National Defense provided a brief outline for the PLA marine organization: "The Marine Corps is organized into marine brigades, and mainly consists of marines, amphibious armored troops, artillery troops, engineers and amphibious reconnaissance troops".

Both marine brigades are almost the same in organizational structure but not in some specific equipment. The organizational structure as well as equipment includes:

- One or two amphibious armored battalions, equipped with amphibious tanks or assault vehicles.
- Four or five infantry battalions, equipped with amphibious infantry fighting vehicles (IFV) [2] or armored personnel carriers (APC) [3].
- An amphibious reconnaissance unit probably composed of a few "frogmen [4]" and special operations teams, including some female scouts.
- An artillery battalion fitted up with self-propelled guns.
- A missile battalion consisting of an anti-tank missile company and an anti-aircraft missile company armed with man-portable surface-to-air missiles.
- An engineering and chemical defense battalion.
- A guard and communications battalion.
- A maintenance battalion.

### Equipment

In the past 30 years, the 1st Marine Brigade has been equipped with different types of

armored personnel carriers/infantry fighting vehicles（APC/IFV）and tanks, for example, Type 77 APC, Type 63 APC , Type 86, and ZBD05 IFV, displayed in the 2009 military parade. The brigade was initially armed with Type 62 non-amphibious, light tanks (based on Type 59 main battle tank) and Type 63 light amphibious tanks. In 2000, Type 63A light amphibious tanks began to serve the PLA, the ZTD05 Amphibious Assault Vehicles followed later. Now new PLZ07 122mm self-propelled howitzers, in addition to Type-89 122mm self-propelled howitzers, have gone into service.

In recent years, Type 075 amphibious assault ships[5], also known as landing helicopter docks, have been launched. These warships with large flat flight decks can make vertical takeoff and landing. Helicopters transport troops much faster than any other transportation means.

Amphibious armored vehicles attached to a brigade of the PLA Navy Marine
Corps make their way to the beachhead during a maritime amphibious assault exercise
(source: http://en.people.cn/n3/2019/0905/c90000-9612400.html)

Training and Operations

Prior to 1999, Marine Corps officers were trained in Army academies. In 1999, the Guangzhou Naval Vessel Academy established the Naval Marine Corps Tactics Command Department[6], which was responsible for training junior (company-level) Marine Corps officers. Through those years, this academy had gone through changes and was renamed Naval Marine Academy in 2011. In 2017 the Naval Marine Academy was transformed into the PLAN marine corps training base.

The Marine Corps has several amphibious warfare training facilities located in several cities for physical, combat tactics, amphibious landing, and joint arms/services operation training and exercises. The marines' physical fitness regimen is extremely challenging, for instance, swimming five kilometers in full combat gear[7] within two and a half hours, running the same distance in 23 minutes, and performing 500 push-ups, sit-ups, and squats daily. Besides, all marines receive hand-to-hand combat[8] instruction.

Marine amphibious reconnaissance and special operations units must join in various kinds of training like parachute drop, helicopter assault, ground support, surface attack, and underwater operation, which will help them acquire "triphibious" capabilities. They also train for underwater demolition to clear obstacles from beaches.

The Marine Corps has conducted actual-combat training in cold regions since 2014. This kind of training covers a number of subjects, such as troops assembly, mobile entry and station keeping, technical search and tactical operation, operational grouping and deployment and actual-troop confrontation in offensive combats on rugged terrains under severe cold conditions.

In recent years, Marine Corps troops have undergone unprecedented tests in fast response and highly-intensive combat exercises carried out in different types of terrain. The exercises included simulated helicopter landing on a pirate ship in the South China Sea, fast boat landings on a hijacked ship in the Gulf of Aden, seizure of an island in the tropical zone by amphibious assault vehicles, infiltration operations on extremely cold grasslands and live ammunition practice in Djibouti. Besides, the Marine Corps sent a group of marines to compete in the International Army Games 2019 in Russia.

In the case of a typical amphibious landing operation, under the cover of initial firepower, marine scouts and engineers will first arrive at the landing zone by submarine and assault boat to clear mines and underwater obstacles. The scouts will provide the battlefield information for the landing ships. Supported by artillery firepower, anti-tank guided missile and air-defense missile attacks, more marines will take amphibious armored vehicles and air-cushion landing craft to land on the beach occupied by the enemy. At the same time, marine troops will be airlifted by helicopters to land on the zones behind the enemy line. After eliminating the guarding troops, the landing troops will establish a beachhead against the enemy's counterattacks before the heavily equipped ground forces arrive.

Apart from primary combat missions, the marines are always prepared to conduct a variety of non-traditional international security missions. In recent years, they have taken

part in several **disaster relief** operations. What is worth mentioning is that they rushed to the stricken area for rescue soon after a powerful earthquake happened in Wenchuan, Sichuan province in 2008. Marine frogmen also provided underwater security for the Olympics and other high-profile events. A Marine Corps special operation **detachment** has become an important part of each of the PLA Navy's task forces against pirates in the Gulf of Aden.

Marines participate in an actual-troop confrontation training at a training base in north China's Inner Mongolia Autonomous Region, March 13, 2014 (source: http://en.people.cn/102774/8565737.html)

*(1177 words)*

**Sources:**

1. http://www.jamestown.org/programs/chinabrief/single/?tx_ttnews%5Btt_news%5D= 37246&tx_ttnews%5BbackPid%5D=25&cHash=b238e0c56e （2020年4月访问）

2. http://www.scio.gov.cn/32618/Document/1545041/1545041.htm

3. http://eng.chinamil.com.cn/news-channels/2015-01/12/content_6305310.htm （2020年5月 访问）

**Notes**

1. the Yijiangshan Island campaign: a combined offensive operation launched in January 1955 by the East China Military Command to attack Yijiangshan Island in eastern Zhejiang province held by the Kuomintang troops 一江山岛战役

2. infantry fighting vehicle (IFV): an armoured personnel carrier, fitted with a gun or cannon, which is designed to transport a group of infantry men to the battlefield and provide them with fire support once they go into action 步兵战车

3. armored personnel carrier (APC): an armoured vehicle used to transport troops 装甲人员输送车

4. frogman: a person equipped with special clothing and breathing apparatus in order to operate underwater "蛙人"突击队

5. Type 075 amphibious assault ship: It has a large flat flight deck for vertical takeoff and landing helicopters to transport troops faster to go into action 075型两栖攻击舰

6. Naval Marine Corps Tactics Command Department: responsible for training junior (company-level) Marine Corps officers 海军陆战队战术指挥系

7. swimming five kilometers in full combat gear: swimming five kilometers with one's weapons 五公里武装泅渡

8. hand-to-hand combat: physical contact with one's opponent in fighting 肉搏战，徒手格斗；短兵相接

## Word Bank

| | |
|---|---|
| infantry[ˈɪnfəntrɪ] | n.（总称）步兵 |
| armour[ˈɑːmə] | n. 盔甲；装甲钢板；装甲部队 |
| disband[dɪsˈbænd] | v. 解散；裁减 |
| vicinity[vɪˈsɪnɪtɪ] | n. 邻近，附近 |
| self-propelled [self prəˈpeld] | adj. 自动推进的；（指火炮）自行的 |
| howitzer[ˈhaʊɪtsə] | n. 榴弹炮 |
| regimen[ˈredʒɪmən] | n.（以增进健康及强身为目的，在饮食、锻炼等方面规定的）生活制度 |
| squat[skwɒt] | n. 蹲坐 |
| demolition [demɒˈlɪʃn] | n. 破坏，毁坏；[军]爆破 |
| simulate [ˈsɪmjʊleɪt] | v. 模仿，模拟，仿真 |
| hijack [ˈhaɪdʒæk] | v. 拦路抢劫 |
| | n. 劫持，绑架；威逼 |
| infiltration [ˌɪnfɪlˈtreɪʃn] | n. 渗透；渗入 |
| airlift [eəlɪft] | v. & n. 空运；空运物资 |
| beachhead [biːtʃhed] | n. 滩头阵地；登陆场 |
| detachment [dɪˈtætʃmənt] | n. 分遣队；小分队 |
| anti-tank missile | [军]反坦克导弹 |
| anti-aircraft missile | [军]防空导弹 |

| surface-to-air missile | [军] 地对空导弹 |
| military parade | [军] 阅兵 |
| main battle tank | [军] 主战坦克 |
| flight deck | [军] 飞行甲板 |
| offensive combat | [军] 进攻战斗 |
| landing zone | [军] 着陆区 |
| assault boat | [军] 攻击艇 |
| landing ship | [军] 登陆舰 |
| landing craft | [军] 登陆艇 |
| disaster relief | [军] 救灾 |

## *Exercises*

## I. Comprehension

**Part A**  Questions

*Answer the following questions in accordance with the text.*

1. What are the components of the Marine Corps?

2. When did the first Marine Division come into being?

3. What do you know about the marine physical fitness regimen from the text?

4. Can you list some forms of the training of the marine amphibious reconnaissance and special operations units? What are they?

5. What subjects does the actual-combat cold region training cover?

**Part B**  Multiple Choices

*Choose the most appropriate answer from the given choices below each question in accordance with the text.*

1. Which of the following descriptions of PLAN marine corps is NOT true?

   A. The PLA formed the 1st Marine Regiment in 1953.

   B. The 1st Marine Brigade was reorganized in Ding'an County, Hainan.

   C. The marine units were disbanded during the military reforms in the early 1950s.

   D. The division participated in the Yijiangshan Island campaign and other island campaigns along the Chinese coast during the late 1950s.

2. When did the Type 63A light amphibious tanks enter the PLA?

    A. In 2009.

    B. Since 2005.

    C. In 2000.

    D. Since 1999.

3. The marine troops have undergone tests in all types of terrain in combat exercises. Which of the following exercise may not be included?

    A. Exercises simulated helicopter landing on a private ship in the South China Sea.

    B. Fast boat landings on a hijacked ship in the Gulf of Aden.

    C. Live ammunition practice in Djibouti.

    D. Competing in the International Army Games 2019 in Russia.

4. Which of the following descriptions of a typical amphibious landing operation is true?

    A. Under the cover of initial firepower, marine scouts and infantry troops will first arrive at the landing zone.

    B. The scouts will provide the battlefield information for the marine infantry troops.

    C. More marines will take amphibious armored vehicles and assault boats to land on enemy beach.

    D. Marine troops will be airlifted by helicopters to land on the zones behind the enemy line.

5. Which of the following missions are not conducted by PLAN marine corps?

    A. Disaster relief mission to Sichuan in 2008 after the Wenchuan earthquake.

    B. Underwater security for the Olympics and other high-profile events.

    C. Navy's anti-piracy task forces in the Gulf of Aden.

    D. Medical services for Djiboutian officers.

## II. Translation

**Part A** Terms & Phrases

*Translate the following terms or phrases from Chinese into English and vice versa.*

1. 快速反应部队        2. 两栖装甲部队

3. 装甲人员运输车       4. 反坦克导弹

5. 警通营             6. 火力支援

7. 登陆舰             8. 陆军学院

9. 两栖作战训练        10. 联合作战

11. 全副武装         12. 徒手格斗

13. 分遣队

14. 空运能力

15. 水下爆破

16. amphibious operation forces

17. combined-arms force

18. infantry fighting vehicles

19. self-propelled artillery battalion

20. surface-to-air missiles

21. light amphibious tanks

22. amphibious assault vehicles

23. sea transport

24. combat tactics

25. new recruit training

26. assault boats

27. landing zone

28. heavily equipped ground force

29. clear mines

30. air cushion landing crafts

## Part B    Paragraph

*Translate the following paragraph from English into Chinese.*

In the case of a typical amphibious landing operation, under the cover of initial firepower, marine scouts and engineers will first arrive at the landing zone by submarine and assault boat to clear mines and underwater obstacles. The scouts will provide the battlefield information for the landing ships. Supported by artillery firepower, anti-tank guided missile and air-defense missile attacks, more marines will take amphibious armored vehicles and air-cushion landing craft to land on the beach occupied by the enemy. At the same time, marine troops will be airlifted by helicopters to land on the zones behind the enemy line. After eliminating the guarding troops, the landing troops will establish a beachhead against the enemy's counterattacks before the heavily equipped ground forces arrive.

## III. Reading Report

What have you learned after reading the text? Have you obtained a better command of PLAN Marine Corps, its organization, and missions? Now create your reading report in no more than 150 words to generalize your achievement in text study.

# Text B
## The United States Marine Corps

The United States Marine Corps (USMC), serving as an amphibious force in readiness, is a branch of the United States armed forces responsible for providing power projection from the sea, utilizing the mobility of the US Navy to rapidly deliver combined-arms task forces to deal with global crises. Administratively, the Marine Corps is a component of the Department of the Navy, but it acts operationally as a separate branch of the military, often working closely with US naval forces for training, transportation, and logistic purposes. In terms of scale, it is the smallest of all the US armed forces under the leadership of the Department of Defense.

### History and Development

The Marine Corps originated from the "Continental Marines" established during the American Revolutionary War[1] by a resolution of the Continental Congress on November 10, 1775. The continental marines were first recruited at Tun Tavern in Philadelphia, Pennsylvania. They served as landing troops for the then Continental Navy. Samuel Nicholas, the first commissioned officer of the Continental Marines, acted as the senior Marine officer throughout the American Revolution. So far, he has been considered to be the first Marine Commandant.

The Continental Marines were disbanded at the end of the war in April 1783 but reorganized on July 11, 1798. For some reasons, Marine Corps worldwide celebrate November 10 as its birthday.

The Marine Corps played insignificant role in the American Civil War[2], but later become prominent due to its participation in small wars around the world. During the latter half of the 19th century, the Marines went into action in Korea, Cuba, the Philippines, etc. During the years before and after World War I, the Marines saw action in some of the Caribbean countries like Haiti and Nicaragua. Those actions were known as "The Banana Wars[3]", and the experience gained in counter-insurgency and guerrilla operations during that period was consolidated into the Small Wars Manual[4].

In World War II, the Marines played a central role in the Pacific War, and meanwhile the Marine Corps grew in strength, expanding from two brigades to two corps with six divisions and five air wings. The notable Navajo code[5] used for security communication by the US

Marines that was difficult to crack by the Imperial Japanese Army is widely regarded as one of the significant factors which led the former to win those battles.

Over the past several decades the US Marines has engaged in fighting against the forces of the Islamic State[6] in Iraq and Syria and the Taliban in Afghanistan. Now, the Corps is expanding its military presence in the Asia-Pacific region, by sending its units to northern Australia in **rotation** for joint training, moving some units to Guam[7], and regrading weapons and equipment for its units in the Western Pacific.

### Mission

Since it was set up in 1775, the Corps' role has been expanding gradually. As a branch of the US armed forces, the Marine Corps carries out its unique mission by promising it "shall, at any time, be liable to do duty in the forts and **garrisons** of the United States, on the seacoast, or any other duty on shore, as the President, at his discretion, shall direct." Acting in this special capacity, on the directives given by the President of the United States, the Marine Corps performs its duties and missions. Now it has developed into an all-purpose, fast-response task force, which can go wherever it is needed to **intervene** in emergencies.

### Chain of command

The Marine Corps has two parallel chains of command. One is the service chain and the other the operational chain. The service chain is from above to below, namely the president, the Secretary of Defense, the Secretary of the Navy and the **Commandant of the Marine Corps** (CMC). The CMC is the most senior Marine officer and also a member of the Joint Chiefs of Staff, responsible for organizing, recruiting, training, and equipping the Marine Corps so that it is ready for operation under the command of the Unified Combatant Commanders from the president to the Secretary of Defense to the commanders of **combatant commands**.

Under the "Forces for Unified Commands" memo, Marine Corps Forces are assigned to each of the regional unified command, at the direction of the Secretary of Defense with the approval of the President.

### Organization

The Marine Corps is organized into four principal subdivisions: headquarters of USMC, the Operating Forces, the Supporting Establishment and the Marine Forces' Reserve. It has three Marine Expeditionary Forces which are the principal and largest war fighting elements in the active force structure of the Marine Corps. A typical Marine Expeditionary Force (MEF) is composed of a Marine Division (MARDIV[8]), a Marine Air Wing and a Marine amphibious assault group.

There are three Marine divisions in the operating forces and one in the Reserve. The 1st Marine Division, stationed at Camp Pendleton, California, is subordinate to the 1st MEF and is the principal division of the USMC. The 2nd Marine Division is subordinate to the 2nd MEF and is stationed at Camp LeJeune, North Carolina. The third Marine Division is subordinate to the third MEF, stationed on Okinawa, Japan[9].

A Marine Expeditionary Brigade (MEB), usually led by a brigadier general, is built on a reinforced infantry regiment, an aircraft group and a service support group. Being able to be rapidly deployed and engaged in fighting by amphibious transport or air lift, MEB is the first echelon of a Marine Expeditionary Force.

The smallest task force unit of the US Marine Corps is the Marine Expeditionary Unit (MEU), which is commanded by a colonel and is routinely deployed with an Amphibious Readiness Group[10].

Marine Air Wing (MAW) is the largest Marine aviation organization of the MEF. Air combat elements are similarly grouped in the first, second and third Marine wings[11]. Each MAW has a unique organizational structure and is commanded by a brigadier general. And a Marine Aircraft Group (MAG) is the smallest aviation unit that is commanded by a colonel and aims at independent operations.

### Training

Every Marine is a rifleman. All Marines must receive strict training so that they can become qualified riflemen. The Marine Corps essentially functions as infantry.

The Marine Corps also has a martial arts training program. The program marks another major step in great efforts to bolster the valuable and matchless "warrior culture".

### Culture

The Marine's motto "Semper Fidelis[12]" means "Always faithful" in Latin. This motto is often called "Semper Fi!" for short. Until 1871 it was "First to Fight", a motto that still applies. It is also the name of the military marches of the Corps, composed by John Phillip Sousa. The colors of the Marine Corps are scarlet and gold, which appear on the flag of the United States Marine Corps and its emblem with patterns of eagle, globe, and anchor (EGA). The eagle represents the United States of America, the globe represents worldwide service, and the

anchor represents sea service and navy relations. The emblem, which began to be adopted in 1868, derives partially from ornaments worn by the Continental Marines and the British Royal Marines, but now it is topped with a ribbon with words "Semper Fidelis".

Marines wear swords in two different styles. The sword worn by a Marine Corps officer is called Mameluke sword[13]; a noncommissioned officer carries a sword in different style, similar to a Civil War cavalry sabre.

Also, marines have several interesting nicknames: "jarhead", "gyrene", "leatherneck", "Devil Dog[14]", "Angels of Death", "blackboots", "whitesleeves", to name but a few.

*(1252 words)*

**Sources:**

1. http://www.montney.com/marine/history.htm（2020年2月访问）
2. http://en.wikipedia.org/wiki/United States Marine Corps（2020年3月访问）
3. https://www.globalsecurity.org/military/agency/usmc/mchq.htm

## *Notes*

1. the American Revolutionary war (1775—1783): also known as the American War of Independence, which took place between the Kingdom of Great Britain and thirteen British colonies on the North American continent 美国独立战争

2. the American Civil War (1861—1865): the four-year war between the United States and 11 Southern states that seceded from the Union and formed the Confederate States of America 美国内战，又称南北战争

3. The Banana Wars: A series of recurring conflicts in Central America and the Caribbean, in which the United States was involved for economic protection. The repeated conflicts lasted from 1898 to 1934 when American troops withdrew from Haiti according to Treaty Paris. They were mainly caused by economic disputes, and the US took advantage of the issues for military intervention so as to protect its own world trade and political interests 香蕉战争

4. the Small Wars Manual: a document about the tactical and operational art and science of small wars or low-intensity conflicts. The manual has recorded some historical events from the Marine Corps' participation in "Banana Wars" to Afghan War 美国海军陆战队手册

5. Navajo code: the Codes designed by the US military during World War II that the Japanese army could never crack 纳瓦荷密码

6. the Islamic State: Full name is ISIS (Islamic State of Iraq and Syria), also known as ISIL (Islamic State of Iraq and the Levant), is a terrorist organization with a particularly violent ideology that calls itself a caliphate and claims religious authority over all Muslims. It was inspired by al-Qaida but later publicly expelled from it. 伊斯兰国（恐怖组织）

7. Guam: the largest and southernmost island in the Marianas which is administered as a territory of the United States; it was ceded by Spain to the United States in 1898 关岛（属于美国，位于西太平洋）

8. MARDIV: an abbreviation of "marine" and "division" 美国海军陆战队陆战师

9. The 1st Marine Division is stationed at Camp Pendleton, California, the 2nd at Camp LeJeune, North Carolina, while the third on Okinawa, Japan: 美国海军陆战队陆战1师驻扎在加利福尼亚州的彭德尔顿营，陆战2师驻扎在弗吉尼亚州诺福克勒兵营，陆战3师驻扎在日本冲绳岛

10. Amphibious Readiness Group(ARG): 两栖戒备大队

11. the first, second and third Marine wings: They are on active duty, respectively belonging to three Marine Expeditionary Forces（美）海军陆战第一、二、三飞行联队

12. Semper Fidelis: Latin expression which means always faithful（拉丁语，永远忠诚）海军陆战队的座右铭

13. Mameluke sword: the US marine corps officer sword 马穆鲁克剑，海军陆战队军官专用佩剑，也称"马穆鲁克弯刀"

14. Devil Dog: a slang used to refer to the marines in US ［美俚］美国海军陆战队员

## Word Bank

| | |
|---|---|
| insurgency [ɪnˈsɜːdʒənsɪ] | n. 起义；造反；暴动；叛乱 |
| guerrilla [gəˈrɪlə] | n. [古] 游击战；游击队 |
| consolidate [kənˈsɒlɪdeɪt] | v. 巩固，加强 |
| Navajo [ˈnævəhəʊ] | n. 纳瓦霍人（美国最大的印第安部落） |
| rotation [rəʊˈteɪʃn] | n. 轮流，循环；换班 |
| garrison [ˈgærɪsn] | n. 守备部队，卫戍部队；要塞，驻防区；<br>v. 守卫；驻防 |
| intervene [ˌɪntəˈviːn] | v. 介入，干涉，干预 |
| echelon [ˈeʃəlɒn] | n.（机构中的）等级，阶层；梯形，梯形编队<br>v. 排成梯队 |

| | |
|---|---|
| rifleman [ˈraɪflmən] | *n.* 步兵 |
| bolster [ˈbəʊlstə(r)] | *v.* 支持；支撑；鼓励；援助 |
| emblem [ˈembləm] | *n.* 象征；徽章；符号 |
| | *v.* 用象征表示 |
| cavalry [ˈkævəlrɪ] | *n.* 骑兵 |
| saber [ˈseɪbə] | *n./v.* (sabre in Ame. E)（用）马刀 |
| gyrene [dʒaɪəˈriːn] | *n.* [美俚] 海军陆战队员 |
| power projection | [军] 兵力投射 |
| task force | [军] 特混（特遣）部队；特混舰队 |
| commissioned officer | [军] 军官 |
| Commandant of the Marine Corps | [军] 海军陆战队司令 |
| combatant command | [军] 作战司令部 |
| brigadier general | [军] 准将 |

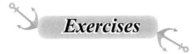

## Exercises

## I. True or False

*Decide whether the following sentences are true or false in accordance with the text.*

1. The Marines Corps is the smallest of the United States' armed forces in the Department of Defense.

2. The Marine Corps' birthday was on July 11, 1798.

3. The Marines played an important role in the American Civil War.

4. The USMC played a key role in the Pacific War in World War II.

5. The Commandant of the Marine Corps is the most senior Marine officer and also a member of the Joint Chiefs of Staff.

6. The second Marine Division is based out of Camp Pendleton, California.

7. Marine Air Wing (MAW) is the largest Marine aviation organization of the MEF.

8. The Marine Corps essentially functions as infantry.

9. The Marine's motto has always been "Semper Fidelis".

10. The emblem of the Marine adopted its present form in 1868.

## II. Word Match

*Match the words/terms/phrases in the left column with its appropriate correspondents in the right column.*

1. chain of command                   A. 战备

2. CMC                               B. 指挥系统

3. task force                       C. （美）海军陆战队司令

4. Department of the Navy       D. 海军部

5. air wing                          E. 混编部队

6. landing force                   F. 兵力投送

7. power projection              G. 两栖战备群

8. readiness                        H. 飞行联队

9. noncommissioned officer      I. 登陆部队

10. amphibious readiness group    J. 士官

## Text C
## Marine Expeditionary Unit

A Marine Expeditionary Unit (MEU[1]), formerly called Marine Amphibious Unit (MAU), is the smallest Marine air-ground task force (MAGTF[2]) in the United States Fleet Marine Force. Each MEU is an expeditionary quick-reaction force, deployed and ready for immediate response to any crisis.

### Introduction

The MEU is a basic unit of the US Fleet Marine force. It comprises a reinforced Marine infantry battalion, an air-combat helicopter squadron, a battalion-sized logistics combat element, and a command element. A typical MEU which has approximately 2,200 Marines and sailors is usually onboard an amphibious assault ship and commanded by a colonel. Currently a MEU is responsible for taking its Marines and equipment board amphibious warfare ships of an Expeditionary Strike Group (ESG[3]) including escort ships and submarines to protect them from air, surface, and submarine threats. For further protection and strong air support, such an ESG is often deployed along with one or more carrier battle groups.

The MEU is unique because its air and ground combat elements are combined with a logistics combat element under one commander; other services do not unite the command of air and ground forces until much higher command levels.

The concept of an air-ground task force concept means exploiting the combat power inherent in air and ground assets by closely integrating them into a single force. The MEU makes full use of all the supplies and logistical support it takes with itself to sustain itself for quick accomplishment of operational mission or to pave the way for follow-up forces. This self-sustaining capability gives the MEU more flexibility in the disposition of forces for operations, and allows it to initiate operations sooner, depending on its own logistical support, without having to wait for other logistical support. US Navy amphibious assault ships are able to deploy MEUs to any seabase around the globe and even at short notice.

### The number of MEUs and their deployment

There are 7 standing MEUs altogether: the 11th, 15th, 16th, 22th, 24th, 26th and 31st MEU, which are subordinate to three Marine Expeditionary Forces respectively.

West Coast MEUs (the 11th, 15th and 16th MEU, headquartered at the Marine Corps Base Camp Pendleton, California) are attached to the first Marine Expeditionary Force. Their main area of operation includes the western Pacific and Indian ocean as well as the Persian Gulf. East Coast MEUs (the 22th, 24th and 26th MEU, headquartered at the Marine Corps Base Camp Lejeune, North Carolina) are subordinate to the second Marine Expeditionary Force, maintaining a military presence in the Atlantic Ocean and Mediterranean Sea. The 31st MEU, also known as Japan MEU, is the only permanently forward-deployed, maintaining a military presence in the Pacific Ocean as part of the third Marine Expeditionary Force. It is headquartered at the Marine Corps Base Camp Smedley D. Butler, Okinawa, Japan.

### Elements

Usually a MEU breaks up into four elements: command element, ground combat element, aviation combat element and logistics combat element.

The command element (CE[4]), composed of the MEU commander and his staff, has operational command and control of the other three elements. It includes special detachments engaging in naval fight and reconnaissance and surveillance, special communications and radio reconnaissance, signal intelligence (SIGINT), electronic warfare, intelligence and counterintelligence and public affairs. It has a total strength of about 200.

The ground combat element (GCE[5]) is based on the battalion landing team (BLT), an infantry battalion reinforced with an artillery battery, amphibious assault vehicle platoon, combat engineer platoon, light armored reconnaissance company, tank platoon, reconnaissance platoon, and other units. It has a total strength of about 1,100 members.

The Maritime Special Purpose Force consists of four basic elements: the assault platoon (a direct action platoon from Force Recon[6]), security platoon (an infantry platoon selected from the battalion landing team), reconnaissance and surveillance platoon, and a headquarters element. It has a total strength of about 350.

The aviation combat element (ACE[7]) is a marine composite unit (reinforced) composed of a medium or heavy helicopter squadron equipped with three different types of helicopters, a detachment with amphibious flight-deck-capable jets, and a marine air control detachment responsible for air traffic control, air support control, and anti-aircraft defense.

The logistics combat element (LCE[8]) (formerly combat service support element, or CSSE) is based on the MEU combat logistics battalion (CLB) (formerly MEU service support group, or MSSG). It has necessary logistics supply and equipment sufficient for the MEU to support

and sustain itself for up to 30 days in an austere expeditionary environment. In addition to the logistics specialists, it has some personnel responsible for service support, medical and dental service, intermediate maintenance, intermediate supply, transportation management, explosive ordnance disposal, utilities management and distribution, bulk fuel storage, internal communication, and technical service. The LCE has a strength of nearly 300.

Recently, MEUs of expeditionary strike groups (ESG) have been deployed in the Mediterranean, the Western Pacific, and periodically, the Atlantic and Indian Oceans. An ESG is composed of three amphibious ships that embark the necessary troops and equipment and are escorted by a guided missile cruiser (CG) and guided missile destroyers (DDG) and submarines (SSN).

Before ESG were established, MEUs, as part of an amphibious readiness group (ARG) were deployed where they were needed.

### The MEU Cycle[9]

MEUs act on a fifteen-month cycle: a nine-month stay stateside (including six months for training), and a six-month deployment aboard ships. This working cycle ensures that at least two of the seven MEUs can be deployed forward at one time. It can be divided into three stages: an interim or build up period, a pre-deployment training period, also called work-up period and a deployment period.

In the interim or build-up period, the MEU assigns training tasks to its major subordinate elements (MSEs) and provides a chance for its command element to rotate and select personnel and make plans for the addition of newly-assigned MSEs and "work-up" training. In the pre-deployment training, the MSEs of the MEU, must receive a six-month various rigorous training. In the deployment period, the MEUs must be well prepared for deployment to any place around world to respond to any sudden serious event.

The training done during the work-up period aims to develop combat and noncombat skills, which include: urban sniping, mechanized and motorized raid, non-combatant evacuation, humanitarian assistance, casualty evacuation, scout activity, jungle and/ or mountain warfare, riot control operations. This kind of training is often referred to as "crawl, walk, run".

What is worthy of note is that during the work-up period, marines must fulfill their training tasks, such as Amphibious Squadron – MEU Integration Training (PMINT[10]), Realistic Urban Training exercise (RUT[11]) which was once called Training in an Urban Environment

Exercise (TRUEX), Expeditionary Strike Group Exercise (ESGEX[12]), Special Operations Capable Certification Exercise (CERTEX or SOCCEX[13]). Prior to deployment, the MEU receives certification as "special operations capable" or "MEU(SOC)" for short.

After the work-up period is ended, the MEU will be deployed to operate for six months under the leadership of regional combatant commanders. During this period of time, the MEU is a forward-deployed, self-sustaining force that the combatant commanders can direct to accomplish a variety of special operations and conventional missions, such as amphibious assaults and raids, tactical recovery of aircraft and personnel (TRAP[14]), humanitarian assistance operation/disaster relief (HAO/DR), noncombatant evacuation operation (NEO[15]) and security operation.

*(1220 words)*

## Sources:

https://military.wikia.org/wiki/Marine_expeditionary_unit（2020年3月访问）

# Notes

1. MEU: (military, US) Marine Expeditionary Unit（美）海军陆战队远征分队

2. MAGTF: (US) Marine Air-ground Task Force. It is a balanced air-ground, combined arms task organization of Marine Corps forces under a single commander that is required to accomplish a specific mission. 海军陆战队陆空特遣队

3. ESG: Expeditionary Strike Group, sometimes called an Expeditionary Strike Force. It is an improved amphibious ready group with the ability to strike targets over a greater range of the force. 远征打击群

4. CE: the Command Element 指挥单元，指挥分队

5. GCE: the Ground Combat Element 地面战队单元，陆战分队

6. Force Recon (FR): armed force of the United States Marine Corps with special operations capable Forces (SOC). Its full name is the US Marine Corps Expeditionary Force Reconnaissance unit. It was founded on June 19, 1957. It provides military intelligence and operational support to the command unit of Marine Air-Ground Task Force (MAGTF). 美国海军陆战队直属侦察连/强侦连

7. ACE: the Aviation Combat Element 空中战斗单元，空战分队

8. LCE: the Logistics Combat Element which used to be the Combat Service Support

Element or CSSE 后勤保障单元，后勤保障分队

9. the MEU Cycle: the pattern of rotation which aims to ensure that at least two of the seven MEUs are deployed forward at any one time. The MEU usually rotates in a 15-month cycle. 远征队兵力轮转/循环

10. PMINT: the acronym for Amphibious Squadron—MEU Integration Training 远征队与两栖中队的集成训练

11. RUT: Realistic Urban Training exercise. It was formerly called Training in an Urban Environment Exercise (TRUEX). 城市环境作战训练

12. ESGEX: Expeditionary Strike Group Exercise, which is an integrated training of the MEU with the ESG 远征队与远征打击群的合成训练

13. CERTEX or SOCCEX: Special Operations Capable Certification Exercise MEU. 认证演习

14. TRAP: acronym for Tactical Recovery of Aircraft and Personnel 飞机和人员的战术救援

15. NEO: noncombatant evacuation operations 非战斗人员撤离行动

## Word Bank

| | |
|---|---|
| self-sustain [selfˌsəˈsteɪn] | v. 自我维持；自给自足 |
| disposition [ˌdɪspəˈzɪʃn] | n. [军] 部署，配置 |
| seabase [səˈbeɪs] | n. 海上基地 |
| | v. 建海上基地 |
| counterintelligence [ˈkaʊntərɪnˌtelɪdʒəns] | n. 反情报 |
| composite [ˈkɒmpəzɪt] | adj. 混合成的，综合成的 |
| | n. 合成物，混合物 |
| austere [ɒˈstɪə(r)] | adj. 严峻的，严厉的 |
| ordnance [ˈɔːdnəns] | n. 军械（如弹药、军车等） |
| stateside [ˈsteɪtsaɪd] | adj. 美国的，美国本土的 |
| | adv. 在美国 |
| interim [ˈɪntərɪm] | adj. 暂时的，临时的；期中的 |
| | n. 间歇，过渡期间；临时协定 |
| snipe [ˈsnaɪp] | v. 狙击 |
| non-combatant [ˌnɒnkəmˈbætənt] | n. 非战斗人员 |
| combat power | [军] 战斗力 |

| | |
|---|---|
| area of operation | [军] 作战地域 |
| radio reconnaissance | [军] 无线电侦察 |
| the Maritime Special Purpose Force | 海上特种用途部队 |
| bulk fuel | 散装燃料 |
| casualty evacuation | 伤员后送 |
| jungle/mountain warfare | [军] 丛林战/山地战 |
| riot control | 防暴，暴乱控制，反暴乱 |

## Exercises

Based on what you have acquired in this text, you are supposed to conduct an online study to explore further into the relevant sphere. Comb and frame what you have found with an online study report in no less than 200 words. In addition, any assistant image, audio, video, or other first-hand material will be preferred when you present your report in class.

# Unit 6  Logistics

**Bridge-in**

*Answer the following questions in accordance with the microlesson "The Super Supply Ship in PLAN".*

1. What is the significance of the Type-901 class in PLAN?
2. Can you introduce its specification in English?
3. What are the advantages of Type-901 compared with other supply ships?

## Text A
## PLA Logistic Supply and Support

Naval logistics is very important to naval forces at sea whether in peace or war because they need to provide essential goods and services to ensure that Naval ships and crews are combat-ready. To update its logistical supply and support, the PLA Navy must make great efforts to add combat-capable **replenishment** ships, build sea lanes in critical waters and secure the supply of fuel, munitions, and repair parts in distant maritime environments.

### Modernizing the Naval Logistic System

It's vital to optimize logistical service and improve maritime integrated support capabilities. For this purpose, the Navy has established a logistical support system which includes the shore-based logistical support used as the foundation and the sea-based logistical support as the **mainstay**. Also, it is stepping up the building of ship bases, **berths**, supply points, docks and airfields. The shore-based support system is responsible for supplying daily necessities, weapons and equipment, especially in wartime. The Navy already had some new-type large integrated supply ships, one hospital ship and ambulance helicopters, and succeeded in developing various types of maritime support equipment and a number of key technologies. All this has greatly promoted the modernization of the maritime support force.

### The PLA Joint Logistic Support Force

The Chinese People's Liberation Army Joint Logistic Support Force (PLAJLSF[1]) was set up in September 2016. On October 1st, 2019, the PLAJLSF made its **debut** in a parade at Tian An Men Square in Beijing marking the 70th anniversary of the founding of the People's Republic of China.

The PLAJLSF comprises warehousing support forces[2], medical service units and transportation troops. Its establishment marks a revolutionary leap in the reform of the PLA.

It owns Wuhan Joint Logistic Support Base and five joint logistic support centers, namely Wuxi Joint Logistic Support Center, Guilin Joint Logistic Support Center, Xining Joint Logistic Support Center, Shenyang Joint Logistic Support Center and Zhengzhou Joint Logistic Support Center.

The establishment of the joint logistic support base and centers is a major strategic measure to deepen the reform of the command system of China's military and construct a modern joint logistic support system with Chinese military characteristics, which is of great and far-reaching significance to building the Chinese military into a first-class army worldwide and winning local modernized wars.

### The PLA Joint Logistic Support Force's Participation in Fighting COVID-19

Since the outbreak of the COVID-19, the Central Military Commission of the CPC has **dispatched** more than 4,000 medical personnel in three batches from multiple military medical units of the Army, Navy, Air Force, Rocket Force, Joint Logistic Support Force and Armed Police to aid Wuhan in Hubei Province, a city hit hardest by the COVID-19 **pandemic**, starting in January 24.

The PLAJLSF has since gone all out for materials urgently needed in the fight against the novel coronavirus pandemic.

In response to the COVID-19, the force immediately sent its purchasers to markets to buy urgently needed materials.

The purchasers asked suppliers to start and expand production as soon as possible and also requested the customs and the transport sector across China to speed up the import and transportation of anti-pandemic and medical materials through simplification of procedures

and formalities.

Vpon finishing the purchase, the PLAJLSF set up a steady supply chain to provide those materials for medics involved in a fight against the highly contagious pneumonia linked to the new coronavirus.

The PLA has fully displayed its quick-reaction and powerful logistical and transportation capabilities of dealing with the COVID-19 crisis in Hubei. Its great efforts can, to a considerable degree, reflect China's latest comprehensive military capability.

### Type-901 Replenishment Ship

The PLA Navy has the largest replenishment ship to accompany CNS[3] Liaoning carrier battle group to seas and oceans.

The CNS Hulun Lake NO.965, the first of the Type-901, which was built by Guangzhou Shipyard International Corp.[4] under China State Shipbuilding Corp[5], has been in commission.

The Hulun Lake is a new-generation, world-class comprehensive supply ship designed by Chinese engineers. Because of its multiple replenishment means and large resupply capacity, it can replenish a carrier battle group or a long-range task force with sufficient supplies.

This state-of-the-art ship demonstrates that China has the capability of designing and manufacturing large replenishment vessels and advanced marine replenishment equipment. This also marks a milestone in the Navy's long-distance logistics support capability.

The ship has a displacement of more than 45,000 tons—almost twice as much as the Type-903, the current pillar of the Navy's replenishment force. Its maximum speed is about 25 knots.

In addition, the PLA Navy has 16 smaller replenishment ships. The largest is the 37,000-ton CNS Qinghai Lake, the only one in the Type-908, which was built in Ukraine as a tanker. It was purchased and refit by China Navy in the early 1990s. Compared with that of the Hulun Lake, the speed of all other replenishment ships is slow, so none of them is not available for service in a fast-moving carrier battle group. Moreover, their supply-loading capacity is not big enough to meet the needs of a carrier group.

However, a large replenishment ship is essential to a carrier battle group for long-distance navigation. It is able to sail fast to follow other combat vessels and capable of carrying sufficient ammunition, fuel and living necessities to support a long-duration operation at sea. By comparison, a smaller ship moves slower and cannot carry enough supplies for a carrier battle group. Ships of the Type-901 are especially important to the PLA Navy that lacks overseas bases. Now, the Type-901 ship Hulun Lake can support a carrier battle group to engage in operations at sea with no need to return to its home port for resupply.

### The PLA Djibouti Logistics Support Base

The PLA Navy Djibouti Logistics Support Base[7] was put into service in August, 2017. It is located in the port city on the Gulf of Aden. It is a product of friendly consultation and cooperation between the governments of China and Djibouti, which is in the interests of both countries.

The base can not only provide material support for the Chinese surface ships to carry out escorting, peacekeeping and humanitarian missions in Africa and western Asia, but also help improve the PLA Navy capabilities in terms of international military cooperation, joint exercises, emergency evacuation and overseas rescue. Furthermore, the base is playing an important role in safeguarding the safety of international strategic maritime passages to other countries.

Since the beginning of its use, the base has provided supplies and equipment for several escort task groups, offered medical service to officers and sailors on board, conducted joint medical exercises with foreign military medical units, and donated teaching aids to local schools.

*(1106 words)*

*Notes*

1. PLAJLSF: People's Liberation Army Joint Logistic Support Force 中国人民解放军联合保障部队

2. warehousing support forces: responsible for supplying or stocking military materiel 仓储部队

3. CNS：Chinese Naval Ship 中国海军舰艇

4. Guangzhou Shipyard International Corp.: affiliated with China State Shipbuilding Corporation Group (CSSC). It is one of the most modern and biggest shipbuilding and repairing companies in the southern part of China. 广州广船国际股份有限公司

5. China State Shipbuilding Corp: a state-owned conglomerate of 58 enterprises engaged in shipbuilding, ship-repair, shipboard equipment manufacturing, marine design and research 中国船舶工业集团有限公司

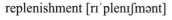

# Word Bank

| | |
|---|---|
| replenishment [rɪˈplenɪʃmənt] | n. 补充；充满 |
| mainstay [ˈmeɪnsteɪ] | n. 支柱；中流砥柱 |
| berth [bɜːθ] | v. （使船）停泊；靠码头 |
| debut [ˈdebjuː] | n. 初次登台；开张 |
| | v. 初次登台 |
| dispatch [dɪˈspætʃ] | v. 派遣，发送；迅速处理 |
| pandemic [pænˈdemɪk] | n.（全国或全球性）流行病，瘟疫 |
| contagious [kənˈteɪdʒəs] | adj. 感染性的；会蔓延的 |
| pneumonia [njuːˈməʊnɪə] | n. 肺炎 |
| tanker [ˈtæŋkə(r)] | n. 油轮；运油飞机 |
| ammunition [ˌæmjʊˈnɪʃn] | n. 弹药；军火 |

# Exercises

## I. Comprehension

**Part A  Questions**

*Answer the following questions in accordance with the text.*

1. What has PLA Navy done to build an integrated logistic support system?

2. What is the significance of the establishment of PLA Joint Logistic Support Force?

3. What role has PLAJLSF played in fighting COVID-19 epidemic?

4. What are the specifications for Hulun Lake?

5. What is the significance of the PLA Djibouti Logistics Support Base?

**Part B  Multiple Choices**

*Choose the most appropriate answer from the given choices below each question in accordance with the text.*

1. Which one is not a modernizing element for PLAN based on text A?

   A. ship bases and berths

   B. shore-based logistical support

C. hospital ships and supply points

D. docks and airfields

2. The PLA Joint Logistic Support Base is located in _____.

A. Zhengzhou

B. Wuhan

C. Xining

D. Guiling

3. Which one of the following is a wrong specification for Hulun Lake?

A. hull NO. 965

B. displacement of 45,000 metric tons

C. maximum speed 25 knots

D. type-903

4. The PLA Djibouti Support Base entered service in _____.

A. 2015

B. 2016

C. 2017

D. 2018

5. Which statements are correct based on text A?

1. In order to curb COVID-19, PLAJLSF purchased medical aids through simplified procedures.

2. Building PLAJLSF is a crucial step to have a first-class Navy for PLA.

3. With the active service of CNS Hulun Lake, PLAN is able to sail further into Oceans.

4. PLA Djibouti LSB is established in the interests of the two countries.

A. 1, 2

B. 2, 3

C. 2, 3, 4

D. 1, 2, 3, 4

## II. Translation

**Part A** Terms & Phrases

*Translate the following terms or phrases from Chinese into English and vice versa.*

1. 补给舰　　　　　　　　　　　2. 联合演习

3. 人道主义任务　　　　　　　　4. 紧急撤退

5. 火箭军

6. 亮相

7. 医疗船

8. 设备维护

9. 武警

10. 岸基后勤保障

11. far-reaching significance

12. automotive troops

13. prepositional stock piles

14. warehousing support forces

15. escort task force

16. tanker

17. international strategic maritime passages

18. long-duration operation

19. overseas rescue

20. long-range task force

## Part B　Paragraph

*Translate the following paragraph from English into Chinese.*

In addition, the PLA Navy has 16 smaller replenishment ships. The largest is the 37,000-ton CNS Qinghai Lake, the only one in the Type-908, which was built in Ukraine as a tanker. It was purchased and refit by China Navy in the early 1990s. Compared with that of the Hulun Lake, the speed of all other replenishment ships is slow, so none of them is not available for service in a fast-moving carrier battle group. Moreover, their supply-loading capacity is not big enough to meet the needs of a carrier group.

## III. Reading Report

What efforts has the PLAN made to build a comprehensive logistics support system? After reading the text, you are supposed to summarize the main points in no more than 120 words.

# Text B
# The US Naval Logistics

In terms of military science, maintaining a country's supply lines while **disrupting** those of hostile country is a crucial element of military strategy. In other words, maritime logistics is extremely important to a nation and its armed forces in wartime. If they cannot get logistics supply in time, the fighting forces will not win a war. The defeat of the British in the American War of Independence and the defeat of the Axis[1] in the African **theatre** during World War II are typical examples. Maritime logistics encompasses naval logistics plus the movement of commodities across the seas to sustain the armed forces, including merchant shipping, manpower, port facilities and so on.

### Naval Logistics

The US Navy has always paid much attention to its naval logistics, which is vital for its naval forces. A strong naval force which carries out tasks such as **deterrence**, sea fight, and other operations cannot do without naval logistics. Naval logistics refers to two levels. At the tactical level, it deals with the readiness of combat forces to fight. Therefore, the responsibility for overall logistics status lies with command, that is, the commanding officer of a ship of aircraft squadron, or the commander of a naval task force. At the theatre level, it includes the entire infrastructure of command and control (C2), the transportation network, stock points, storage, and production that provide logistical support for operating naval forces at locations required to execute a strategic plan.

Naval logistics plays a vital role in sustaining US naval forces whether in peace or war. It can ensure that naval forces are able to maintain continuous forward presence, conduct routine patrols, perform deterrent operations, and quickly respond to any crisis in various complex maritime environments.

With the support of naval logistics, the US navy is capable of fulfilling daily tasks and missions. Its **credibility** hinges on the capability of effective logistic support for the naval forces in peace or war. Such support comes from a multitude of sources and is essential to the naval forces combat readiness and operations, which is an important factor generally recognized and taken seriously by other navies.

Daily missions require US naval forces to operate in the oceans and the **littorals** of

other countries. Naval logistics also can ensure that the expeditionary, naval forces carry out complex missions around the world to maintain the national interests and accomplish their objectives. To sustain the striking force of the Navy and Marine Corps, powerful logistic support is essential, that is to say, a reliable support system needs to be established that includes stock points, logistic support ships, advanced supply bases, airlift, and sealift.

Sustained forward-deployed operations allow the US sea power to engage in regional coalition and collective-security efforts. Once a major conflict breaks out, it can be dealt with by joint and multinational forces. Therefore, the naval logistic structure needs to be designed to provide support to them. Of course, the US naval forces also benefit from the mature logistic infrastructure in the theatre, for example, getting additional support from multinational partners and host nations. Wherever they are deployed, the naval forces can be given logistic support immediately.

Naval logistic operations are conducted much the same in peace as they are in war. The major differences in war are that there will be an increase in the magnitude of personnel-support functions and the quantity of materiel and supplies needed and the requirements of corresponding airlift and sealift, and that the logistical support systems may be subjected to disruption by the enemy and the fog (friction and uncertainty) of war resulting in erroneous assumptions and deficient planning.

**NAVAL LOGISTICS**

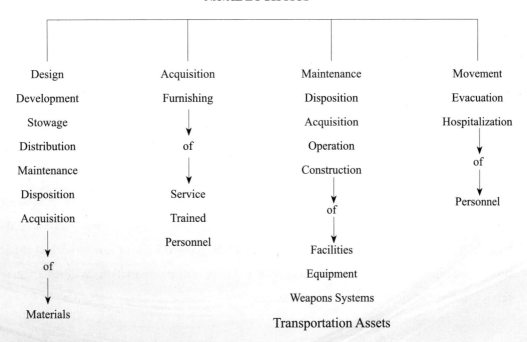

In peace or war, the purpose of naval logistics is to provide logistical support for naval forces anywhere and anytime and keep them in operational readiness. In peace, operational readiness needs getting everything ready for a possible conflict or war. In war, operational readiness means getting ready to fight.

### Levels of Logistic Support

Logistic support is provided at the strategic, operational and tactical levels, and involves some interrelated and overlapping functions and capabilities.

Strategic logistics encompasses the nation's ability to deploy and sustain its operating forces according to the national military strategy. It refers to requirements determination, personnel recruiting and training stations, acquisition, management of airlift and sealift for strategic mobility, and support of forces operating in distant theaters. It also includes the role of prepositioned equipment and materiel—both afloat and ashore—and the nation's ability to maintain the required support levels for operations of short or long. Long-term sustainment is tied directly to the foundation of the national economy, which refers to many areas such as industry (including military industry), agriculture, communications and transport, and health services.

Operational logistics involves coordinating and providing logistic resources for intratheater operating forces, which are commanded by the unified combatant commanders[2] and the service component commanders[3].

Tactical logistics focuses on planning and supporting the combat units of a task force or battle group. The tactical commander of logistics at the tactical level is responsible for dealing with resources which are made available at the operational level. Navy tactical logistics encompasses the logistic support for a carrier battle group, amphibious readiness group and other naval elements ashore, from both afloat platforms—including the Combat Logistics Force[4]—and shore-based logistic support facilities.

The logistic support at three levels depends on manufacturers, training facilities, and depots, and also on trained personnel, transportation facilities, and services support systems. To sum up, the interrelated strategic, operational and tactical logistics can guarantee the continuity of logistic support, which means providing the US naval forces with constant flow of supplies, ammunition, fuel, maintenance equipment, transportation facilities, medical service, combat engineer and personnel transport.

### Principles of Logistics

● **Responsiveness**. Providing the right support at the right time at the right place. This is the most important of all the principles of logistics. To Ensure that logistic resources can responsively meet the operational needs, emphasis shall be first put on logistic planning. Such planning requires to be made by the commanders and planners and also to be implemented by the operations support officers and those responsible for providing logistic support.

● Simplification. Avoiding unnecessary complexity in preparing, planning and conducting logistic operations. It is never easy to provide logistic support smoothly and safely, but the full use of basic standard support systems according to the established logistic plans usually stands a good chance for success. Following the mission-oriented logistic support concept and standardized procedures, the operational commanders can simplify the complicated operation flow of logistic tasks according to priorities, and demands on current and accurate available data.

● Flexibility. Adapting logistic support to changing conditions. Flexibility is an important factor in logistics. As missions change with conditions, it is necessary to ensure logistical support in a flexible way.

● Economy. Utilizing logistic support assets effectively. The naval forces should be economized in their use of logistic resources even when they carry out missions. Generally speaking, the allocation and distribution of logistic assets is based on the logistic planning and practical needs. How to employ the logistical resources economically and effectively is up to the operational commander to decide.

● Attainability. Trying to attain the objective combat operations with essential logistic support. Perhaps, there may be a risk when the absolute minimum logistic support can not fit in with what the commander desires to satisfy mission requirements. In this case, the commander must reasonably utilize the minimum essential logistic in an attempt to attain his objective of combat operations.

● Sustainability. Providing logistic support for sustained operations. Providing essential logistic supply to sustain the committed forces for the duration is a major challenge to logisticians. So, it is necessary to take every means to sustain naval forces with essential logistic support at all times.

*(1288 words)*

**Sources:**

https://news.usni.org/2021/02/02/kathleen-hicks-current-navy-shipbuilding-plan-needs-future-analysis

## Notes

1. the Axis: axis powers, coalition headed by Germany, Italy, and Japan that opposed the Allied powers in World War II 轴心国

2. unified combatant commander : a commander responsible for joint operations 联合作战指挥官

3. service component commander: a commander responsible for organzing individuals, units, detachments, organizations, and installations under the command 军种部队指挥官

4. combat logistics force: a key component to carry out the command's mission to sustain forces at sea 作战后勤部队

## Word Bank

| | |
|---|---|
| disrupt [dɪsˈrʌpt] | v. 破坏；使瓦解 |
| theatre [ˈθɪətə(r)] | n. 战区 |
| deterrence [dɪˈterəns] | n. 威慑；妨碍物 |
| credibility [ˌkredəˈbɪlətɪ] | n. 可信性；确实性 |
| littoral [ˈlɪtərəl] | adj. 沿海的；海滨的 |
| | n. 沿海地区 |
| expeditionary [ekspɪˈdɪʃ(ə)n(ə)rɪ] | adj. 远征的；探险的 |
| magnitude [ˈmægnɪtjuːd] | n. 大小；量级 |
| materiel [məˌtɪərɪˈel] | n.（法）物资；军备 |
| encompass [ɪnˈkʌmpəs] | v. 包含；包围 |
| afloat [əˈfləʊt] | adj. 漂浮的，不沉的 |
| ashore [əˈʃɔː(r)] | adv. 在岸上；向岸 |
| depot [ˈdepəʊ] | n. 仓库；补给 |
| | v. 把……存放在储藏处 |
| responsiveness [rɪˈspɒnsɪvnəs] | n. 响应能力 |
| logistician [ˌləʊdʒɪˈstɪʃən] | n. 物流师；军需官 |

## I. True or False

*Decide whether the following sentences are true or false in accordance with the text.*

1. Sustained forward deployed operations allow the US navy to engage in regional coalition-building and collective-security efforts.

2. In war, operational readiness means getting ready for war.

3. Strategic logistics encompasses the nation's ability to deploy and sustain its operating forces in executing the national military strategy.

4. Long-term sustainment is tied directly to the regional industrial bases, which include the nation's manufacturing, agriculture, transportation, and health services sectors.

5. The logistic support at three levels depends on manufacturers, training facilities, and depots, and also on trained personnel, transportation facilities, and services support systems.

6. Effective employment further requires the operational commander to decide which resources must be committed immediately and which should be kept in reserve.

7. Effectiveness is defined as the difference between the commander's desired level of support and the absolute minimum needed to satisfy mission requirements.

8. Providing essential logistic supply to sustain the committed forces for the crisis is a major challenge to logisticians.

## II. Word Match

*Match the words/terms/phrases in the left column with its appropriate correspondents in the right column.*

| | |
|---|---|
| 1. operation commander | A. 危机应对 |
| 2. erroneous assumption | B. 行动指挥官 |
| 3. striking power | C. 后勤基础设施 |
| 4. long-term sustainment | D. 预备役部队 |
| 5. combat readiness | E. 错误的假设 |
| 6. logistic infrastructure | F. 战备 |
| 7. forward presence | G. 前沿部署 |
| 8. reserve forces | H. 打击力量 |
| 9. crisis response | I. 长期保障能力 |
| 10. deterrence operation | J. 威慑行动 |

# Text C
# The US Navy Programs for Improving Quality of Life

Personnel are the most valuable asset to the Navy. Various programs made for improving quality of life aim at the rational and effective use of the Navy's human assets. The programs can help officers and ratings to further improve their military qualities and develop their capabilities. And what's more, the enhancement of leadership skills can contribute greatly to strengthen the chain of command[1]. Led by the chain of command, the naval personnel must act on the following principles and programs.

- Management
- Order and discipline
- Acceptance of responsibility
- Authority and accountability
- Pride and professionalism
- Motivation

The major program initiated for quality of life includes:

- Personal excellence
- Family support
- Equal opportunity
- Health and physical readiness
- Navy family housing

### Personal Excellence Program

The purpose of this program is to promote the personal development of Navy members so as to raise their individual morale, sense of satisfaction and quality of life. The personal excellence program focuses on four principal aspects: education, fitness, citizenship, and partnership. Personal excellence marks an individual's fine performance of his highest potential in education, health/fitness, and citizenship.

### Education

Education refers to two aspects. One is that education provides Navy personnel with multiple avenues to personal intellectual growth and success. The other is that education helps

improve the personnel's professional skills and develop their competence for various tasks under the guidance of Navy Skill Enhancement Program (SEP)[2].

### Fitness

Health promotion programs involve the activities that promote healthy lifestyle. These programs include physical fitness, sports, nutrition, weight/body fat control, inhibition of alcohol and drug abuse, smoking prevention or cessation, stress relief, back injury prevention, and high blood pressure check and control.

### Citizenship

The goal of personal excellence is the development of core values, which are the fundamental qualities of morally and socially responsible members of American society, including the Navy personnel and their families. The citizenship included in the Personal Excellence Program refers to the following:

Integrity-honesty, honor, and responsibility

Professionalism-competence, teamwork, and loyalty

Tradition-concern for people, patriotism, courage, and personal values

### Navy Personal Excellence Partnership Program

The Navy Personnel Excellence Partnership Program also aims at cultivating the above-mentioned values. In addition, it also considers its effects on American society. And, the program highlights a person's responsibility for his or her acts, justice, compassion, self-respect and respect for others, and community service.

In order to achieve personal excellence partnership, the program emphasizes the importance of cooperation, and schools or youth organizations. Its purpose is to make full use of manpower and material resources to bring the youth up to personal excellence.

### Family Support Program

The Navy family matters! Harmonious families are a reliable backing for naval personnel and beneficial to their military career. To raise the living standard of families in the Navy, the Navy formulated Family Support Program in 1979. The program aims to provide necessary resources and services supporting and enriching the life of Navy families as well as single sailors. The Program includes Family Service Centers[3] Program, Family Advocacy Program[4],

Family Home Care Programs[5], and Casualty Assistance Calls Program[6].

### Family Service Centers

All bases, each with 500 or more active-duty personnel, have Family Service Centers (FSCs). They are located throughout the United States and overseas. FSCs offer a variety of services for single and married sailors and their families. While individual FSCs tailor services and programs to the needs of the local military community, all the centers offer 13 core programs. These programs fall into three categories: (1) information and consultation, (2) education and training, and (3) counseling.

### Military Cash Awards Program

The Military Cash Awards Program (MILCAP)[7] was developed to encourage individuals to give good suggestions about how to reduce costs and improve productivity concerning the Navy, Department of Defense[8], and other federal government operations. The MILCAP provides for payment of cash incentives based on the amount of money saved by a suggestion. If you propose a better, or more efficient way to do that, you will be awarded a sum of money. The program gives all the details on how to submit suggestions and inventions to the Navy for consideration. You may help the Navy to improve its way of doing business and get a cash reward as well.

### Navy Family Housing Program

The Navy Family Housing Program aims at tackling the housing, which is and will be a priority, for improvement in quality of life. The navy ensures that the military members have houses to relieve them of their family worries so that they can better fulfil their missions. According to the housing policies made by the congress and Department of Defense , the civilian housing market cannot meet the needs of the naval personnel. The Navy will solve the housing problem on its own by constructing houses for their families.

### Summary

The main purpose of these programs is to help promote the Navy's combat readiness and capability using all its human and material resources. All naval personnel benefiting the program can concentrate on their work and bring their capabilities into full play. All this is of great significance to the building-up and development of the Navy.

*(860 words)*

**Notes**

1. chain of command: the way in which military executive positions traditionally structure their reporting relationships 指挥体系

2. Skill Enhancement Program (SEP): a pragram to improve basic competencies of Navy personnel. 技能提升项目

3. Family Service Centers (FSCs): a place to tailor services and programs to fit the needs of the local military community 家庭服务中心

4. Family Advocacy Program (FAD): a program dedicated to domestic and child abuse prevention, education, prompt reporting, investigation, intervention and treatment 家庭宣传项目

5. Family Home Care Program (FHCP): a program to fund various supports that help family and informal caregivers care for older adults 家庭居家护理项目

6. Casualty Assistance Calls Program (CACP): a program which ensures that military families have support in their time of need, including understanding all benefits and other forms of assistance 受害者援助电话项目

7. Military Cash Awards Program (MILCAP): a special incentive awards program designed to find new ideas to effectively increase performance within the Department of the Navy 军事现金奖励项目

8. Department of Defense：the federal department responsible for safeguarding national security of the United States; created in 1947 美国国防部

**Word Bank**

| | |
|---|---|
| accountability [əˌkaʊntəˈbɪlətɪ] | *n.* 有义务；有责任 |
| morale [məˈrɑːl] | *n.* 士气，斗志 |
| cessation [seˈseɪʃn] | *n.* 停止；中止 |
| compassion [kəmˈpæʃn] | *n.* 同情；怜悯 |
| incentive [ɪnˈsentɪv] | *n.* 动机；刺激 |
| | *adj.* 激励的；刺激的 |

## *Exercises*

Based on what you have acquired in this text, you are supposed to conduct an online study to explore further into the relevant sphere. Comb and frame what you have found with an online study report in no less than 200 words. In addition, any assistant image, audio, video, or other first-hand material will be preferred when you present your report in class.

# Unit 7  Navigation

**Bridge-in**

*Answer the following questions in accordance with the microlesson "An Introduction to Red-to-red Passage in Collision Prevention".*

1. What kind of lights should a power-driven vessel underway display at night?

2. What does it imply when you see a red light and a green light of a ship at the same time at sea?

3. What's the significance of complying with COLREGS for the navy?

## Text A
### Navigation Basics

Navigation is the science of directing a ship or craft by determining its position, course, and distance travelled. Navigation is concerned with finding the way, avoiding collision, conserving fuel, and keeping time. The main purpose of navigation is to find the way from one point to another.

To acquire knowledge of navigation, it is necessary to learn some navigation basics or basic nautical terms such as position, direction, bearing, course, distance, and depth. The following marine navigation basics will help understand how to navigate at sea with the help of nautical charts.

### Navigation by Nautical Chart

#### ● Latitude and Longitude

The position of a naval ship can be determined by its latitude and longitude. According to the angle they form at the center of the earth, lines of latitude and longitude are measured in degrees (°), minutes ('). One degree (1°) is equal to 60 minutes (60').

The latitude and longitude scales are printed at the edge of the navigational map with grid lines crossing them, allowing positions to be measured and plotted. Positions are described, as latitude being the first in °N or °S, followed by longitude in °E or °W, e.g., 53° 42' N, 5° 20' W.

● **Direction**

During the voyage, it is easier for a navigator to know his exact position on the sea according to the direction and distance from his ship to a landmark than according to latitude and longitude. Direction is measured clockwise as an angle relative to north. The direction of an object related to a ship's position can be determined by taking a bearing on the object. And the direction in which the ship sails is also known as heading.

● **North**

"North" is referred to when defining a direction. "North" maybe have three interpretations: True north (°T), which means north according to the earth's axis but not magnetic north, represents the direction of the geographic North Pole, being the alignment of the longitude lines on a chart; Magnetic north (°M), which means the northerly direction indicated by a magnetic needle, represents the direction of the magnetic North Pole; the divergence between magnetic and true north is known as variation, altering slightly each year with the movement of the magnetic North Pole.

Compass north (°C) is the northerly direction at which the compass points. The compass will point to magnetic north if there is no local magnetic interference. The direction of navigation is in the variation between true, magnetic, and compass north.

● **Distance and Speed**

The nautical mile, or sea mile is the unit of distance. A nautical mile is equal to one minute (1') of arc of latitude, that is, 6,076 ft or 1,852 m. In the past years of exploration by sea, a ship's speed was roughly measured by throwing overboard a small log tied to a knotted line. As the log drifted astern, the line was played out; the number of knots that passed while a sandglass emptied gave the speed of the ship in knots. Now, a knot is defined as one nautical mile per hour.

● **Depth and Height**

The depth and height of the sea is measured in meters. Depth as shown on a nautical chart is relative to a datum point and is usually the lowest Astronomical Tide[1] representing the lowest water level ever expected. The water depth is higher than what is practically shown because of the height of tide. The datum level from which the height is measured depends on

the type of object measured.

### Nautical Terms

A lot of nautical terms such as bearing, heading, course and position are used in recording information or data on a nautical chart. Moreover, the following are the nautical terms universally recognized, which can help us have a better understanding of navigation.

- °T =Degrees true

  The suffix letter attached to a direction measured is relative to true north, e.g., 095°T.

- °M = Degrees magnetic

  The suffix letter attached to a direction measured is relative to magnetic north, e.g., 135°M.

- °C = Degrees compass

  The suffix letter attached to a direction measured by the compass, e.g., 110°C.

- nm = Nautical mile

  A nautical mile is equal to one minute of arc of latitude, or 6,076 feet (1,852 meters), and is divided into 10 cables (ca), each being 185m (200yd).

- Kn = Knot

  The unit of speed concerning navigation. A knot is one nautical mile per hour.

- M = Meter

  Meter is the unit of length in the metric system. It is used to indicate depth and height on nautical charts. One meter is equal to 10 decimeters or 100 centimeters. For example, 7.1m is shown on the nautical chart as 71 dec or 710 cm.

- Fm = Fathom

  A Fathom, which is a measure of the depth of water, is equal to 6ft (1.829m). Sometimes, it is found on old nautical charts. The word fathom is not used as commonly as the word foot representing measure of length. For example, the harbor is 30 feet (5 fathoms) deep.

### Nautical Charts

A nautical chart is a detailed map used to help navigation at sea. It shows coasts, rocks, the depth of the sea, etc. By the aid of the nautical chart, a navigator can know his ship's exact positions on the sea, determine the bearing and follow the desired course. Besides, using the aids to navigation[2] and other devices such as compass, radio beacon, sextant and gyroscope, the navigator can avoid shoals and treacherous areas marked on the sea chart and safely reach his destination.

● **Chart Scale**

Various scaled charts are available for use in navigation.

Small-scale charts which cover the whole seas or oceans are used for planning and plotting positions on long passages. Medium-scale charts usually mark sections of a coastline and provide information about coastal and offshore features for the departure and arrival points. Large-scale charts which describe small areas in greater detail are essential for a ship when it enters the intricate waters or sails into an unfamiliar harbour. In short, the chart scale along with other details plays a very important role in navigation.

Marine Chart Plotter[3]

Marine charts made in the electronic form and by plotters as well as data given by other instruments can be shown on a screen. They are available for the preparation of navigation.

The marine chart plotter displays on the screen the details of planned navigation such as positions, courses and distances indicated by the cursor. It has a zoom function[4] to show the position by the GPS. Its plotted chart is comparable with a radar image. Its disadvantages are costly and susceptible to power failure.

Navigators should be proficient in the use of navigational devices and can accurately interpret the navigational information or data. Accurate information about navigation needs to be provided not only by digital navigational systems but also by nautical charts. Now, electronic charts are commonly used for navigation, but it is also essential to keep paper charts on board a ship for urgent use.

*(1157 words)*

**Sources:**

https://www.working-the-sails. com/navigation_basics.html

## Notes

1. Astronomical Tide: also called gravitational tide, which is influenced by the gravitation of the sun and the moon 天文潮汐

2. aids to navigation: facilities such as lighthouses, buoys, and beacons 助航设备

3. Marine Chart Plotter: a device used to plot charts for navigation in combination with GPS 海图标绘仪

4. zoom function: the function of magnification 放大功能

## Word Bank

| | |
|---|---|
| navigation [ˌnævɪˈɡeɪʃn] | *n.* 航行；航海 |
| course [kɔ:s] | *n.* 航向 |
| nautical [ˈnɔ:tɪkl] | *adj.* 航海的，海上的；船员的 |
| bearing [ˈbeərɪŋ] | *n.* 方位，方向；轴承；关系 |
| latitude [ˈlætɪtju:d] | *n.* 纬度 |
| longitude [ˈlɒŋɡɪtju:d] | *n.* 经度；经线 |
| clockwise [ˈklɒkwaɪz] | *adj. / adv.* 顺时针方向的（地） |
| alignment [əˈlaɪnmənt] | *n.* 队列，成直线 |
| divergence [daɪˈvɜ:dʒəns] | *n.* 差异，偏差，偏向；发散 |
| knot [nɒt] | *n.* （绳等的）结；海里/小时（航速单位） |
| cable [ˈkeɪbl] | *n.* 链 |
| fathom [ˈfæðəm] | *n.* （测量水深的长度单位，相当于6英尺）英寻 |
| sextant [ˈsekstənt] | *n.* 六分仪 |
| gyroscope [ˈɡaɪərəskəʊp] | *n.* 陀螺仪 |
| shoal [ʃəʊl] | *n.* 海的浅水处，浅滩 |
| treacherous [ˈtretʃərəs] | *adj.* 危险的 |
| cursor [ˈkɜ:sə] | *n.* （显示器）光标 |
| susceptible [səˈseptəbl] | *adj.* 易受影响的 |
| nautical chart | 海图 |
| grid line | 网格线 |
| true north | 真北 |
| magnetic north | 磁北 |
| compass north | 罗盘北 |
| nautical mile | 海里 |
| datum point | （测量）基准点，参考点，原点 |
| datum level | （水深）基准面 |

radio beacon　　　　　　　无线电信标
chart scale　　　　　　　　*海图比例尺*

# Exercises

## I. Comprehension

**Part A**　Questions

*Answer the following questions in accordance with the text.*

1. How should the position of a naval ship be described?

2. How is direction measured at sea?

3. What's the difference among true north, magnetic north and compass north?

4. What are the units of distance and speed used at sea?

5. What is the function of nautical charts?

**Part B**　Multiple Choices

*Choose the most appropriate answer from the given choices below each question in accordance with the text.*

1. Which of the following descriptions of the position of a naval ship is NOT true?

    A. 60° 41' N, 15° 30' W

    B. 5° 10' S, 20° 40' W

    C. 34° 20' E, 15° 30' N

    D. 34° 20' N, 15° 30' E

2. Which of the following definition of true north is true?

    A. True north is the direction of the geographic North Pole.

    B. True north is the direction of the magnetic North Pole.

    C. True north is the direction at which the compass points.

    D. True north is the alignment of the latitude lines on a chart.

3. What can be defined as the unit of speed?

    A. Nautical mile.

    B. Meters.

    C. One minute of latitude.

    D. One nautical mile per hour.

4. Which of the following term is equivalent to one nautical mile?

    A. 10 decimeters

    B. 10 cables

    C. 185 meters

    D. 6 feet

5. Which nautical chart covers whole seas or oceans?

    A. Small-scale charts.

    B. Medium-scale charts.

    C. Large-scale charts.

    D. All the above.

## II. Translation

**Part A**　**Terms & Phrases**

*Translate the following terms or phrases from Chinese into English and vice versa.*

| | |
|---|---|
| 1. 海图 | 2. 经度 |
| 3. 纬度 | 4. 海里 |
| 5. 节 | 6. 链 |
| 7. 分米 | 8. 英寻 |
| 9. 度 | 10. 分 |
| 11. true north | 12. magnetic north |
| 13. compass north | 14. magnetic interference |
| 15. astronomical tide | 16. radio beacon |
| 17. datum point | 18. aids to navigation |
| 19. chart scale | 20. marine chart plotter |

**Part B**　**Paragraph**

*Translate the following paragraph from English into Chinese.*

    A nautical chart is a detailed map used to help navigation at sea. It shows coasts, rocks, the depth of the sea, etc. By the aid of the nautical chart, a navigator can know his ship's exact positions on the sea, determine the bearing and follow the desired course. Besides, using the aids to navigation and other devices, such as compass, radio beacon, sextant and gyroscope, the navigator can avoid shoals and treacherous areas marked on the sea chart and safely reach his destination.

## III. Reading Report

What have you learned after reading the text? Have you obtained a better command of navigation basics? Now create your reading report in no more than 150 words to generalize your achievement in text study.

# Text B
# Weather Report

As we know, strong winds and huge waves often affect boats and ships, even modern large vessels sailing on the sea. And the sea state including winds and waves as well as changes in the environment has a certain influence on dead reckoning[1]. Poor visibility is an impediment to a ship's navigation. Unusual atmospheric conditions have an unfavorable effect on electronic navigation and radio communication. If it is overcast, celestial observation will be affected, and the refraction and dip angle will be disturbed under certain conditions. As the wind is a primary motive power, knowledge of wind force scale or different types of wind is of great importance. Obviously, a weather report is vital to ships at sea.

The weather report usually includes three parts: Gale Warning[2], Synoptic Situation and forecast.

The most important of all the three parts is Gale Warning, which refers to wind force, central position, speed and direction of a gale, storm and hurricane[3]. If there are no such strong winds, then the report just says: no warning or no storm.

A gale warning is an advisory or warning issued by the local meteorological stations in coast countries, announcing the gale-force wind. For example, a gale of force 8 on the scale is imminent at sea. The purpose of gale warnings is to allow sailors to take precautions against danger at sea.

In the United States, warnings are issued by the National Weather Service[4] to ships in related maritime areas about the gale, for example, a strong wind of 39 to 54 miles per hour or 63 to 69 kmph (approximately 34 to 48 knots) as well as the wind of 31-39 mph that blows at least one hour and the gust—a sudden rush of wind, which gusts up to 46-57 mph.

In Britain, gale warnings are issued by the Meteorological Office[5]. They are broadcast by radio four times a day at fixed times on 198KHz[6] to provide forecast for ships at sea. Part of them is broadcast by BBC Radio 4. If there is a considerable time left before the next Shipping Forecast[7], an extra gale warning is issued and read out between the broadcast programs. Weather stations often warn ships in the sea areas surrounding the UK that a gale of force 8 or above on the Beaufort Scale[8] is coming. Even the forecast can be sent as far as the north of Iceland and as far as the south of Spain.

Strong winds, which are related to low pressure centers, can also arise from anticyclone, or high area in the continental interior. In this case, it is necessary to issue a gale warning to coastal areas to let ships be prepared for gale-force winds which will cause serious damage. The term High Wind Warning (HWW) is substituted for "gale warning" (severer "storm warning") and used in non-marine settings in the United States for indicating winds between 39 and 71mph. The high wind can cause a dust storm[9], or sandstorm.

Two red triangular flags, one placed above the other, are the insignia for a gale warning.

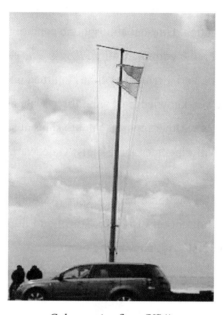

*Gale-warning flags (USA)*

As for Synoptic Situation (Synopsis), it presents important data concerning high- or low-pressure systems.

In a report, mbs, Kts and pd stand for millibars, knots and period, respectively. The abbreviated word pd is added to the end of a statement to stress its completeness. But sometimes, there is no pd added to the end of a statement.

As for the third part—forecast, it is about what kind of weather is going to appear in the following hours or days and about how long this forecast keeps valid. For example, *PART THREE FORECAST VALID FOR 12 HRS FRM 110100Z STOP*. It is the weather station that is responsible for providing the brief weather information for the main areas.

Military weather forecast aims to present weather information to the armed forces. Weather information is extremely important to air forces and naval forces. For example, military weather warning centers provide pre-flight and in-flight weather briefings for pilots and real-time weather information for military installations. Naval weather service units

provide information about oceanic climate and tide for ports and ships.

The US Navy Joint Typhoon Warning Center[10] offers special weather service to the naval forces and the federal government departments concerned by issuing typhoon warnings, for instance, forecasting when a tropical cyclone will sweep across the Pacific and Indian Oceans. The US Air Force weather observation and forecasting system provides accurate weather information for the Air Force units so that they can prepare for peacetime or wartime operations as well as operations supporting the ground forces. The US Coast Guard weather forecasters also provide weather forecasts for vessels, for example, ice breakers[11] and ships carrying out various missions. The Marine Corps weather forecasters often provide weather information for marines whose duty is to fight on land or sea. All the enlisted personnel to be engaged in weather forecast must take their initial technical training on meteorology at Keesler Air Force Base[12]. Military forecasters often closely cooperate with civilian forecasters in collecting, analyzing, creating and evaluating meteorological data for accurate weather forecast.

*Emblem of JTWC (Joint Typhoon Warning Center)*
The following is a complete sample of weather report.

**Sample: Weather Report**[13]

SINGAPORE WX BULLETIN FOR SHIPPING STOP

PART ONE NO STORM STOP

PART TWO GENERAL SITUATION WEAK SOUTHWEST MONSOON STOP

PART THREE FORECAST VALID FOR 12 HRS FROM 280100Z STOP

PUKET SOUTHWESTERLY 15 KTS ISOLATED SHOWERS AND THUNDE-RSTORMS SEA SLIGHT TO MODERATE STOP

MALACCA AND TIOMAN SOUTHSOUTHEASTERLY 5/10 KTS ISOLATED

SHOWERS AND THUNDERSTORMS SEA SLIGHT STOP

CONDORE SOUTHWERSTERLY 10/15 KTS SCATTERED SHOWERS AND THUNDERSTORMS SEA SLIGHT TO MODERATE STOP

REEF (NORTH) SOUTHWEST/WESTSOUTHWESTERLY 5/10 KTS ISOLATED SHOWERS AND THUNDERSTORMS SEA SLIGHT STOP

BUNGURAN SOUTHEAST/SOUTHERLY 5/10 KTS ISOLATED SHOWERS AND THUNDERSTORMS SEA SLIGHT STOP

*(963 words)*

## Notes

1. dead reckoning: calculation of one's position by log or compass (when visibility is bad) 航位推算法，推算定位法

2. Gale Warning: warning about very strong wind (force 7—10) on the Beaufort Scale 大风警报

3. hurricane: wind force 12 or more on Beaufort Scale 飓风

4. National Weather Service: also known as the Weather Bureau, which is a branch of the National Oceanic and Atmospheric Administration (NOAA) of the United States government, and is headquartered in Silver Spring, Maryland. 美国国家气象局

5. Meteorological Office: the United Kingdom's National Weather Service 英国气象局

6. KHz: abbreviation of kilohertz 千赫

7. Shipping Forecast: a BBC Radio broadcast of weather reports and forecasts to ships around the coasts of the British Isles 航运行情预测

8. Beaufort Scale: scale for measuring wind speed ranging originally from 0 (calm) to 12 (hurricane) 蒲福风级（最初将风速划为0—12级，即由无风到飓风的等级）

9. dust storm: also called sandstorm, which happens when a gust front or other strong wind blows loose sand and dirt from a dry surface 沙尘暴

10. Joint Typhoon Warning Center: Located in Pearl Harbor, Hawaii, it is responsible for issuing tropical cyclone warnings about the North West Pacific Ocean, South Pacific Ocean and Indian Ocean. 联合台风警报中心

11. ice breaker: strong ship designed to break a passage through ice 破冰船

12. Keesler Air Force Base: A United States Air Force base located in Biloxi, a city in Harrison County, Mississippi, which is named in honor of aviator 2d Lt Samuel Reeves Keesler, Jr.,

a Mississippi native killed in France during the First World War 基斯勒空军基地

13. A sample of weather report: 气象报告范例译文:

新加坡对海上船舶发布的气象公告。

第一部分：无风暴。

第二部分：天气形势，弱西南信风。

第三部分：从28日0100Z时起12小时内有效的天气预报。

普吉岛：西南风15节，局部阵雨和雷雨，轻浪到中浪。

马六甲海峡和雕门岛：东南偏南风5—10节，局部阵雨和雷雨，轻浪。

昆仑岛：西南风10—15节，零星阵雨和雷雨，轻浪到中浪。

曾母暗沙（北）：西南风到西南偏西风5—10节，局部阵雨和雷雨，轻浪。

朋古兰岛：东南风到南风5—10节，局部阵雨和雷雨，轻浪。

 **Word Bank**

| visibility [ˌvɪzɪˈbɪlɪtɪ] | n. 能见度；清晰度 |
| overcast [ˈəʊvəkɑːst] | adj. 阴天的；阴暗的 |
| celestial [səˈlestɪəl] | adj. 天体的，天文的，天空的 |
| refraction [rɪˈfrækʃən] | n. 折射作用；折射度 |
| dip [dɪp] | n. 倾斜 |
| synoptic [sɪˈnɒptɪk] | adj. 天气的 |
| advisory [ədˈvaɪzərɪ] | n.（气象）报告，通报，（风沙）警报 |
| meteorological [ˌmiːtjərəˈlɒdʒɪkl] | adj. 气象（学上）的 |
| imminent [ˈɪmɪnənt] | adj. 即将来临的；即将发生的 |
| gust [gʌst] | n. 阵风 |
| anticyclone [ˈæntɪˈsaɪkləʊn] | n. 反气旋；高气压 |
| insignia [ɪnˈsɪgnɪə] | n. 徽章；标志，标记 |
| synopsis [sɪˈnɒpsɪs] | n. 概要，梗概，一览；天气图 |
| millibar [ˈmɪlɪbɑː] | n. 毫巴（气压单位） |
| installation [ˌɪnstəˈleɪʃən] | n. 军事设施；安装；设置 |
| cyclone [ˈsaɪkləʊn] | n. 暴风；旋风；气旋 |
| meteorology [ˌmiːtjəˈrɒlədʒɪ] | n. 气象学 |
| wind force | 风力 |
| central position | （台风的）中心位置 |

## I. True or False

*Decide whether the following sentences are true or false.*

1. Due to the development of science and technology, modern vessels will not be affected by wind and sea at all.

2. Nowadays even if the skies are overcast, celestial observations are still available.

3. The first and the most important part of a weather report is gale warning.

4. The purpose of gale warning is to allow mariners to take precautionary actions to ensure their safety at sea.

5. Gale warning is most commonly issued in coastal areas and is primarily directed at land-based interests rather than marine.

6. The insignia for a gale warning is two red triangular flags, one placed beside the other.

7. The second part of a weather report is synopsis, which presents to you the important data concerning high- or low-pressure systems.

8. The third part of a weather report is forecast, which tells what kind of weather is going to occur in the following hours or days.

9. Naval forecasters cover the waters and coastal areas forecasts.

10. Within the United States, Air Force Weather provides weather forecasting for the Navy.

## II. Word Match

*Match the words/terms/phrases in the left column with its appropriate correspondents in the right column.*

| | |
|---|---|
| 1. hurricane | A. 台风 |
| 2. gale warning | B. 台风中心位置 |
| 3. gust | C. 沙尘暴 |
| 4. dead reckoning | D. 风力 |
| 5. central position | E. 蒲福风力等级 |
| 6. wind force | F. 气象形势 |
| 7. typhoon | G. 大风警报 |
| 8. synopsis | H. 航位推测法 |
| 9. Beaufort Force | I. 阵风 |
| 10. dust storm | J. 飓风 |

### Text C
## International Regulations for Preventing Collisions at Sea

When a country's vessels, warships and seaplanes meet with another country's on the open sea, or in territorial waters[1], contiguous zones[2], Exclusive Economic Zones (EEZ)[3] and around the waters of an archipelagic state, collisions are likely to happen. Because of the necessity for collision avoidance and safety of vessels, navies are encouraged to comply with the 1972 International Regulations for Preventing Collisions at Sea (COLREGS)[4].The regulations shall apply to all vessels upon the high seas and in all waters connected therewith navigable by seagoing vessels. When vessels meet at sea, they must abide by the following Rules.

### Rule 1 Application
Rules in this section apply to vessels which meet one another at sea.

### Rule 2 Action of Collison Avoidance
When two vessels are approaching one another, one shall make way for the other so as to avoid risk of collision.

### Rule 3 Overtaking
● A vessel overtaking another one shall keep out of the way to avoid colliding with the overtaken vessel.

● A vessel shall be deemed to be overtaking when coming up with another vessel from a direction more than 22.5 degrees abaft her beam. When overtaking at night, she will only see the stern light of that vessel but not any side lights.

● When a vessel is in doubt about whether she is overtaking another, she shall make a correct judgement and act accordingly.

● Any subsequent alteration of the bearing between the two vessels shall not make the overtaking vessel a crossing vessel or relieve the overtaking vessel of her duty of keeping clear of the overtaken vessel until she finally goes past.

### Rule 4 Head-on Situation[5]

● When two power-driven vessels[6] are meeting on the reciprocal or nearly reciprocal course, one shall alter her course to starboard and pass the other so as to eliminate risk of collision.

● In a head-on situation, when one vessel finds the other ahead or nearly ahead at night by seeing the latter's head lights and/or both side lights and in the daytime by observing the other vessel's corresponding conditions, she shall act on the regulations of collision avoidance.

● When a vessel is not sure about such a situation, she shall assume that it does exist and act accordingly.

### Rule 5 Crossing Situation

When two power-driven vessels get into crossing situation, one shall keep out of the way and shall not cross ahead of the other vessel so as to avoid risk of collision.

### Rule 6 Action by Give-way Vessel[7]

One vessel which is prepared to keep out of the way of another vessel shall take substantial action as early as possible to give way.

### Rule 7 Action by Stand-on Vessel[8]

● When two vessels sailing in opposite directions meet each other, either of them shall evade and keep her course and speed.

● The stand-on vessel, a vessel which is kept out of the way, can safely pass when the give-way vessel takes action to avoid collision.

● If the give-way vessel finds herself so close to the stand-on vessel that collision will possibly occur, she shall take quick action or rapid maneuver to avoid collision.

● A power-driven vessel which takes action in a crossing situation to avoid collision with another one shall not alter her course and speed.

● According to the rule, the give-way vessel is obliged to keep out of the way.

### Rule 8 Responsibilities of Vessels

● A power driven vessel shall keep out of the way of:

i. A vessel out of control;

ii. A vessel limited in maneuver capability;

iii. A vessel engaged in fishing;

iv. A sailing vessel;

● A sailing vessel shall keep out of the way of:

i. A vessel out of control;

ii. A vessel limited in maneuver capability;

iii. A vessel engaged in fishing;

● A fishing vessel shall keep out of the way of:

i. A vessel out of control;

ii. A vessel limited in maneuver capability.

● Any vessel other than a vessel not under control or a vessel limited in maneuver capability shall, as the case may be, avoid impeding the safe passage of a vessel constrained by her draft, in compliance with the relative rule.

● A vessel constrained by her draft shall navigate with extreme caution by practical consideration.

● A seaplane[9] on the water shall, in general, keep clear of all vessels and avoid impeding their navigation. In case of risk of collision, she shall comply with the Rules of this Part.

● A WIG craft[10] shall, when taking off, landing and flying near the surface, keep clear of all other vessels and avoid impeding their navigation;

● A WIG craft operating on the water surface shall comply with the Rules of this Part.

*(788 words)*

**Sources:**

https://www.storming.ca/marine/colregs/

## Notes

1. territorial waters: the sea near a country's coast (12 nautical miles from the coast) and under its control 领海

2. contiguous zone: adjacent zone, that's, a zone which is adjacent to the territorial waters 毗连区

3. Exclusive Economic Zone (EEZ): economic waters not more than 200 nautical mile, measured from the baseline of the territorial sea's breadth, which is defined by the 1982 United Nations Convention on the Law of the Sea 专属经济区

4. 1972 International Regulations for Preventing Collisions at Sea (COLREGS): maritime traffic rules made by the International Maritime Organization in order to avoid collision at sea 国际海上避碰规则

5. head-on situation: a situation in which the bows of two vessels meet each other in opposite directions （两船）对遇局面，相遇情势

6. power-driven vessel: any vessel propelled by machinery 机动船

7. give-way vessel: the vessel which keeps out of the way of another vessel in a crossing situation 让路船

8. stand-on vessel: the vessel which is kept out of the way in a crossing situation 直航船，被让路船

9. seaplane: any aircraft designed to maneuver on the water 水上飞机。

10. WIG craft: Wing-In-Ground craft, a kind of air-cushion craft, which flies in close proximity to the surface by use of surface effect, or wing-in-ground effect 地效翼船

## Word Bank

| | |
|---|---|
| archipelagic [ɑːkɪpɪˈlædʒɪk] | *adj.* 群岛的 |
| therewith [ðeəˈwɪθ] | *adv.* 同时，随之；于是，随即 |
| seagoing [ˈsiːˌgəʊɪŋ] | *adj.* 航海的；从事航海业的 |
| abaft [əˈbæft] | *prep.* 在……之后；在……后的方向；<br>*adv.* 向（往）船尾；在船尾 |
| reciprocal [rɪˈsɪprəkl] | *adj.* 相互的；互易的；反方向的 |
| maneuver [məˈnuːvə] | *n.* 调遣；策略；（pl.）演习；操纵 |
| impede [ɪmˈpiːd] | *v.* 阻碍；妨碍 |
| constrain [kənˈstreɪn] | *v.* 强迫；压制；束缚；拘束 |
| draft [drɑːft] | *n.* （船的）吃水（深度） |
| comply with | 遵守 |
| stern light | 尾灯 |
| side light | 舷灯 |
| head light | 前桅灯 |

## *Exercises*

Based on what you have acquired in this text, you are supposed to conduct an online study to explore further into the relevant sphere. Comb and frame what you have found with an online study report in no less than 200 words. In addition, any assistant image, audio, video, or other first-hand material will be preferred when you present your report in class.

# Unit 8  Operations and Joint Exercises

**Bridge-in**

*Answer the following questions in accordance with the microlesson "RIMPAC".*

1. How many countries and vessels have participated in RIMPAC-2014/16?

2. Which Chinese ships have participated in RIMPAC-2014/16?

3. What's the objective of RIMPAC?

### Text A
### RIMPAC[1] 2014, with China's Participation

The Rim-Pacific Joint Exercise, or RIMPAC for short, is the world's largest naval exercise. In 2014, 47 ships, 6 submarines, more than 200 aircraft, and 25,000 officers and sailors from 23 nations joined in the RIMPAC which took place around the Hawaii Islands. It was the first time that China's Navy ships took part in the joint exercises.

Ships participating in the RIMPAC sailed to Hawaii ahead of time. They were the vessels from the US, Brunei[2], Singapore and China (sending four PLAN ships: missile destroyer Haikou, missile frigate Yueyang, supply ship Qiandaohu and hospital ship Peace Ark at the invitation of Pentagon[3]). The Chinese ships, with 1,100 sailors, arrived in Hawaii. The task force was second in size only to that of the host nation, the United States.

RIMPAC was first held in 1971. RIMPAC 2014 was the 24th joint exercise. Now, it is held biennially. Besides China and Brunei participated for the first time.

In RIMPAC 2014 hosted by the US Pacific Fleet[4], Thailand was refused participation after the US State Department responded to the military coup which took place on May 22 in this country. During the RIMPAC, forces from China, the US, France, Mexico and Brunei practiced

joint drills which included weapons firing, logistical support, damage control, fighting piracy, disaster relief, coordinated interception, landing operation, and joint assaults by warships and helicopters.

In addition, Chinese sailors participated in other exchanges or activities from June 25 to July 8, for example, attending press conferences, visiting warships, holding basketball and football matches and running a 5-kilometer cross-country race. The former spokesman of China's Ministry of National Defense, Yang Yujun said in Beijing, "China has sent several advanced vessels to help forge a new era in the Sino-US military relationship, because both the countries have shared interests in spite of differences in some aspects. China holds that the two countries should enhance exchanges and mutual understanding to overcome those differences."

"The multinational naval exercises have provided a wonderful opportunity to establish working and personal relationship with the navies from Brunei, China and Singapore participating in RIMPAC," said Captain Patrick Kelly, commanding officer of the guided-missile cruiser USS Chosin sailing from Guam to Hawaii.

Zhang Junshe, a naval expert at PLA Naval Military Studies Research Institute[5], said that China would have a good opportunity to manifest its transparent military policy and determination to maintain peace by joining in international military exercises and displaying its strength.

The Chinese People's Liberation Army (PLA) Navy replenishment ship Qiandaohu 886 sails past the PLA Navy hospital ship Peace Ark berthed at the Joint Base Pearl Harbor Hickam in Hawaii to participate in RIMPAC 2014. (Picture from www.chinadaily.com.cn)

### China Navy is RIMPAC "Highlight"

The Chinese flotilla, which consists of four ships, joined the multinational forces from the United States, Singapore and Brunei in Guam. They spent 10 days sailing in formation from Guam to the islands of Hawaii, during which they had good teamwork and conducted a series of exercises, including personal exchanges, weapons firing, ships' deployment, maneuvering, and communication.

"Such activities themselves are a very successful exchange and help promote friendship and mutual understanding," Zhao Xiaogang, drill director of the Chinese task force, told reporters. He said, "attending many receptions hosted by the navies of participating nations is also a good opportunity for friendly exchanges and mutual understanding." The Chinese navy hosted a deck reception during the period of RIMPAC to entertain officers from the participating nations and senior officers from the US Pacific Fleet.

"I think it (RIMPAC) is an important platform for military exchanges and friendly cooperation," Zhao said. He revealed that the PLA navy also paid attention to exchanges with the Japanese and Philippine navies. Both US allies currently have maritime territorial disputes with China. Zhao said it was natural for the Chinese flotilla participating in RIMPAC for the first time to carry out exercises under the command of the US side. He said the PLA navy's participation in RIMPAC was primarily aimed at promoting the steady and healthy development of a new type of relationship between the Chinese and US militaries as well as at enhancing exchanges and deepening cooperation with the navies from the participating nations, and meanwhile he made clear the Chinese Army's positive and sincere attitude towards world peace and regional security and stability. Zhao made such remarks at the opening ceremony of RIMPAC, at which Vice-Admiral Kenneth Floyd, commander of the US Third Fleet was present, highlighting China's participation.

Floyd, who acted as commander of the 2014 RIMPAC Combined Task Force[6], said that China and Brunei participated in RIMPAC for the first time, and so did two hospital ships in the history of RIMPAC.

The two hospital ships Floyd mentioned were the US Navy hospital ship the USS Mercy and the Chinese PLAN hospital ship the Peace Ark. He visited the Peace Ark in Pearl Harbor. These two ships conducted exchange of programs during RIMPAC.

Floyd highly appreciated the friendly and cooperative relationship established during RIMPAC. "If you ask veterans who once participated in RIMPAC, they'll tell you that what has deeply impressed them is the chance to work along with sailors of different navies, learning

from each other by military exchange and enhancing trust. Based on the close cooperation, we can unite to any crisis or disaster at any time no matter where it may happen."

RIMPAC 2014 was the largest joint exercise in the naval history and ended with success on August 1.

*(943 words)*

*Sources:*

www.chinadaily.com.cn

## Notes

1. RIMPAC: RIM-Pacific Joint Exercise 环太平洋联合军演（由美国第三舰队倡议的国际上规模最大的多国海上联合军演，始于1971年）

2. Brunei: a sultanate in northwestern Borneo; became independent of Great Britain in 1984 文莱（东南亚苏丹国）

3. the Pentagon: the five-sided building that is the place of the US Department of Defence in Washington D.C. 五角大楼（美国国防部的代称）

4. the US Pacific Fleet: the main US military force in the Asia-Pacific region 美国太平洋舰队

5. PLA Naval Military Studies Research Institute: PLAN's institute which is a functional department of the Navy's military academic research 中国人民解放军海军军事学术研究所（研究海军军事学术的实体和组织领导海军军事学术研究工作的职能部门）

6. Combined Task Force: formed by a large number of multinational warships for a specific operation 多国特混编队

## Word Bank

| | |
|---|---|
| rim [rɪm] | *n.* 边，边缘 |
| biennially [baɪˈenɪəlɪ] | *adv.* 每两年；两年一次地 |
| coup [kuː] | *n.* 政变 |
| piracy [ˈpaɪrəsɪ] | *n.* 海盗 |
| interception [ˌɪntə(ː)ˈsepʃən] | *n.* 拦截 |
| assault [əˈsɔːlt] | *n.* 攻击，袭击 |
| cross-country [krɒsˈkʌntrɪ] | *adj.* 越野的 |

| multinational [ˌmʌltɪˈnæʃənl] | adj. 多国的 |
| --- | --- |
| Captain [ˈkæptɪn] | n. 海军上校 |
| Vice-Admiral [vaɪsˈædmərəl] | n. 海军中将 |

# *Exercises*

## I. Comprehension

### Part A Questions

*Answer the following questions in accordance with the text.*

1. How many vessels have participated in RIMPAC-2014?

2. Which Chinese ships have participated in RIMPAC-2014?

3. What countries have participated in RIMPAC-2014 for the first time?

4. What drills did the Chinese fleet conduct?

5. According to the drills director of the Chinese fleet, what is the primary aim of China's participation?

### Part B Multiple Choices

*Choose the most appropriate answer from the given choices below each question in accordance with the text.*

1. How many nations have participated in RIMPAC-2014?

   A. 21

   B. 22

   C. 23

   D. 24

2. What drills will be conducted by forces from China, the US, France, Mexico and Brunei?

   A. Weapons firing, supply transportation, damage control.

   B. Anti-piracy and disaster relief.

   C. Coordinated interceptions and landings and joint assaults.

   D. All of the above.

3. Which one is not the opinion of China's Ministry of National Defense spokesman about Sino-US military relations?

   A. China wants to forge a new era in the Sino-US military relationship.

   B. The two countries have shared interests but face differences.

C. China believes they should work together to strengthen communication and handle those differences.

D. It was natural for the Chinese fleet to be put under the command of the US side.

4. What are the aims of the PLA navy's participation?

A. Promoting the steady and healthy development of a new type of Sino-US relationship.

B. Uniting navies to strengthen exchanges and deepen cooperation.

C. Demonstrating China's positive attitude in maintaining world peace and promoting regional security and stability.

D. All of the above.

5. Which is not a "first" in RIMPAC-2014?

A. China's participation.

B. Norway's participation.

C. Thailand's participation.

D. Two hospital ships are taking part.

## II. Translation

**Part A**  **Terms & Phrases**

*Translate the following terms or phrases from Chinese into English and vice versa.*

1. 导弹驱逐舰                      2. 导弹护卫舰

3. 补给舰                          4. 医院船，医务船

5. 东道国，主办国                  6. 武器射击

7. 补给运输                        8. 损管演习

9. 灾难援助                        10.协同拦截

11. joint assault                  12. commanding officer

13. guided-missile cruiser         14. maneuvering drills

15. communications drills          16. deck reception

17. senior officers                18. maritime territorial disputes

19. regional security              20. Combined Task Force

**Part B**  **Paragraph**

*Translate the following paragraph from English into Chinese.*

The Chinese fleet, which consists of four ships, joined multinational forces from the United States, Singapore and Brunei in Guam. They spent 10 days in a group sail from Guam to the islands of Hawaii, during which they refined their interoperability and conducted a number of exercises including personnel exchanges, weapons firing, ship-handling and maneuvering drills and communications drills.

## III. Reading Report

Why is the Chinese fleet RIMPAC-2014's highlight? After reading the text, you should summarize the main points in no more than 120 words.

## Text B
## NATO's BALTOPS-2019 and Russia's Response

Around 8,600 US and European troops from 18 nations took part in the annual BALTOPS[1] naval exercise, which began on Sunday (9 June, 2019) in Germany's Baltic Sea port of Kiel[2] and ended on 21 June. The 47th BALTOPS exercise involved naval, air and ground forces with about 50 ships and submarines and 40 aircraft. The exercise included finding and destroying sea mines and submarines, and deploying air-defense and landing troops to strike hostile targets.

"The Baltic Sea is of vital strategic importance for the Alliance because it is bordered by six NATO countries", said NATO[3] spokesperson Oana Lungescu. "BALTOPS is now in its 47th year and is not directed against anyone – but clearly the security environment in the region has deteriorated after Russia's illegal annexation of Crimea[4]." She added, "BALTOPS tests how well our forces work together and shows that NATO can defend itself against any adversary."

BALTOPS is the largest exercise series in the Baltic Sea. Participating troops come from Belgium, Denmark, Estonia[5], Finland, France, Germany, Latvia[6], Lithuania[7], the Netherlands, Norway, Poland, Portugal, Romania, Spain, Sweden, Turkey, the United Kingdom, and the United States. Russia used to participate in the exercise but has not been invited since its illegal annexation of Crimea in 2014 and its beginning to destabilize eastern Ukraine[8].

The US Navy's 2nd Fleet command[9] in Norfolk, Virginia was responsible for BALTOPS 2019, marking its first major role in Europe. The 2nd Fleet command was re-established last year in response to Russia's growing naval activities in the Atlantic. Vice Admiral Andrew Lewis directed BALTOPS from the USS Mount Whitney command ship. Lewis said: "It is imperative that allies and partners unite to confront today's challenges. Our combined efforts during BALTOPS demonstrate our commitment to regional peace and prosperity. Our exercise aims at improving our joint operational capability and preparing for future strategic challenges. We will become stronger."

US Navy Rear Adm. Brad Skillman, the commander of Expeditionary Strike Group 2, said that a major exercise generally needs one amphibious task force, but BALTOPS requires two full-sized amphibious task forces, which often try out the new tactics, for example, personal movement between the task forces as needed.

Involved in BALTOPS 2019 were these two amphibious task forces. One was the British-led Joint Expeditionary Force including a landing unit, which was set up last year for participating in the exercise. The other was a task group composed of US **dock** landing ship USS Fort McHenry (LSD-43), Spanish **flagship** ESPS Juan Carlos I (L-61) and air defense frigate ESPS Cristobol Colon (F-105), Polish landing ship ORP Gniezno (822), and a multinational landing force.

In BALTOPS 2019, reconnaissance aircraft from Sweden and the US conducted formation flight near Russia's Kaliningrad[10] region. After taking off from the Mildenhall air base in the UK, a US Air Force reconnaissance aircraft RC-135V cruised along the southern border of the Kaliningrad region and then in Polish airspace for about two and a half hours. At the same time, a Swedish reconnaissance Gulfstream 4 aircraft flew over the international waters of the Baltic Sea near the Kaliningrad region's maritime border. Although it is a **non-aligned** country, Sweden has recently taken an active part in NATO drills. This time it sent two **corvettes** (Nyköping K34 and Karlstad K35) and a submarine.

In the exercise, the German, Norwegian, Danish, and US Navy sailors made joint efforts to clear World War II-era bottom mines near the Bundeswehr Military Training Area in Todendorf, Germany.

Another highlight was that the US Helicopter Sea Combat Squadron 28 first used the Airborne Laser Mine Detection System (ALMDS)[11] and Airborne Mine Neutralisation System-Archerfish (AMNS-AF)[12] in the Baltic region.

In the exercise, the Marines performed amphibious operations at several locations in the Baltic Sea region. All air operations were directed by the NATO's Air Operations Centre in Uedem. Aircraft, along with naval forces, provided air defence, surveillance and cover for amphibious operations. After the exercise was over, most ships sailed to Kiel to participate in the Kielerwochen naval parade.

At the time the Russian Navy was holding a military exercise in close **proximity** to the NATO's maneuver area. Russia **claimed** that three warships (two corvettes and one small missile ship) of its Baltic Fleet had tracked and monitored the BALTOPS 2019 naval exercise.

According to the news **bulletin** of Russia's Baltic Fleet press office, several naval groups comprising corvettes, small missile ships and an anti-submarine warfare (ASW) vessel were then in the Baltic Sea practice ranges for maritime maneuvers.

The press office said in a statement, "As part of planned drills, the hunter-killers and surface ships including corvettes Boiky and Stoiky, small missile ships Serpukhov, Zelyony

Dol, Liven and Passat as well as ASW ship Aleksin, have held a series of exercises, which involve practicing ASW measures, missile strikes against target ships, artillery and torpedo attack on air and sea targets."

The Russian Defense Ministry admitted that from June 10th on, its Baltic Fleet had been watching out for NATO's BALTOPS 2019 performed by the troops from the US and 17 other European nations, and taking a series of measures so as to rapidly react to possible emergencies in the Baltic Sea. At that time, Russian Baltic Fleet's warships, aircraft and Bastion coastal missile defense systems[13] were ordered to get into a state of combat readiness.

*(882 words)*

---

*Sources:*
- - - - - - - - - - - - - - - - - - - - - - - - - - - - - - - - - - - - - - - - - - - - - - - - - - - - - - - - - -

1. www.chinadaily.com.cn

2. www.xinhuanet.com

*Notes*

1. BALTOPS (Baltic Operations): an annual military exercise in the Baltic Sea and the regions surrounding it which has been commanded by US Naval Forces in Europe since 1971波罗的海演习

2. Kiel: a port city in Germany 基尔（德国港市）

3. NATO: North Atlantic Treaty Organization, an international organization created in 1949 by the North Atlantic Treaty for the purpose of collective security 北大西洋公约组织

4. Crimea: a peninsula between the Black Sea and the Sea of Azov（亚速海）克里米亚；克里米亚半岛

5. Estonia: a republic in northeastern Europe on the Baltic Sea 爱沙尼亚

6. Latvia: a republic in northeastern Europe on the eastern coast of the Baltic Sea 拉脱维亚

7. Lithuania: a republic in northeastern Europe on the Baltic Sea 立陶宛

8. Ukraine: a republic in southeastern Europe which was an allied republic of the Soviet Union but now is independent 乌克兰（苏联一加盟共和国，现已独立）

9. the US Navy's 2nd Fleet command: the organization which directs the US Navy's 2nd Fleet at strategic level 美国海军第二舰队司令部（美国海军第二舰队是美国海军的主力舰队，于2011年撤编，撤编前曾执行过1962年对古巴海上封锁和1989年入侵巴拿马任务。2018年5月，美国海军重启这一舰队，主要目的是遏制俄罗斯海上力量扩张。）

10. Kaliningrad: a city in Russia 加里宁格勒

11. the Airborne Laser Mine Detection System (ALMDS): 机载激光水雷探测系统

12. Airborne Mine Neutralisation System-Archerfish (AMNS-AF): 机载反水雷系统—射水鱼型

13. Bastion coastal missile defence systems: a Russian mobile costal defense missile system 俄罗斯"堡垒"海岸导弹防御系统

## Word Bank

| | |
|---|---|
| deteriorate [dɪˈtɪərɪəreɪt] | v. 恶化 |
| annexation [ˌænekˈseɪʃn] | n. 合并 |
| destabilize [ˌdiːˈsteɪbəlaɪz] | v. 使动摇 |
| imperative [ɪmˈperətɪv] | adj. 必要的，不可避免的 |
| amphibious [æmˈfɪbɪəs] | adj. 两栖的，水陆两用的 |
| full-sized [ˈfʊlˈsaɪzd] | adj. 全尺寸的 |
| tactics [ˈtæktɪks] | n. 策略；战术；用兵学 |
| dock [dɒk] | n. 船坞 |
| flagship [ˈflæɡʃɪp] | n. 旗舰 |
| non-aligned [ˌnɑːn əˈlaɪnd] | adj. 不结盟的；中立的 |
| corvette [kɔːˈvet] | n. 轻型护卫舰 |
| proximity [prɒkˈsɪmətɪ] | n. 接近，邻近 |
| claim [kleɪm] | v. 声称 |
| bulletin [ˈbʊlətɪn] | n. 新闻简报 |

## Exercises

### I. True or False

*Decide whether the following sentences are true or false in accordance with the text.*

1. Around 8,600 US and European troops from 18 nations are taking part in the annual BALTOPS naval exercise that starts on Sunday (9 June) in Germany's Baltic Sea port of Kiel.

2. The training includes finding and destroying sea mines and submarines, the use of air

defence and landing troops onshore as well as defence against attack from enemy navy vessels.

3. Russia used to participate in the exercise but has refused to participate.

4. Unlike other major exercises, the BALTOPS command structure included two amphibious task forces.

5. To this year's edition of BALTOPS, Sweden is sending two corvettes and an aircraft.

6. Upon conclusion of the exercise, most ships will sail to Kiel to participate in the Kielerwochen naval parade.

7. The Russian exercise will see the warships practising anti-submarine warfare measures, missile strikes against simulated enemy ships, artillery and torpedo firing and targeting of sea targets.

8. The Russian Defence Ministry confirmed that its Baltic Fleet is monitoring the NATO naval drills.


## II. Word Match

*Match the words/terms/phrases in the left column with its appropriate correspondents in the right column.*

| | |
|---|---|
| 1. dock landing ship | A. 海岸导弹防御系统 |
| 2. air defense frigate | B. 执行作战任务 |
| 3. multinational landing force | C. 火炮和鱼雷发射 |
| 4. reconnaissance aircraft | D. 猎潜艇 |
| 5. bottom mines | E. 演习范围 |
| 6. practice ranges | F. 沉底水雷 |
| 7. hunter-killer | G. 侦察机 |
| 8. artillery and torpedo firing | H. 跨国登陆部队 |
| 9. coastal missile defence  system | I. 防空护卫舰 |
| 10. assume combat duty | J. 海滩登陆舰 |

## Text C
## Development of China's Naval Communication Network: Present and Future

Whether in naval exercises or in military operations like escorting in the Gulf of Aden, network communication data are extremely important for the Chinese naval forces, including useful data from satellites and land stations and intelligence data from radar, sonar and other electronic sensors. They can make full use of those data to perform their assigned tasks and missions ashore, at sea, and in the air. And what is worth mentioning is that the Chinese naval communication system of today has been incorporated into the network composed of multiple communication satellites. Furthermore, the success of quantum communication technical test in 2017 will open up broad prospects for the Navy's future development.

### Long-range Diagnosis Done For Chinese Naval Escort Ship

When the warship "Yantai" attached to the PLA Navy's 11th escort task force was performing an escort mission in the Gulf of Aden on the morning of May 24, 2012, its automatic radar plotting device (ARPD)[1] suddenly went on "strike". The technicians conducted repeated checks but could not identify the cause of the malfunction. Then, they started the diagnosis system of "Long-range Maintenance and Technical Support for Ship Equipment" and made contact with the technical experts of an electronic science and technology department in Shanghai. Through the video diagnosis, the fault was removed at last.

According to the then briefing, it was the first time that the PLAN North China Sea Fleet had conducted its escort mission. Under the active coordination by the PLAN Equipment and Technology Department, the Fleet had established a cooperative relationship of long-range equipment support with 400-plus military and civilian experts from dozens of academies, science and technology research institutes, equipment manufacturers as well as various leading organs and troop units prior to its departure.

Ever since the escort mission began, technical experts of the collaborative units have been carrying out timely cross-ocean diagnosis to deal with malfunctions in ship equipment by using such methods as video guidance, telephone consultation and network communication. Such troubleshooting is so useful for the ships of each Navy task force that they will be able to successfully perform escort missions in the Gulf of Aden.

### 11th China Navy Escort Task Force Holding Communication Drill

In order to meet the requirements of actual combat, the 11th China Navy escort task force held a communication drill in the waters of the Gulf of Aden on June 26, 2012. Reporters on the scene saw the task force make various plans rapidly and send them to each warship for implementation, which was attributed to the advanced communication network and new command system.

Xu Guangjin, communication officer of the task force, told the reporters that during the period of convoying merchant ships, the sophisticate satellite communication network could play a crucial role in rapid reaction to emergencies and successful accomplishment of escort missions. The drill further verified high-quality technical performance of the task force's communication network system, which was helpful to its implementation of escort missions.

For the escort ships' communication of today, a system composed of multiple satellite communication networks has been used instead of the original single short-wave communication system. At the press briefing Rear Admiral Yang Junfei, commander of the 11th China Navy escort task force, said: "the task force has greatly improved its efficiencies of carrying out escort missions through various means and methods such as situation report, exchange of information with foreign ships, timely communication with the convoy and effective organization and command. And our capability of escort has been further enhanced."

History has seen the development of naval intracommunication means since the idea of ships used as force projection[2] came into being. At first, flag signal and flashing signal served as the main communication means, then followed by more advanced technological means such as wireless radio and satellite communication. With the advent of miniaturization and the latest technologies, the military communication networks have developed greatly, but they have not yet caught up with the commercial networks. As mobile phones and other mobile devices become popular, new commercial networks will find application. Now, the commonly-adopted bandwidth has greatly outstripped what is available to the military. So it is natural for the naval forces to utilize commercial communication systems.

### Experimental Result of Quantum Communication Technology

Chinese scientists successfully experimented on undersea quantum communication, which marks a great breakthrough in quantum communication technology. It was Jin Xianmin and his team from Shanghai Jiao Tong University that conducted the experiment, in which they applied quantum mechanics to securing communication between two underwater points several hundred meters apart. Jin told the *Global Times* on Monday that his team also could manage the communication with satellites and aircraft from a point several meters under the sea.

Quantum communication is of high security because the quantum **photon** can neither be separated nor **duplicated**. Accordingly, the information it transmits is difficult to **wiretap**, **intercept** or **crack**. Once it is mature, the quantum communication technology will be used in the field of military affairs, finance, and public communications, according to Jin.

To carry out the experiment, the team collected samples of saltwater from six sites in the Yellow Sea and kept them in containers to see whether variations in the water affect experimental results, Jin said. A beam of light was then made to penetrate through a crystal to split it into pairs of photons, which are connected at sub-atomic, or quantum, level. This means that the performance of the pair of particles now linked theoretically over any distance allows data to be transmitted between the two. Jin said that although the floating substances and salt in the sea can result in the loss of photons, his team discovered a window which would enable the photons to travel and hence preserve enough photons for secure communication.

"Such a window can be spotted by means of commercial photon **detectors**," said Jin, "If the seawater, which covers more than 70 percent of the Earth, cannot be dealt with, the global quantum communication will remain impossible." "The quantum communication is highly secured and free from interruption, thereby solving the problem of underwater quantum communication. This is a good news for the Navy," said Li Jie, a Beijing-based naval expert. Jin added that the experiment was just the first step toward underwater quantum communication, so there would be still a long way to go before the construction of a quantum communication network covering the sea and sky.

China is striving to set up the first global quantum communication network by around 2030, by linking a satellite **constellation** consisting of dozens of quantum satellites with ground-based quantum communication networks, according to the Xinhua News Agency.

*(1101 words)*

**Sources:**

1. www.en.people.cn
2. www.xinhuanet.com

## Notes

1. automatic radar plotting device (ARPD): 自动雷达标绘仪

2. force projection: the capability of a state to conduct expeditionary warfare 兵力投送

## Word Bank

| | |
|---|---|
| sensor [ˈsensə(r)] | n. 传感器 |
| quantum [ˈkwɒntəm] | n. 量子 |
| long-range [ˌlɒŋˈreɪndʒ] | adj.（飞机、火箭等）远程的 |
| diagnosis [ˌdaɪəgˈnəʊsɪs] | n. 诊断 |
| collaborative [kəˈlæbərətɪv] | adj. 合作的，协作的 |
| troubleshooting [ˈtrʌblʃuːtɪŋ] | n. 故障判断与排除 |
| advent [ˈædvent] | n. 到来；出现 |
| miniaturization [ˌmɪnɪətʃərɪˈzeʃən] | n. 微型化 |
| bandwidth [ˈbændwɪdθ ˈbændwɪtθ] | n. 带宽 |
| outstrip [ˌaʊtˈstrɪp] | v. 超过；胜过 |
| photon [ˈfəʊtɒn] | n. 光子 |
| duplicate [ˈdjuːplɪkeɪt] | v. 复制 |
| wiretap [ˈwaɪətæp] | v. 搭线窃听 |
| intercept [ˌɪntəˈsept] | v. 拦截； |
| crack [kræk] | v. 阻止、破解 |
| detector [dɪˈtektə(r)] | n. 探测器；检测器 |
| constellation [ˌkɒnstəˈleɪʃn] | n. 星群，一系列（相似的事物） |

## Exercises

Based on what you have acquired in this text, you are supposed to conduct an online study to explore further into the relevant sphere. Comb and frame what you have found with an online study report in no less than 200 words. In addition, any assistant image, audio, video, or other first-hand material will be preferred when you present your report in class.

# Unit 9  Ship Building and Handling

## Bridge-in

*Answer the following questions in accordance with the microlesson "The Chinese Navy's Dream in Shipbuilding".*

1. Can you list the major achievements in shipbuilding in the New Era of the PLA Navy?

2. What's the significance of the first domestically-built aircraft carrier in PLAN?

3. What's your reflection on the development path of the PLA Navy in terms of shipbuilding?

## Text A
### Stealth Zumwalt-Class Destroyers at Different Stages of Development

Evading the detection from radar, quietly sailing into the enemy waters and launching long-range precision attacks from undetectable positions all give a vivid picture of how "stealthy" offensive destroyers can change modern naval warfare. Can a large destroyer equipped with Tomahawk missiles[1], deck-mounted guns, sensors, antennas and power systems be considered truly stealthy? Sure! Because of its tall and vertical masts, protruding antennas and hull-mounted sensors, a ship can be easily identified and attacked by the enemy. This shows that stealthiness is vital to surface ships.

Stealthiness is just one of the remarkable characteristics of the new-generation Zumwalt-class warships[2] that have been much discussed. This class is perceived as the pivot which can play an important role in modern warfare by use of laser weapons, artificial intelligence systems, expanded networks, advanced sonars and electrically-driven devices.

All the three high-tech Zumwalt destroyers are now in the ordinary course of things, Capt. Kevin Smith, Zumwalt-Class Program Manager, said at the Navy League's Sea, Air, Space Symposium. Smith went into details about how each destroyer is at different stages of development. The first one of USS Zumwalt-Class is in the process of weapons setting-up before its final delivery later in 2019. The Zumwalt is now test-firing its weapon systems, according to the preset operational scenario during the transit from Alaska to Hawaii, and what's more, its crew get a chance of receiving advanced tactical training so as to prepare for its maiden deployment. The practice involving the use of weapons, sensors and networks is a vital step towards the actual combat capability the destroyer needs. The second, PCU[3] Michael Monsoor (DDG 1001), has begun to show its combat availability, and the third, PCU Lyndon B. Johnson (DDG 1002) is under building according to the Hull, Mechanical and Electrical (HM&E) plan and will be delivered in time. The Johnson has already been 85 percent built since its launch in December, 2018. Smith explained the reason for the separate delivery of the three ships. By convention, they will get to a home port of San Diego[4] for further preparation before going into commission. Although there are small differences in some aspects such as deck layout, all the three ships are basically the same in structure and operational performance. Their developmental approaches are of great value and worthy of reference.

When it comes to the term "stealth", people often think of stealth aircraft, stealth bomber and stealth fighter-bomber. But now, the Zumwalt-Class destroyers with stealth characteristics have come into being as a result of the technical application of what constitutes "stealth".

Several years ago, when the Zumwalt-Class was at the early stage of development, there were many reports about its development according to the news released by the Naval Sea Systems Command[5]. It was claimed the Zumwalt looked like a small fishing boat through radar observation. The result obtained from radar is just what is expected. It seems that the Zumwalt has features of stealth. A large destroyer like the Zumwalt is very likely to generate returning echoes to be picked up by enemy radar or sonar, but its configuration is designed to produce a return object quite different than what it actually is, with the aim of confusing enemy radar. This is, in concept, fully aligned with the intended effect of Air Force stealth jet fighters and stealth bombers. They are designed to appear in the air like a "bird" or "insect" to practice deception on enemy radar.

As for its external shape, the Zumwalt lends itself to a discussion of some of these fundamentals regarding stealth properties. First and foremost, it is quite different from other surface ships in shape. The Zumwalt has fewer edges, no conspicuous protrusions or varied contours, and its left and right sides seamlessly connected with the edge of the deck are straight, flat and linear yet slightly angled. The Zumwalt's front exterior has only a few rounded edges without multiple sharp, intertwined steel panels and structures, which is requisite for stealthy purpose. Its wave-cutting Tumblehome[6] hull is narrower than the existing destroyers, making it less detectable to enemy sonars.

Most current destroyers have multiple deck-mounted sensors, weapon systems and angular staircases visibly positioned on the deck, but none of those facilities are mounted on the deck of the Zumwalt except the only entirely-enclosed superstructure and gun turret. Some of its weapons are housed in the seemingly rounded cone-shaped structures.

For example, a DDG 51 has multiple antennas, sensors, masts and other narrow, vertical structures with definable contours, but the Zumwalt does not. In addition, the Zumwalt's electric-drive propulsion system not only helps generate more electrical power for weapons, but is also much quieter, with less noise to be monitored by enemy sensors and even submarines. Interestingly, there are other "conceptual" parallels between the Zumwalt and stealthier jet fighters. From the ship's exterior can be seen very few sensors, weapons, antennas or other structures. This design is based on the advanced technology used for building stealth aircraft. Many sensors and antennas in stealth aircraft are embedded or woven "into" the skin of the aircraft according to the design requirements. For the Zumwalt, there are no visible "seams" or shaped "bolts" holding parts of the ship together. Considering these technological concepts, it does not seem surprising at all that many of the Zumwalts sensors, radars, sonars and other key devices have been deliberately placed or buried in the hull or exterior of the Zumwalt, as is the case for the Air Force stealth B-2. The B-2 has engines internally buried to cover the signs of its heat emission. Because of its rounded horizontal shape with no hard edged, steep angles or perpendicular structures, the stealth B-2 is more difficult to recognize by enemy radar. For the stealth aircraft, special materials have been to used for radar absorption. Although something specific about what materials are used for the Zumwalt is not released for security reasons, it is certain that the building materials of the ship have radar absorption characteristics.

According to Capt. Kevin Smith, the Zumwalt-class destroyer has technical and tactical advantages. Its new-type integrated power system (IPS) consists of main and auxiliary gas turbine generators and advanced induction motors, with total generating capacity of 78 megawatt[7]. The IPS is used to supply electricity to the propulsion system, high-power detection devices and high-energy weapons. Take the laser weapon for example. It is quite significant for a stealth surface ship because it has the advantage of silent attack. In such an

attack, the laser weapon gives out less detectable traces than missiles do.

As is known to all, ships have difficulties sailing in stealth on the surface. For this reason, technicians and engineers have done their best to apply stealth techniques to designing and building the stealthy Zumwalt-class destroyers for the purpose of keeping them invisible or undetectable by confusing the enemy radar sensors while they sail on the sea or in a sea fight.

*(1167 words)*

**Sources:**

https://www.foxnews.com/tech/3-new-stealthy-navy-destroyers-now-in-the-water

**Notes**

1. Tomahawk missile: a long-range, all-weather, jet-powered, subsonic cruise missile primarily used by the US Navy and Royal Navy 战斧式巡航导弹

2. Zumwalt-class warships: three US Navy guided missile destroyers belonging to Zumwalt-class and designed as multi-purpose stealth ships 朱姆沃尔特级战舰（美国海军新一代多用途对地打击宙斯盾舰）

3. PCU: Pre-Commissioning Unit, used for the US Navy ships that are not in commission yet 在建

4. San Diego: a city in the US state of California on the coast of the Pacific Ocean, approximately 120 miles south of Los Angeles and immediately adjacent to the border with Mexico 圣迭戈（亦作"圣地亚哥"，美国加州西南部城市）

5. Naval Sea Systems Command: the largest of the US Navy's five "systems commands", or material organizations. NAVSEA consists of four shipyards, ten "warfare centers", four major shipbuilding locations and the NASEA headquarters, located at the Washington Navy Yard, in Washington 海军海上系统指挥部

6. Tumblehome: a term describing the narrowing of a ship's hull as it rises above the water-line. In naval architecture it is present when a ship's beam is wider than its uppermost. 船舷内倾

7. megawatt：a unit of power equal to one million watts 兆瓦，百万瓦特（电能计量单位）

## Word Bank

| | |
|---|---|
| evade [ɪˈveɪd] | v.（尤指机敏地）避开 |
| undetectable [ˌʌndɪˈtektəbl] | adj. 看不见的，察觉不出的；探测不到的 |
| stealthy [ˈstelθɪ] | adj. 隐身的；不声张的；秘密的 |
| sensor [ˈsensə(r)] | n.（探测光、热、压力等的）传感器，敏感元件，探测设备 |
| antenna [ænˈtenə] | n. 天线 |
| protrude [prəˈtruːd] | v. 突出；伸出；鼓出 |
| pivot [ˈpɪvət] | n. 支点；枢轴；中心点；最重要的人（或事物）；核心 |
| symposium [sɪmˈpəʊzɪəm] | n. 专题讨论会；研讨会 |
| scenario [səˈnɑːrɪəʊ] | n. 设想；方案 |
| maiden [ˈmeɪdn] | adj. 首次的；初次的 |
| configuration[kənˌfɪɡəˈreɪʃn] | n. 布局；结构；构造；形状 |
| align [əˈlaɪn] | v. 排整齐；校准；（尤指）使成一条直线；使一致 |
| conspicuous [kənˈspɪkjʊəs] | adj. 易见的；明显的；惹人注意的 |
| contour [ˈkɒntʊə(r)] | n. 外形；轮廓 |
| seamless [ˈsiːmləs] | adj. 无（接）缝的；（两部分之间）无空隙的 |
| linear [ˈlɪnɪə(r)] | adj. 直线的；线性的； |
| intertwine [ˌɪntəˈtwaɪn] | v.（使）缠结，缠绕在一起；紧密相连 |
| requisite [ˈrekwɪzɪt] | adj. 必需的：必备的；必不可少的 |
| angular [ˈæŋɡjələ(r)] | adj. 有棱角的；有尖角的 |
| staircase [ˈsteəkeɪs] | n.（建筑物内的）楼梯 |
| cone [kəʊn] | n.（实心或空心的）圆锥体 |
| mast [mɑːst] | n. 桅杆；船桅；旗杆 |
| definable [dɪˈfaɪnəbl] | adj. 可辨别的 |
| seam [siːm] | n.（合在一起的两块木板等之间的）接缝，缝隙 |
| bolt [bəʊlt] | n.（门窗的）闩，插销；螺栓 |
| perpendicular [ˌpɜːpənˈdɪkjələ(r)] | adj. 垂直的 |
| induction [ɪnˈdʌkʃən] | n. 感应，电感 |

| | |
|---|---|
| deck-mounted | *adj.* 甲板安装式的 |
| hull-mounted | *adj.* 船体安装的 |
| generating capacity | 发电量 |
| high-power | *adj.* 大功率的 |
| high-energy | *adj.* 高能的 |

## I. Comprehension

**Part A**  Questions

*Answer the following questions in accordance with the text.*

1. When it comes to "stealthy" destroyers, what picture occurs in your mind?

2. Why is Zumwalt-class perceived as the pivot in modern warfare?

3. Can you give a description of three high-tech Zumwalt destroyers' development stages?

4. What's the difference between Zumwalt-Class and other surface ships in shape?

5. What's the function of the Zumwalt's electric-drive propulsion system?

**Part B**  Multiple Choices

*Choose the most appropriate answer from the given choices below each question in accordance with the text.*

1. Which of the following descriptions of Zumwalt destroyers is NOT true?

   A. The first one of USS Zumwalt class is now test-firing its weapon systems.

   B. The second one of USS Zumwalt class has begun to show its combat availability.

   C. The third one of USS Zumwalt class is under building according to the Hull, Mechanical and Electrical (HM&E) plan.

   D. All three ships are entirely different in structure and operational performance.

2. In the past, when it comes to the term "stealth", people usually think of the following except _____.

   A. stealth aircraft

   B. stealth bombers

   C. stealth fighter-bombers

   D. stealth destroyer

3. Which of the following facilities are mounted on the deck of the Zumwalt?

    A. weapon systems

    B. deck-mounted sensors

    C. angular staircases

    D. entirely-enclosed superstructure

4. According to Capt. Kevin Smith, which of the following is wrong?

    A. The Zumwalt-class destroyer only has tactical advantages.

    B. The new-type integrated power system consists of main and auxiliary gas turbine generators and advanced induction motors

    C. The IPS is used to supply electricity to the propulsion system, high-power detection devices and high-energy weapons.

    D. Laser weapon is quite significant for a stealth surface ship because it has the advantage of silent attack.

5. Which of the following descriptions concerning Air Force stealth B-2 is NOT true?

    A. The B-2 has engines externally buried to cover the signs of its heat emission.

    B. The B-2 has rounded horizontal shape with no hard edged, steep angles or perpendicular structures.

    C. The stealth B-2 is more difficult to recognize by enemy radar.

    D. The technological concepts of stealth B-2 and the Zumwalt-class destroyer is somewhat similar.

## II. Translation

**Part A** Terms & Phrases

*Translate the following terms or phrases from Chinese into English and vice versa.*

| | |
|---|---|
| 1. 甲板布局 | 2. 散热 |
| 3. 吸收雷达 | 4. 综合电力系统 |
| 5. 总发电量 | 6. 推进系统 |
| 7. 大功率探测装置 | 8. 高能武器 |
| 9. 隐形战斗轰炸机 | 10. 全封闭的上层建筑 |
| 11. stealthy | 12. sensor |
| 13. antenna | 14. configuration |
| 15. maiden deployment | 16. deck-mounted |

17. preset operational scenario

18. return object

19. separate delivery

20. gun turret

**Part B** **Paragraph**

*Translate the following paragraph from English into Chinese.*

Its new-type integrated power system (IPS) consists of main and auxiliary gas turbine generators and advanced induction motors, with total generating capacity of 78 megawatt. The IPS is used to supply electricity to the propulsion system, high-power detection devices and high-energy weapons. Take the laser weapon for example. It is quite significant for a stealth surface ship because it has the advantage of silent attack. In such an attack, the laser weapon gives out less detectable traces than missiles do.

## III. Reading Report

What have you learned after reading the text? Have you obtained a clear understanding of stealth Zumwalt-class destroyers? Now create your reading report in no more than 150 words to generalize your achievement in text study.

## Text B
## Fiscal Year[1] (FY) 2020 Annual Long-Range Plan for Construction of Naval Ships

The National Defense Strategy[2] and the Navy Strategy determine the **overarching** high-level requirements for the US Navy. The Navy's long-term plan aims at building up and sustaining a powerful maritime force through balanced investments in shipbuilding, and weaponry and equipment for improving the readiness capability and operational capacity. This 30-year shipbuilding plan for the Navy's future development presents the following highlights:

- Continuing to increase the production capacity and efficiency of shipyards and improve the **seaworthiness** and **maneuverability** of ships, and pursuing the Secretary of the Navy's[3] reform initiatives that require considerable improvements in **procurement** and program management.

- Acting on the FY2018 National Defense Authorization Act (NDAA[4]), supporting the Navy's **validated** minimum requirement of 355 warships of different types and following the FY2019 NDAA which involves budget for sustaining a larger fleet in the context of the balanced investment plan.

- Predicting the significant combined effect of stable and timely funding on shipbuilding, and the potential unfavorable impact of Budget Control Act[5] on the fulfillment of this plan.

- Procuring 55 warships according to the Future Years Defense Program (FYDP[6]) and attaching importance to service life extension (SLE[7]) in an effort to attain the ultimate goal of 355 about 20 years ahead of the plan made last year. It is possible to predict that the acquisition programs will be better implemented and efforts will be made to carry out reforms in the aspects of shipbuilding, maintenance, and personnel management.

- Saving $4 billion (18%) through negotiation for the procurement of two aircraft carriers and by suspending the **overhaul** of the refueling facility of one aircraft carrier. The savings can help balance the investments in the next-generation naval equipment.

- Taking the fiscal challenge in carrying out the shipbuilding plan while starting serial production of the new Columbia-class SSBN[8].

- Taking challenges from commercial shipbuilding and **recapitalizing** the funds for auxiliary fleet[9] according to the concept of Distributed Maritime Operations (DMO[10]).

The National Defense Strategy puts emphasis on how the United States military will compete with, deter and defeat any adversary by deploying a more powerful and rapid-reaction joint force. With the rapid development of technology and the increasing complexity of operating environments, the Navy pays more attention to adaptability, maneuverability and quick reaction capability. The Navy Strategy made in accordance with the National Defense Strategy includes the major elements of readiness capability and operational capacity, which must be attainable and sustainable so as to build up a credible naval power.

The FY2020 shipbuilding plan needs to be implemented in combination with the reform initiatives proposed in the 2018 Shipyard Infrastructure Optimization Plan[11], the Long-Range Plan for Maintenance and Modernization of Naval Vessels[12], the Sealift that the Nation Needs[13] and the Navy strategy in order to improve the naval forces' combat efficiency and self-sustaining capability. The following framework defines the three major imperatives for shipbuilding:

- Steady and sustainable Growth. Sustaining the minimum-leveled acquisition to develop the force at a steady and affordable rate while implementing a balanced military investment strategy. Keeping the industrial base at a healthy level is of particular importance to supporting the affordable acquisition, predictable and efficient main-tenance and modernization, and more aggressive growth of an appropriate-scale naval force on condition that additional resources become available. Steady and sustainable growth can ensure the strength of naval forces in the long run.

- Aggressive Growth. Accelerating the production by taking advantage of available industrial capacity and additional resources and expanding on basis of long-term steady growth if possible without harm to the overall balance of the military investment plan— the upper boundary of what can be attained (aggressive growth) and what must be sustained (steady growth).

- Service Life Extension (SLE). SLE is very valuable in the ship management inventories, but it must complement (not replace) the long-term development program discussed above so as to have a desired positive effect on inventory objectives. There are two kinds of SLE: collective SLE based upon engineering analysis of performance metrics over time, and individual SLE of a specific ship being imminently out of commission. Collective SLE is more valuable for long-term planning, sustainment, and inventory management. Two notable examples of successful collective SLE are the service life of the Ohio-class SSBN[14] is extended to the 42nd year and that of the recent Arleigh Burke-class DDG[15] is extended to the 45th year.

The PB2020 30-year Shipbuilding Plan[16] includes procurement of 55 warships in accordance with the FYDP. Overall inventory will reach 314 ships by FY2024 and 355 ships in FY2034. The blueprint now provides a predictable bright future for fleet planners, shipbuilders and numerous supporting acquisition programs as well as competent contributors—maintainers, trainers etc. The mix of ships has a bias towards DDG before coming up to the standards and objectives of other ships types. In the inventory of ships, SSN[17] and CVN[18] are lacking in number. So, SSNs need the expansion of production. Although the existing DDGs can not completely compensate for that shortage, they still have powerful combat capability and lethality, realizing the balance of the force. 355 ships in the inventory are **capped** beyond FY2034, so the present operating and sustainment costs must be managed well, and meanwhile additional DDGs are needed for service if possible. Achieving these objectives depends on the required conditions, practicable shipbuilding plan, sufficient funds, and updated inventory requirements. In addition to an increase in the number of DDGs, the most notable adjustments made according to the plan of 2019 include:

- Procuring two aircraft carriers (CVN 80 and CVN 81), which results in saving $4B to be spent on CVN 81—its procurement to be advanced from FY2023 to FY2020. The Ford-class[19] represents Navy's enduring commitment to the construction of a new type of aircraft carrier.

- Considering its previously funded Refueling Complex Overhaul (RCOH[20]), CVN-75 is allowed to be out of commission. This adjustment is **in concert with** the Defense Department's pursuit of a more appropriate balance between **high-end**, survivable platforms (e.g. CVNs) and complementary capabilities resulting from novel technologies. Timely and effective operations analysis and threat study can keep the naval forces informed of operational environments and specific requirements. So, the Navy has been paying much attention to these studies. In order to get an increase in the number of warships, the Navy plans to do the following things:

- Adding a third SSN in FY2020, procuring one DDG in FY2020 but not in FY2021, and adding a second FFG(X)[21] in FY2021.

- Delaying the procurement of LPD[22] aims at balancing shipbuilding costs in support of near-term priorities determined in the National Defense Strategy. The Navy decided to **defer** its procurement in FY2024 to a later date according to the FYDP.

- Extending the service life of the entire DDG-51 class, and adding two Los Angeles-class attack submarines[23]. Also, five additional SSNs are needed for SLE.

- Accelerating the process of getting mine countermeasure ships (MCMs[24]) out of commission. The Navy focuses on both future MCM capability and near-term improvement of operational availability (Ao[25]) of the aging Avenger-class MCMs, giving priority to the forward deployed naval force (FDNF[26]).

*(1192 words)*

**Sources:**

https://news.usni.org/2019/03/21/fy-2020-u-s-navy-30-year-shipbuilding-plan

## Notes

1. Fiscal Year (FY): a one-year period that companies and governments use for financial reporting and budgeting 财政年度（财年）
2. NDS: National Defense Strategy 国防战略
3. The Secretary of the Navy: (or SECNAV) a statutory officer and the head (chief executive officer) of the Department of the Navy, a military department (component organization) within the Department of Defense of the United States of America 美国海军部长
4. NDAA: National Defense Authorization Act 《美国国防授权法案》
5. Budget Control Act: a federal statute for controlling the budget that was passed by the Congress and signed into law by the President 预算控制法案
6. FYDP: Future Years Defense Program 未来多年防御计划
7. SLE: service life extension, which means extending the service life of ships, systems, equipment,etc 使用寿命延长
8. Columbia-class SSBN: The Columbia-Class ballistic missile submarine will be powered by an electric-drive propulsion system that includes an electric motor driving the propeller of the boat and use a nuclear reactor to produce the necessary electrical energy to supply the electric propulsion motor. 哥伦比亚级战略核潜艇
9. auxiliary fleet: a group of support or supply ships that accompany a main fleet 辅助舰队
10. DMO: Distributed Maritime Operations 分布式海洋作战
11. Shipyard Infrastructure Optimization Plan: a comprehensive, 20-year, $21-billion effort to optimize the infrastructures at the four naval shipyards by repairing and maintaining critical dry docks, restoring the facilities to working order and removing the aging and out-of-date equipment 船厂基础架构优化计划

12. the Long-Range Plan for the Maintenance and Modernization of Naval Vessels: A plan which complements the FY2020 Annual Long-Range Plan for Construction of Naval Vessels to effectively maintain investments in the Navy. 海军舰船维修和现代化远程计划

13. the Sealift that the Nation Needs 国家需要的海上运输

14. Ohio-class SSBN: The Ohio-Class submarines serve the US Navy as virtually undetectable undersea launch platforms of intercontinental missiles. 俄亥俄级战略核潜艇

15. Arleigh Burke-class DDG: the Arleigh Burke class of guided missile destroyers (DDGs) 阿利·伯克级导弹驱逐舰

16. PB2020 30-year Shipbuilding Plan: PB denotes President's Budget. 总统2020年预算30年造船计划

17. SSN: a nuclear-powered general-purpose attack submarine 攻击型核潜艇

18. CVN: Nucear Powered Aircraft Carrier 核动力航空母舰

19. Ford-class: which means a Ford-class aircraft carrier 福特级航母

20. RCOH: Refueling Complex Overhaul 加油综合检修

21. FFG(X): guided missile frigate, which represents the most capable and modern frigate in the world. It delivers needed capabilities to the US Navy with enhanced lethality, survivability, safety, maintainability, habitability, and cybersecurity. 新一代导弹护卫舰

22. LPD: Landing Platform Dock 船坞登陆舰

23. Los Angeles-class attack submarine 洛杉矶级攻击潜艇

24. MCMs: mine countermeasures ships 反水雷舰艇

25. Ao: operational availability 作战有效性

26. FDNF: forward deployed naval force 前沿部署的海军部队

## Word Bank

| | |
|---|---|
| fiscal [ˈfɪskl] | adj. 财政的；国库的；国家岁入的 |
| overarching [ˌəʊvərˈɑːtʃɪŋ] | adj. 非常重要的；首要的 |
| seaworthiness [ˈsiːwɜːðməs] | n. 适航性 |
| maneuverability [məˌnuːvərəˈbɪlɪtɪ] | n. 机动性 |
| procurement [prəˈkjʊəmənt] | n.（尤指为政府或机构）采购，购买 |
| validate [ˈvælɪdeɪt] | v. 批准；认可；使有法律效力 |
| overhaul [ˈəʊvəhɔːl] | n. 检修；大修；改造 |
| recapitalize [ˌriːkəˈpɪtəlaɪz] | v.（对……）进行资本重组 |

| sealift [ˈsiːlɪft] | *n.*（尤指紧急）海上运输，海上补给 |
|---|---|
| imperative [ɪmˈperətɪv] | *n.* 重要紧急的事；必要的事 |
| inventory [ˈɪnvəntrɪ] | *n.*（建筑物里的物品、家具等的）清单；库存 |
| metrics [ˈmetrɪks] | *n.* 衡量指标；量度 |
| cap [kæp] | *v.*（政府）限制（组织或地方议会的支出），限定（预算），限定金额 |
| high-end [ˌhaɪˈend] | *adj.* 高档的；高端的；价高质优的 |
| defer [dɪˈfɜː(r)] | *v.* 推迟；延缓 |
| in concert with | 与……一致；与……合作；相呼应 |

## *Exercises*

## I. True or False

*Decide whether the following sentences are true or false in accordance with the text.*

1. The National Defense Strategy and the Navy Strategy determine the overarching high-level requirements for the US Navy.

2. The Navy Strategy puts emphasis on how the United States military will compete with, deter and defeat any adversary by deploying a more powerful rapid-reaction joint force.

3. One of the three major imperatives for shipbuilding is to sustain the maximum level acquisition to develop the force at a steady and affordable rate while implementing a balanced military investment strategy.

4. SLE is valuable in the ship management inventories, but it must replace the long-term development program.

5. There are two kinds of SLE: collective SLE and individual SLE.

6. In the inventory of ships, SSNs and CVNs are sufficient.

7. Although the existing DDGs can not completely compensate for that shortage, they still have powerful combat capability and lethality, realizing the balance of the force.

8. The Ford class represents Navy's enduring commitment to the construction of a new type of aircraft carrier.

9. The Navy decided to continue its procurement of LPD in FY2024 to a later date according to the FYDP.

10. The Navy focuses on both future MCM capability and long-term improvement of

operational availability of the aging Avenger-class MCMs, giving priority to the forward deployed naval force.

## II. Word Match

*Match the words/terms/phrases in the left column with its appropriate correspondents in the right column.*

1. Fiscal Year
2. National Defense Strategy
3. readiness capability
4. operational capacity
5. auxiliary fleet
6. seaworthiness and maneuverability
7. operational availability
8. forward deployed naval force
9. overhaul
10. sealift

A. 辅助舰队
B. 备战能力
C. 适航性和机动性
D. 检修
E. 前沿部署的海军部队
F. 作战能力
G. 国防战略
H. 海上运输
I. 作战有效性
J. 财年

## Text C
## Damage Control

Damage Control is considered to be absolutely essential for a ship. It is defined as taking precautions, measures or actions to minimize or eliminate damage in order to save a ship or maintain its own survivability. If damage occurs, measures must be taken quickly to deal with it. After it is controlled, investigation is needed to be made on the causes of the damage, such as shipboard fire and flooding. In most cases, damage results from short-circuits, collision, hit, or munitions explosion. Besides, a hidden danger of damage can never be ignored, which includes abnormal power loss, inexplicable smoke, a slight leak in the seam and excessive heat of bulkhead.

As is known to all, damage sustained by ships in peacetime accidents is often similar to the effect of wartime enemy action; a peacetime collision with possible attendant fires and explosions may be just as enemy hits. Therefore, all seamen must be trained in damage control. A course in firefighting is given to every recruit in basic training. Most are also introduced to at least the basics of first aid. In the battle training, every crewman on board has a station, and a part in damage control operations. The Damage Control Assistant is attached to the engineering department. He supervises the training of the crew in damage control measures and checks the ship's emergency preparations. In battle, he mans the Damage Control Center, keeping track of casualties, damage to the ship and remedial measures taken. Generally, there are eight repair parties on board a ship, each responsible for a different station of the ship. When damage happens, the repair parties must take measures or actions to overcome it as soon as possible.

All Damage-Control personnel should understand that damage is sometimes more serious than expected. For example, a projectile or bomb obliquely pierces Compartment A of a vessel and then explodes in Compartment B, as shown in Fig. Thorough check should be conducted on all spaces along the path of the projectile, including all systems and structures in every compartment adjacent to B and even two or three compartments below. The purpose is to find out the degree and magnitude of damage caused by explosion shock and fragments and to determine the boundaries around the damaged area.

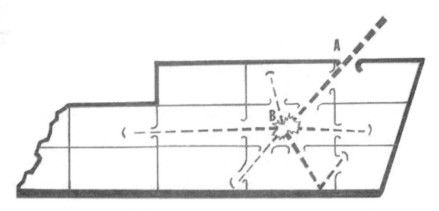

**Figure**  Schematic drawing of a bomb piercing Compartment A obliquely and exploding in Compartment B

After that, measures must be taken to remove the obvious damage and to locate latent faults causing damage. Repairmen should be provided with protective equipment, lighting and ventilating facilities to cope with damage.Numerous facts confirm that fire and flooding are the severest threats to the safety of a ship.

As for shipboard fire, it may bring about a great disaster to a ship if it is uncontrolled. Although modern construction techniques and materials have reduced the danger of shipboard fire, consumable supplies such as paint stores and dry and liquid cargo pose an ever-present threat. Once started, big fires are difficult and sometimes impossible to extinguish. What is worthy of note is that even small fires may disrupt essential circuits, causing a loss in power and communications.

In case of fire, the fire fighters should take actions immediately to save the ship from grave danger. Men should wear breathing apparatus while fighting fires in interior spaces. No repairs can be done until the fire is put out.

The electric circuits in the damaged area must be cut off or de-energized to prevent a short circuit. The reason is that a short circuit will lead to an electrical accident which may cause a fire.

The pipe lines in the damaged area are subject to rupture and the valves to breakdown. If the lines are so badly damaged as not to be repaired at once, the sections where they are in must be isolated from the others.

The air in a damaged area is certain to be fouled with smoke, fumes and gases, many of which will be injurious to personnel. If a compartment may be so hot that repairmen cannot remain there, they must be provided with fresh air through the regular ventilation system, or by means of air bleed[1] and portable blowers[2]. Hot compartments can be cooled by using the fog

nozzles for spraying and men can be cooled by drenching their clothing or using streams of water to get themselves wet through. And breathing apparatus should be worn in time of need.

When the compartment is not on fire and before it needs to be repaired, fire extinguishers should be brought to the scene, and the air should be tested for its explosive vapors and oxygen content before repair work is begun. Tests of poisonous fumes should also be made to prevent personnel from being overcome by them.

The detailed information about the damage obtained from the investigation should be reported to the officers in charge of their respective repair parties, who study and judge it and then pass it on to the damage control officer of the damage control center. The damage control center is an important department of a ship that is responsible for directing emergency repairs after the ship is damaged so as to maintain the ship's operational capacity.

Moreover, after serious damage, the captain must be informed of his ship's existing power, buoyancy and stability, weapons effectiveness, and related casualties.

For a ship, serious flooding is very terrible. Whenever it suffers damage like that flooding, the damage is so extensive that the ship never stops listing or settling in the water, going down within a few minutes. Sometimes, a ship may suffer a hit or collision which makes a large hole opened in the side. Immediate flooding occurs through the hole, giving the ship her initial list, trim, and reduced stability. This structural damage must be taken seriously.

The personnel concerned should investigate and assess the structural damage and propose useful plans for emergency repairs. If flooding comes about below the waterline, it is necessary to curb the flooding in order to keep the ship from sinking, and to discharge flooding water as much as possible in order to restore its buoyancy and stability.

In addition to structural damage, there may be a certain amount of subsidiary damage, with riddled or warped bulkheads and decks, opened seams, leaking doors and hatches, etc. These permit slow leakage and progressive flooding pour the boundaries of the damage. The slow flooding is aggravated if sailors escaping from the damaged area leave doors or scuttles open behind them.

In order to limit or minimize damage to a ship, precautions against damage must be prepared beforehand. If damage suddenly happens to a ship, the precautions will determine whether efforts to save the ship afterwards can be successful or not. To be sure, with effective precautions available for use, warships are more capable of dealing with damage than merchant ships because they are usually fully compartmented and have more men and equipment to get over the damage. Now, merchant ships have a tendency to improve their capability of resisting damage. In short, well-prepared precautions will certainly play a vital role in damage control.

Generally speaking, the precautions include:

- Utilizing the designed hull safety features at all times when a ship is at sea(for example, ensuring that watertight boundaries are reliably maintained).
- Ensuring that the ship is not overloaded.
- Ensuring that deck loads are not exceeded.
- Ensuring proper amount and distribution of liquid and other cargo and ballast.
- Ensuring that crew members are trained in damage control to correctly take measures against damage once it occurs.

In addition, two important decisions must be made immediately after serious damage. These two decisions are (1) whether all hands should remain aboard, all but the salvage party should be evacuated, or all hands should abandon ship, and (2) what corrective measures will improve the situation instead of making it worse. The first decision is made by the captain, but his conclusions must be based on information he receives from the engineer. The second decision is up to the engineer to make according to his judgement of the situation.

In order to further the capability of damage control, navies of many countries are making great efforts to research and develop advanced control damage training simulation software and land simulation systems for crewmen to use in peacetime training.

*(1390 words)*

---

**Sources:** - - - - - - - - - - - - - - - - - - - - - - - - - - - - - - - - - - - - - - - - - - - - -

https://maritime.org/doc/dc/part8.htm#pg245l

## Notes

1. air bleed: a slow escape or admission of air provided for in a mechanical system (as for equalizing pressure) 通气器（引出空气）
2. portable blower: an easy-to-carry facility with fans which move air to ventilate wherever a breeze is required 便携式鼓风机

## Word Bank

| | |
|---|---|
| precaution [prɪˈkɔːʃn] | n. 预防措施；预防；防备 |
| survivability [səˌvaɪvəˈbɪlɪtɪ] | n. 生命力；生存能力 |
| short-circuit [ˌʃɔːtˈsɜːkɪt] | n.（电）短路 |

collision [kəˈlɪʒn]     *n.* 碰撞（或相撞）事故

munition [mjuːˈnɪʃn]     *n.* 军用品（尤指枪、炮、弹药）；军火

inexplicable [ˌɪnɪkˈsplɪkəbl]     *adj.* 不能说明的；无法解释的

bulkhead [ˈbʌlkhed]     *n.* （船舱或机舱的）舱壁

attendant [əˈtendənt]     *adj.* 附带的

remedial [rɪˈmiːdɪəl]     *adj.* 旨在解决问题的；补救的；纠正的

projectile [prəˈdʒektaɪl]     *n.* （武器发射的）投射物；枪弹；炮弹

compartment [kəmˈpɑːtmənt]     *n.* 舱室

    *v.* 分割，划分

adjacent [əˈdʒeɪsnt]     *adj.* 与……毗连的；邻近的

fragment [ˈfrægmənt]     *n.* 爆炸碎片

latent [ˈleɪtnt]     *adj.* 潜在的；隐藏的

ventilate [ˈventɪleɪt]     *v.* 使（房间、建筑物等）通风

de-energize [diːˈenədʒaɪz]     *v.* 切断，断电，停电

rupture [ˈrʌptʃə]     *n.* 断裂，破裂

valve [vælv]     *n.* 阀；阀门

nozzle [ˈnɒzl]     *n.* 管口；喷嘴

vapor [ˈveɪpə(r)]     *n.* 蒸汽，水气

buoyancy [ˈbɔɪənsɪ]     *n.* 浮力

list [lɪst]     *v.* （船）（向一侧）倾斜；横倾

settle [ˈsetl]     *v.* （使）沉降，下陷

trim [trɪm]     *v.* 纵倾

riddled [ˈrɪdld]     *adj.* 布满窟窿的

warped [wɔːpt]     *adj.* 弯曲的；扭曲的；变形的

scuttles [ˈskʌtlz]     *n.* 舷窗

 **Exercises**

Based on what you have acquired in this text, you are supposed to conduct an online study to explore further into the relevant sphere. Comb and frame what you have found with an online study report in no less than 200 words. In addition, any assistant image, audio, video, or other first-hand material will be preferred when you present your report in class.

# Unit 10  Power Plant

**Bridge-in**

*Answer the following questions in accordance with the microlesson "A Brief Introduction to the Electromagnetic Aircraft Launch System".*

1. Why is EMALS necessary for aircraft taking off from aircraft carriers?
2. What are the major components of EMALS?
3. What is the significance of China's achievement on EMALS?

## Text A
## Electromagnetic Aircraft Launch System (EMALS)[1]

The Electromagnetic Aircraft Launch System (EMALS) is a complete carrier-based launch system designed to expand the operational capability of Ford-class carriers[2], providing the Navy with capability for launching all current and future carrier air wing[3] platforms – lightweight **unmanned** to heavy strike fighters. The mission and function of EMALS remains the same as traditional steam **catapult**; however, it employs entirely different technologies. EMALS uses stored kinetic energy[4] and **solid-state** electrical power conversion. This technology permits a high degree of computer control, monitoring and automation.

The US Navy demonstrated initial integration of future naval aircraft on 18 November 2011 when it launched F-35C[5] test aircraft CF-3[6] with its new EMALS. Testing the F-35C using EMALS provided a good opportunity to evaluate technical risks, and began the process to integrate the carrier variant Joint Strike Fighter[7] with the future carrier fleet aircraft launch system.

The US Navy has begun using electromagnetic launch (EML) technology instead of the existing steam catapults on current and future aircraft carriers. The steam catapults are

large, heavy, without feedback control[8]. They transfer large transient loads[9] to the airframe, so they are difficult and time-consuming to maintain. The steam catapult is also approaching its operational limit with the present complement of naval aircraft. The **inexorable** trend towards heavier, faster aircraft will soon lead the launch energy requirements to exceed the capability of the steam catapult. An EML system offers higher launch energy capability and better performance characteristics as well as substantial improvements in other areas. These include reduced weight, volume and maintenance costs, and increased controllability, availability, reliability and efficiency.

### EMALS Benefits

The introduction of EMALS will have an overall positive impact on the ship. The launch engine is capable of a high **thrust density**, as shown by the half-scale model[10] with 1322 psi[11] over its cross section, as compared with the relatively low 450 psi of the steam catapult. The same is true of energy storage devices, which is **analogous** to the steam catapult's steam **accumulator**. The low energy density of the steam accumulator will be replaced by high energy density **flywheels**. These flywheels provide energy densities of 28 KJ[12]/KG. The increased densities can reduce the system's volume and allow for more room for vital support equipment on the host platform.

Another advantage of EMALS is that it may reduce manual requirements by inspecting and troubleshooting itself. This is a significant improvement over the present system, which requires substantial manual inspection and maintenance. EMALS, however, requires a transition from mechanical technology to electrical/electronic technology.

EMALS is not so complex as the present system composed of different subsystems. The steam catapult uses about 614 kg of steam for launching; it extensively uses **hydraulics**, water for braking, and electromechanics. These subsystems, along with their associated pumps, motors and control systems, tend to make the whole launch system complex. But for EMALS, its launch motor can function well in launching, braking, and **retraction**, with the reduction of **auxiliary** components and the simplification of the overall system as a result. EMALS is an independent system, completely independent of the ship's main plant. This will allow greater flexibility in the design of a ship and its more efficient propulsion system schemes.

One of the major advantages of EML is the ability to be integrated into the all-electric ship. The US Navy has directed substantial research into its Advanced Surface Machinery Program that aims at developing electric-drive propulsion technology for the next generation of surface combatants. There has also been a good deal of work in high-power electric weapon systems. As such, a ship's systems will evolve from old mechanical systems into electric-drive ones. The average power required by EMALS is only 6.35 MVA[13]. Taking these power levels off the **grid** should not be a problem in an all-electric ship, considering multi-megawatt pumps already exist on carriers for various applications.

Perhaps the most interesting aspect of EML is the flexibility it offers in the way of future aircraft and ship designs. An electromagnetic (EM) launcher can easily be sized down to perform as a launch-assist system, contributing to the short takeoff of a STOVL aircraft[14]. It can also be easily incorporated into the contour of a ramp, which provides a more efficient fly-away angle for the aircraft being launched. This reduces the commensurate energy supplied and the stress on the airframe. Overall, an EM launcher offers a great deal of flexibility to future naval requirements and ship designs.

Due to the inherent high level of elegant control of electronic equipment, it is possible to reduce the stress imparted to the aircraft. The present steam catapult has relatively high peak-to-mean[15] acceleration profiles (nominally 1.25, with **bias** up to 2.0). This results in high stress on the airframe and generally poor performance. With an electromagnetic system, it is possible to correct the **deviations** in the acceleration profile in typically hundreds of milliseconds, which will result in low peak-to-means. This low peak-to-means can reduce the stress on the airframe. To quantify the effect of a reduced peak-to-mean, a Fracture Mechanics[16] analysis has been conducted on the airframe with both the steam catapult and EMALS peak-to-means. The results from this analysis show that a peak airframe life extension is up to 31% due to the reduced stress on the airframe. This is becoming more important as tight budgets are forcing the US Navy to procure fewer aircraft. In addition, when EMALS meets with any unforeseen problems during a launch, it has the capability of quick adjustment and solution, even if a component fails during the launch.

EMALS offers the increased energy capability necessary to launch the next generation of carrier-based aircraft. This will provide a means of launching all present naval carrier-based aircraft and those in the foreseeable future.

### EMALS Drawbacks

On the other hand, there are drawbacks to EMALS. One of these is that high-power electromagnetic motors create electromagnetic interference (EMI) with electronic equipment. As in the case of an EM launcher, there is sensitive aircraft equipment sitting directly above

the launch motor. Along with the aircraft equipment is the ship's own equipment, which may be affected by the electromagnetic emissions[17]. Through the proper EMC[18] design and "magnetically closed" motor design, EMI will be minimized.

All prospective EMALS designs must meet the requirements for launching present and future naval fixed-wing aircraft from the deck of an aircraft carrier. The designs involve 30% reduction in manning, 20% reduction in life-cycle cost, 20% improvement in operational availability, and up to a 50% reduction in installed size and weight as compared with the current steam catapults. The EMALS performance requirements are: 90,000,000 ft-lbs[19] of power capability, an end speed[20] of 55 to 200 knots, a peak-to-mean acceleration of 1.05 for launching various aircrafts (including lightweight aircraft such as Unmanned Air Vehicles and Unmanned Combat Air Vehicles), and a 45-second cycle time.

*(1136 words)*

*Sources:*

*Time Magazine*, May, 2017. https://www.globalsecurity.org/military/systems/ship/systems/emals.htm

**Notes**

1. Electromagnetic Aircraft Launch System: EMALS 电磁弹射系统

2. Ford-class carriers: Gerald R. Ford-class aircraft carriers 福特级航空母舰

3. carrier air wing: a carrier-based administrative and tactical combat unit 舰载机联队

4. kinetic energy: energy generated by a moving body 动能

5. F-35C: a type of joint strike fighter designed and made in the US F-35C 型战斗机

6. CF-3: a type of F-35C fighter CF-3 型战斗机

7. Joint Strike Fighter: a type of fighter of wide use, advanced performance and affordable price jointly developed by the US various services 联合攻击战斗机

8. feedback control: controlling the process of returning the output information of a system to its source so as to modify the output 反馈控制

9. transient load: load in transient time, which is the load with higher loading rate 瞬（时荷）载，瞬变负载

10. half-scale model: a model established to a 1/2 scale of the real object 比例为1/2的模型

11. psi: pounds per square inch 磅/英寸$^2$，每平方英寸磅数（1psi=0.068大气压力=0.70kg/cm$^2$）

12. KJ: kilojoule 千焦耳（能量、热量、功的单位）

13. MVA: megavolt-ampere 兆伏安

14. STOVL aircraft: short take-off and vertical landing aircraft 短距起飞垂直降落飞机

15. peak-to-mean: the ratio of peak value to mean/average value 峰均比

16. Fracture Mechanics: a branch of the science of motion and force concerning the study of the propagation of cracks in materials 断裂力学

17. electromagnetic emission: electromagnetic wave emitted by the interaction between electric field and magnetic field 电磁辐射，电磁发射

18. EMC: electromagnetic compatibility 电磁兼容性

19. ft-lbs: foot-pounds 英尺磅（功的单位）

20. end speed: instantaneous velocity of an object at the end of its motion 末速

## *Word Bank*

| | |
|---|---|
| unmanned [ˌʌnˈmænd] | *adj.* 无人的；无人操纵的 |
| catapult [ˈkætəpʌlt] | *n.* （航母上的弹射飞机的）弹射器 |
| solid-state [ˌsɒlɪdˈsteɪt] | *adj.* （电子器材）使用晶体管或硅片的 |
| inexorable [ɪnˈeksərəbl] | *adj.* 不可阻挡的；无法改变的 |
| analogous [əˈnæləɡəs] | *adj.* 类似的；可比拟的 |
| accumulator [əˈkjuːmjəleɪtə(r)] | *n.* 蓄能器 |
| flywheel [ˈflaɪwiːl] | *n.* [机]飞轮，惯性轮；调速轮 |
| hydraulics [haɪˈdrɒlɪks] | *n.* 液压技术；水力学 |
| retraction [rɪˈtrækʃn] | *n.* 收回；撤回，撤销 |
| auxiliary [ɔːɡˈzɪliəri] | *adj.* 辅助的；附加的；（发动机、设备等）备用的 |
| grid [ɡrɪd] | *n.* 电网；网格 |
| bias [ˈbaɪəs] | *n.* 偏移；偏差 |
| deviation [ˌdiːvɪˈeɪʃn] | *n.* 偏差；偏离 |
| thrust density | 推力密度 |

**Exercises**

## I. Comprehension

**Part A** Questions

*Answer the following questions in accordance with the text.*

1. What is the design objective of the Electromagnetic Aircraft Launch System (EMALS)?

2. What is the significance of the US testing the F-35C on EMALS?

3. Why is EMALS not so complex as the present system composed of different subsystems?

4. How does an EM launcher offer a great deal of flexibility to future naval requirements and ship designs?

5. How can electromagnetic interference (EMI) be minimized?

**Part B** Multiple Choices

*Choose the most appropriate answer from the given choices below each question in accordance with the text.*

1. When did the US Navy launch F-35C test aircraft CF-3 with its new EMALS?

   A. On 18 September, 2011.

   B. On 18 November, 2011.

   C. On 19 November, 2011.

   D. On 19 September, 2011.

2. Which of the following descriptions of the existing steam catapults is NOT true?

   A. They are large and heavy.

   B. They operate without feedback control.

   C. They impart large transient loads to the airframe.

   D. They use stored kinetic energy and solid-state electrical power conversion.

3. Which of the following is NOT included as the substantial improvements of EMALS?

   A. Reduced weight.

   B. Reduced availability.

   C. Increased controllability.

   D. Increased efficiency.

4. What does the result of the Fracture Mechanics analysis conducted on the airframe show?

    A. The performance of airframe is impaired.

    B. The peak-to-mean ratio is reduced.

    C. The lifespan of airframe is extended.

    D. The stress on the catapult is reduced.

5. Which of the following descriptions of EMALS and steam catapult is true?

    A. It employs entirely different technologies from the traditional steam catapult.

    B. Its mission and function is entirely different from the traditional steam catapult.

    C. It aims to reduce 30% of required personnel and life-cycle cost compared with steam catapults.

    D. It aims to improve 20% of operational availability and 50% of size and weight compared with steam catapults.

## II. Translation

### Part A Terms & Phrases

*Translate the following terms or phrases from Chinese into English and vice versa.*

1. 舰载机联队
2. 轻型无人战斗机
3. 重型攻击机
4. 蒸汽弹射器
5. 动能
6. 固体电子学
7. 航母编队
8. 全电力驱动舰
9. 水面战斗部队
10. 发射辅助系统
11. 断裂力学
12. 舰载机
13. 固定翼飞机
14. 无人战斗机
15. Electromagnetic Aircraft Launch System
16. Joint Strike Fighter
17. feedback control
18. transient load
19. thrust density
20. cross section
21. host platform
22. STOVL aircraft
23. peak-to-mean ratio
24. life extension
25. EMI
26. electromagnetic emission
27. EMC

**Part B**　Paragraph

*Translate the following paragraph from English into Chinese.*

Another advantage of EMALS is that it may reduce manual requirements by inspecting and troubleshooting itself. This is a significant improvement over the present system, which requires substantial manual inspection and maintenance. EMALS, however, requires a transition from mechanical technology to electrical/electronic technology.

## III. Reading Report

What have you learned after reading the text? Have you obtained a better command of EMALS, its technologies, advantages and drawbacks? Now create your reading report in no more than 150 words to generalize your achievement in the text study.

# Text B
# Marine Nuclear Propulsion

Many observers deny that the success of nuclear propulsion for warships has any relationship to the possibility of success in a commercial endeavor. They claim that the costs are far too high, that merchant ships do not obtain much benefit from high speed endurance, or that the public will not accept nuclear powered shipping.

However, there is undeniable evidence that ships using nuclear power for propulsion have covered hundreds of millions of miles for over 40 years.

### Proven Truths

Nuclear propulsion[1] is reliable. Even single reactor submarines routinely operate under the Arctic Ice cap[2] where a loss of power can be fatal. No nuclear-powered ship has been lost because of a power failure.

Nuclear propulsion is clean. A nuclear engine can push a sealed submarine for months at a time without affecting the atmosphere in the ship.

Nuclear engines can provide sufficient power for the propulsion of oversized ships. A nuclear engine able to drive an 80,000-ton aircraft carrier at 35 knots into the wind while launching aircraft with steam-driven catapults has a significant power capacity[3].

As for the amount of payload on nuclear carriers, compared with carriers using fossil fuel as driving force, nuclear engines occupy less space and are lighter than the oil-burning steam turbines.

Purely on capability, nuclear power is worth notice. Cost is a hurdle which needs to be overcome, considering aircraft carriers and large submarines are several-billion-dollar machines.

### Overcoming Hurdles

There are some approaches to the reduction of cost. Cost reduction can start by doing away with Rickover's[4] idea that "everything has to be made special." The establishment of military technology systems often needs to go through a long-time design process. Digital technology, for example, is just now being introduced into naval nuclear propulsion plants, ten to twenty years after its introduction into competitive commerce.

Military marine power plants must also be built with the characteristics of shock resistance[5] and low noise, which are different from the commercial standard. If many of the extra steps taken to meet these criteria have nothing to do with safety, reliability or capability, they can be eliminated to reduce the cost.

There is even a good way to improve upon military propulsion technology by replacing the 45-year-old pressurized water steam plants with a nuclear engine that combines a low-capital-cost gas turbine heat engine with a low-fuel-consumption nuclear engine.

### Fuel

Nuclear ships differ from conventional ships in the use of types of fuel. Instead of fuel oil which is liquid in nature, a kind of solid metal is used. Instead of piping the fuel from the bunker in the ship, the nuclear fuel elements are, all in one, built into a reactor "core". Instead of atomizing the fuel through a spray burner to mix it with oxygen for combustion, nuclear fission is utilized with no need of oxygen. Instead of combustible gases weaving through bundles of water-filled tubes which subsequently produce steam, a working material is pumped from the hot core to a second device – a heat exchanger – which subsequently produces steam. For both an oil ship and a nuclear ship, the end product of the fuel consumed is the same: it is steam.

In general, nuclear propulsion is closely related to nuclear fission. The Marine Nuclear Propulsion system is a main energy system that consumes nuclear fuel to generate heat energy and ensuing from heat, meanwhile to turn it into mechanical energy or output power essential to the propeller driven by steam turbines. Marine nuclear reactors consume the maximum level of burn-up fuels, for example, uranium-zirconium, uranium-aluminum, and metal ceramic fuels, while land-based reactors consume uranium dioxide $(UO_2)$[6]. Using nuclear reactors, it is possible for naval vessels to take a long voyage and carry out missions for a long time. Now, nuclear reactors are considered to be of great advantage for marine propulsion.

### Small Modular Reactors (SMR)[7]

Since the 1970s, consideration given to the size of nuclear power plants has aroused a lot of interest in the design of smaller ones that have intrinsically safe features. With the development of nuclear technology, there is the need for a technical revolution in the field of marine power, especially advanced marine propulsion.

Novel technologies contribute greatly to the production of propulsion systems that are capable of driving vessels at high speed and are characterized by more efficiency, improved maneuverability, less vibration, and low noise. Nowadays, nuclear power plants for marine propulsion are mainly used in aircraft carriers and submarines. What's more, some schemes have been proposed for designing a new generation of compact-type nuclear power plants.

The application of the advanced Small Modular Reactor (SMR) nuclear technology to sea-going ships will probably open up new bright prospects. At present, there is growing interest in SMRs and their perfect applications. In current years, some reactor manufacturers have dynamically improved designs for SMRs with highly safe features. The designs include removing specific accident initiators from the SMRs and taking more effective measures to prevent various accidents or mitigate their consequences.

SMRs are the updated reactors designed to produce electric power up to 300 MW[8]. Their components and systems can be shop-fabricated and then transported as modules to the sites for installation as there is an increase demand. Most of the designs consider SMR reliability and safety, and even the reasonable configuration of a single or multi-module plant. SMRs under development include: water-cooled reactors[9], high-temperature gas-cooled reactors[10], liquid-metal[11], sodium and gas-cooled reactors with fast neutron spectrum[12], and molten salt reactors[13].

The driving force of the SMR can meet the needs for power capacity which is supplied to users. SMRs which are substituted for the aging fossil-fired units are capable of operating in a more economical and safer way. In a word, SMRs have advantages of modular construction, cost-effectiveness, safety, and operational flexibility.

Although important advances have been made in SMR technology in recent years, there are still some issues which need to be taken seriously. They include staffing the control room, securing human operation of multi-module SMR plants, preparing for emergency disposal and developing new technical standards.

To sum up, the use of nuclear reactors for marine propulsion is greatly promising because the reactors such as SMR are not only economical and serviceable, but also safe and reliable.

*(1044 Words)*

**Sources:**

1. *Marine Nuclear Propulsion: The Undeniable Facts.* (https://atomicinsights.com/marine-nuclear-propulsion-undeniable-facts/)
2. *Design and Comparative Analysis of Small Modular Reactors for Nuclear Marine*

*Propulsion of a Ship. World Journal of Nuclear Science and Technology*, August, 2018, 136-145. (http://www.scirp.org/journal/wjnst)

3. *Crouch, Holmes F. NUCLEAR SHIP PROPULSION [J]*. 1970. (https://energyfromthorium.com/pdf/NSP_chap00.pdf)

## Notes

1. nuclear propulsion: the use of nuclear reactors for marine propulsion 核动力推进

2. Arctic Ice cap: the thick layers of ice and snow that cover the North Pole 北极冰冠

3. power capacity: capacity of power 电力电容，功率电容；发电量

4. Rickover: Hyman Rickover (1900—1986), a United States admiral who advocated the development of nuclear submarines and was known as the Father of the Nuclear Navy 海曼·里科弗，美国海军上将，人称"核动力海军之父"

5. shock resistance: the ability to resist shock 抗震能力，抗冲强度

6. uranium dioxide ($UO_2$): a type of nuclear fuel widely used in power reactors 二氧化铀（燃料）

7. small modular reactor (SMR): a new kind of small nuclear power built on modules 小型模块化反应堆

8. MW: megawatt 兆瓦，百万瓦特

9. water-cooled reactor: a nuclear reactor cooled by water 水冷反应堆

10. gas-cooled reactor: a nuclear reactor cooled by gas 气冷反应堆

11. liquid metal: a kind of metal which can flow like liquid without definite shape 液态金属

12. neutron spectrum: spectrum of a particle carrying no electric charge, with about the same mass as a proton, and forming part of the nucleus of an atom 中子能谱

13. molten salt reactor: a kind of nuclear reactor with molten salt as primary coolant 熔盐反应堆

## Word Bank

| | |
|---|---|
| hurdle [ˈhɜːdl] | *n.* 障碍；困难 |
| bunker [ˈbʌŋkə(r)] | *n.* 燃料舱 |
| atomize [ˈætəmaɪz] | *v.* 使分裂为原子；使雾化 |
| combustion [kəmˈbʌstʃən] | *n.* 燃烧，氧化 |

| | |
|---|---|
| fission [ˈfɪʃn] | n. 裂变；分裂 |
| ensue [ɪnˈsjuː] | v. 随即发生，因而发生 |
| propeller [prəˈpelə(r)] | n. 螺旋桨；推进器 |
| uranium [juˈreɪniəm] | n. 铀 |
| zirconium [zɜːˈkəʊniəm] | n. 锆 |
| ceramic [səˈræmɪk] | n. 陶瓷 |
| maneuverability [məˌnʊvəˈbɪləti] | n. 可操作性；机动性 |
| mitigate [ˈmɪtɪgeɪt] | v. 缓解；减轻 |
| shop-fabricated [ʃɒp-ˈfæbrɪˌkeɪtɪd] | adj. 车间预制的；工厂组装的 |
| sodium [ˈsəʊdɪəm] | n. 钠 |
| sea-going ship | 远洋船 |

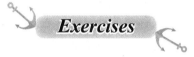

# Exercises

## I. True or False

*Decide whether the following sentences are true or false in accordance with the text.*

1. Many observers deny that merchant ships do not obtain much benefit from high speed endurance.

2. No nuclear-powered ship has been lost because of a power failure.

3. A nuclear engine can push a sealed submarine for months at a time without affecting the atmosphere in the ship.

4. The nuclear engines occupy more space and weight than oil-burning steam turbines.

5. Nuclear engines can provide sufficient power for the propulsion of oversized ships.

6. The establishment of military technology systems often needs to go through a long-time design process.

7. The requirements of shock resistance in military marine power plants are similar to the commercial standard.

8. Conventional ships use a kind of solid metal as fuel.

9. New propulsion systems can drive vessels at high speed.

10. SMRs have advantages of modular construction, cost-effectiveness, safety, and operational flexibility.

## II. Word Match

*Match the words/terms/phrases in the left column with its appropriate correspondents in the right column.*

1. nuclear propulsion                                         A. 电力电容

2. power failure                                              B. 抗震能力

3. sea-going ship                                            C. 熔盐反应堆

4. high-temperature gas-cooled reactor          D. 远洋船

5. molten salt reactor                                     E. 核动力推进

6. power capacity                                           F. 中子能谱

7. SMR                                                           G. 电路中断

8. neutron spectrum                                       H. 火力发电机组

9. fossil-fired unit                                          I. 高温气冷反应堆

10. shock resistance                                       J. 小型模块化反应堆

## Text C
## Ship Electric Propulsion

The ship electric propulsion system (EPS) includes such devices as frequency converter[1], propulsion motor[2] and propeller. Compared with traditional diesel-powered ships, ships with electric propulsion have small prime movers[3], which have advantages of small mass, low noise, high efficiency and convenient speed regulation. The electric propulsion technology converts the mechanical energy of the prime mover into electric energy first, and then directly drives the propeller through electric energy. This propulsion mode obviously improves the efficiency of the ship driving. With the development of ships in the direction of intelligence, integration and digitalization, the electric propulsion technology still has great potential of application.

### Composition

● Power Equipment

The power generation equipment in the EPS is mainly a generating set driven by diesel engines for power generation. Also, some driving equipment includes gas engine, gas turbine or steam turbine. The diesel engines used in the EPS are medium- and high-speed engines. The diesel engine using AC or DC generators is more economical than those used in the traditional mechanical propulsion system.

● Power Distribution Unit

Its function is to receive and distribute electric energy during the normal operation and to quickly remove the failure by manual or automatic control when it occurs so as to restore its normal operation, adjust the generator in time, and conduct scientific measurements.

● Motor Frequency Converter

The motor frequency converter is also a commonly-used device in the electric propulsion system. It is classified as voltage source[4] type inverter, circulating frequency converter, current source type frequency converter, and DC frequency converter. Among them, the voltage source type inverter is most widely used for its adaptability and good performance.

● Propellers

The ship electric propulsion involves the shaft propeller propulsion, the omnidirectional propeller propulsion and the pod propulsion. The shaft propeller propulsion device uses a variable-speed motor as a driving source to connect the horizontal motor[5] to the propeller

shaft[6]. Its structure is simpler and more stable. The omnidirectional propulsion device is a freely movable device, generating thrust in any direction. The pod propulsion device[7] is also free to rotate, but it integrates the motor and propeller shaft into the enclosed compartment.

● Control System

The control system is a core part of the ship EPS. It includes a propulsion remote-control system, a power management system, and a ship management system. The power management system mainly aims at meeting the power demand of the ship's actual operation and carrying out the real-time monitoring of the generating set. The ship management system is mainly used to assist the ship's operation. It can conduct manual control and semi-automatic control, which refers to various valves, HVAC[8] systems, load-bearing systems and cargo handling. The control system also contains the alarm system and safety system.

Advantages

Reasonable Configuration to Save Space

Generally speaking, almost all marine diesel engines are installed in the lower part of the stern. They are used to drive the propellers. The EPS generator is closer to the propeller. Without the transmission shaft used, a lot of space can be saved. The devices in the EPS can be reasonably configured according to the actual needs of the ship.

● Energy Saving

The traditional diesel propulsion system is characterized by high mechanical efficiency, but its fuel consumption and long-term operating costs are high. The EPS has the advantages of energy saving.

● High Maneuverability

Ship maneuver generally depends on the adjustment of the machine speed and the manipulation of the rudder angle to change direction. The speed of the ship EPS mainly depends on the drive control device to adjust and change. The drive controller can control the running speed of the motor. The nacelle unit can make a 360° rotation, and it is easier to change the speed of the propeller. This advantage is especially obvious when the ship is moving.

● Low Noise and Less Vibration

As the ship uses an EPS instead of rudder and drive shaft, its overall weight is reduced by more than 30% compared to that of a conventional diesel-powered ship, and its capacity is also reduced. As a result, the EPS will make low noise and less vibration when it is running.

● Ship Safety

For a traditional diesel propulsion system, its steering gear and transmission shaft are apt to malfunction. But for the EPS, multiple generators can be used. Even if an individual unit fails, a ship's navigation will not be affected. In general, ships depending on electric propulsion are equipped with more than two sets of EPSs, so remedial measures can be taken in time when there is a fault in one system.

### Disadvantages

The EPS has advantages as described above, but it also has some disadvantages. For example, there is an urgent need for a large amount of investment in the construction and installation of EPS. However, the investment has not met the demand as yet. Besides, the energy conversion during the operation of the generating set and the propeller is a problem of complexity, which needs to be further studied and solved.

### Direction of EPS Development

The present EPS consisting of a DC motor, an AC motor or a synchronous motor will certainly be improved in the future. With advances in the EPS technology, some new-type motors are being and have been developed, such as permanent magnet (PM) motor and superconducting machine[9]. In recent years, some developed countries have developed PM synchronous motors[10], which are small in size and high in quality, but run at a faster speed. The development of superconducting machine which is lighter in weight and higher in working efficiency than the conventional electric propulsion device is in progress, with attention paid to exploiting the nitrogen equipment. The gradual maturity of low-temperature technology in China also helps to research and develop the superconducting propulsion system.

### Prospects

At present, AC electric propulsion, superconducting propulsion, fuel cell[11] propulsion and all-electric propulsion are the trend of key technologies in this field. Although there are still some problems with the existing electric propulsion system, researchers, engineers and technicians are making great efforts to develop the power system with high efficiency, energy saving and economical application, which will promote the rapid development of China's ship electric propulsion.

*(1024 words)*

*Sources:*

*IOP Conference Series: Earth and Environmental Science.* (https://www.researchgate.net/publication/340083792_Research_on_ship_electric_propulsion)

## Notes

1. frequency converter: a power control device of AC motor controlled by changing the frequency of motor power supply 变频器

2. propulsion motor: a rotating motor used for propulsion 推进电机

3. prime mover: an important driving part of mechanical equipment 原动机

4. voltage source: the source which controls the output voltage 电压源

5. horizontal motor: a motor with its base parallel to the rotor shaft 卧式电机

6. propeller shaft: a revolving shaft to which two or more spiral blades are fixed for propulsion 传动轴，螺桨轴

7. pod propulsion device: a new type of marine propulsion device integrating propulsion and steering device 吊舱式推进器

8. HVAC: high voltage alternating current 高压交流电

9. superconducting machine: a motor characterized by superconductivity 超导电机

10. PM synchronous motor: permanent magnet synchronous motor 永磁同步电动机

11. fuel cell: a kind of cell containing fuel, which can convert chemical energy into electric energy directly through electrochemical reaction 燃料电池

## Word Bank

| | |
|---|---|
| inverter [ɪnˈvɜːtə] | *n.* 逆变器 |
| omnidirectional [ˌɒmnɪdəˈrekʃənl] | *adj.* 全方向的 |
| pod [pɒd] | *n.* 吊舱 |
| compartment [kəmˈpɑːtmənt] | *n.* 舱室；隔间 |
| rudder [ˈrʌdə(r)] | *n.* 船舵 |
| nacelle [nəˈsel] | *n.* 引擎舱；吊舱 |
| synchronous [ˈsɪŋkrənəs] | *adj.* 同步的；同时的 |
| superconducting [ˌsjuːpəkənˈdʌktɪŋ] | *adj.* （低温）超导的 |
| nitrogen [ˈnaɪtrədʒən] | *n.* 氮 |

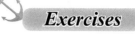

**Exercises**

Based on what you have acquired in this text, you are supposed to conduct an online study to explore further into the relevant sphere. Comb and frame what you have found with an online study report in no less than 200 words. In addition, any assistant image, audio, video, or other first-hand material will be preferred when you present your report in class.

# Unit 11   Network-centric Warfare

**Bridge-in**

*Answer the following questions in accordance with the microlesson "Behind the Scenes: The 5G Battle".*

1. How is 5G technology utilized in hypersonic weapons?

2. What changes can 5G bring to the network on battlefields?

3. Why did the US government take an illegal action against Huawei?

## Text A
## The Electronic Warfare and Cyber War

### Electronic Warfare

Electronic warfare (EW) means military actions whose aim is either to intercept communications or, particularly in wartime, to disrupt operation of adversary sensors or communication links by use of electromagnetic spectrum(EMS) — radio wave, radar wave, infrared radiation, visible light, etc.

Nowadays, military operations are executed in an increasingly complex environment that is closely related to EMS. EMS refers to the entire distribution of electromagnetic (EM) radiation according to frequency or wavelength. Devices whose functions depend upon EMS are used by the military for intelligence, communication, positioning, navigation and timing (PNT)[1], sensing, command and control (C2)[2], attack, ranging, data transmission, and information storage and processing. EW is essential for maritime forces to achieve offensive and defensive purposes.

### Three Categories of Electronic Warfare

EW falls into three categories: electronic attack (EA), electronic protection (EP) and electronic warfare support (ES). The following figure gives an overview of EW, which involves EA, EP and ES as well as their relations with principal EW activities.

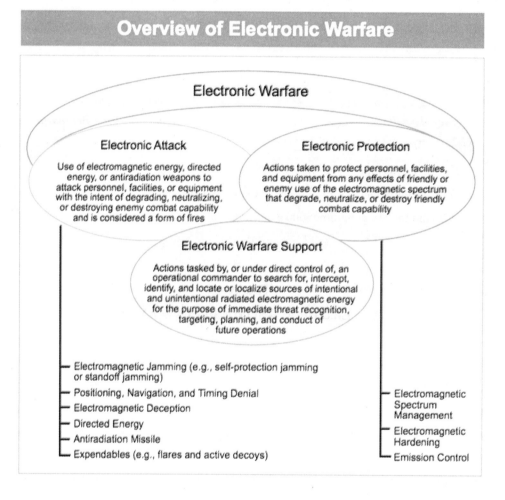

**Figure** Overview of Electronic Warfare

EA means employing new weaponry which includes electromagnetic or directed energy (DE)[3], or anti-radiation weapons to attack enemy personnel, facilities and equipment with the intent of degrading, neutralizing or destroying an enemy combat capability. It can be used in both offensive and defensive operations. Offensive operations are generally conducted to suppress a threat for only a limited period of time. Examples include employing self-propelled decoys, jamming an enemy's radar or C2 systems, launching anti-radiation missiles to destroy its air defenses, using electronic deception techniques to confuse its intelligence, surveillance

and reconnaissance (ISR)[4] systems, and applying DE weapons to disable or destroy the hostile personnel, facilities, equipment, massed ground installations and other devices such as satellites on orbit and airborne optical sensors[5]. Defensive operations aim to protect friendly personnel, facilities, capabilities and equipment by use of EMS and other protective measures.

EP involves passive and active means taken to protect personnel, facilities, and equipment from any effects of friendly or enemy employment of EW that degrade, neutralize or destroy friendly combat capability.

ES refers to the tasks assigned and directed by an operational commander that include searching for, intercepting, identifying, and locating the sources of intentional and unintentional radiated EM energy for the purpose of immediate threat recognition, targeting, planning and conduct of future operations. ES helps the commander to perform operational missions. ES measures have an important intelligence function. It refers to the use of jammers and deception devices. Jammers destroy the information content of enemy signals, radio or radar, by covering them in meaningless noise.

Deception devices, on the other hand, produce misleading signals which include electronic items such as blip-enhancers, deception transponders and also radar-reflecting decoys such as chaff. ES data can be used to produce signal intelligence (SIGINT)[6] and provide targets for electronic or destructive attack.

All in all, EW applications play a vital role not only in support of homeland defense but also in the deterrence, detection, prevention, and conquest of external threats, i.e., hostile ballistic missiles, aircraft (manned and unmanned), warships, space systems, cyberspace, and domestic/international terrorism.

Navy EW

Navy EW is executed by surface ships, shipboard aircraft, and submarines that are organized into a strike group. For the strike group, the information operations warfare commander (IWC)[7] is responsible for coordinating and integrating EW, typically through the strike group electronic warfare officer (EWO)[8], into naval and joint operations. EW personnel are required to continually monitor EW execution. It is delegated to the EW control ship, usually an aircraft carrier or large amphibious ship in the strike group. The whole strike group is equipped with a variety of shipboard EW systems. Their main functions are further emphasized as following:

(a) ES for detecting, identifying, and locating potential threats and friendly forces, and enhancing situational awareness.

(b) EA for self-protection and principally destroying incoming anti-ship missiles and denying the enemy's use of EMS.

(c) Maintaining friendly force availability of EMS and space resources to ensure robust communication, surveillance, reconnaissance, data correlation, and navigation capabilities.

### Cyber War

Cyber war, or cyber warfare, means using computers and the Internet for a war in cyberspace. A cyber warrior[9] is a good example. He is the person who is highly skilled in the art of cyber warfare. In other words, he is an expert in information security technique, hacking, espionage, and computer forensics[10].

Governments, military forces, law enforcement agencies and private sectors around the world are making great efforts to train personnel to engage in cyber warfare. The Internet security company McAfee stated in its 2007 annual report that approximately 120 countries have been developing methods to use the Internet as a weapon, targeting financial markets, government computer systems and utilities.

There are several commonly-used ways in cyber warfare. One of them is cyber espionage. It means exploiting computer networks to gain illegal access to secret or classified information that is held by adversaries, governments and organizations. Cyber espionage is mainly used for military, political or economic purposes. Web vandalism refers to attacks that deface web pages, or denial-of-service attacks[11]. Cyber propaganda is also a common tactic. Political messages can be spread through the network or to anyone with access to the Internet or any device like cell phones, PDAs[12] that receives digital information. Gathering data by espionage is to intercept and even modify the classified information that is not handled securely. There are also distributed denial-of-service attacks. Military activities need to be coordinated by the aid of computer and satellite communications. If the computer system or network is disrupted or hacked, orders and communications can be intercepted, so that the coordinated military actions will fail and even the troops will be at risk. Attacking critical infrastructure and using compromised counterfeit hardware are also tactics in cyber war.

Cyber warfare and EW have always been interrelated. However, the tools used for the two kinds of warfare need to be fully interoperable and integrated on the battlefield. In the future, the focus is on using advanced information technology — computers, high-speed data links, and networking software — to connect naval ships, aircraft, and shore installations to

highly integrated local and wide-area networks. Within these networks, Navy and Marine Corps personnel will share large amounts of critical information simultaneously and rapidly. Additionally, in the next phase of development, naval forces will draw on the power of big data[13], machine-to-machine communications, and AI[14]-powered algorithms to identify the potential threats across the spectrum in real time. All these advances will dramatically improve naval combat capability and efficiency.

*(1082 words)*

**Sources:**

Joint Publication 3-13.1Electronic Warfare, February 2012

## Notes

1. positioning, navigation and timing (PNT): PNT is a technology evolved from traditional satellite navigation. It is used for both civilian and military purposes. 定位导航定时

2. command and control (C2): the exercise of authority and direction by a properly designated commanding officer over assigned and attached forces in the accomplishment of a mission 指挥控制

3. directed energy (DE): directional energy transmitted through subatomic, particle or electromagnetic wave to produce damage effect on the target 定向能

4. intelligence, surveillance, and reconnaissance (ISR): ISR is the coordinated and integrated acquisition, processing and provision of timely, accurate, relevant, coherent and assured information or intelligence. 情报、监视、侦察

5. airborne optical sensors: optical sensors installed on aircraft 机载光学传感器

6. signal intelligence (SIGINT): SIGINT is the interception, collection and analysis of transmitted information. 信号情报

7. information operations warfare commander (IWC): IWC is responsible for information warfare operations. 信息作战指挥官

8. electronic warfare officer (EWO): officer in charge of EW 电子战军官

9. cyber warrior: an individual engaging in cyberwarfare or the sabotage of computer systems 网络战士

10. computer forensics: an interdisciplinary science in the field of computer science and law. It is used to solve a large number of computer crimes and accidents, including network

intrusion, intellectual property theft and network deception. 计算机取证

11. denial-of-service attack: DoS attack, a cyber attack in which the perpetrator seeks to make a machine or network resource unavailable to its intended users by temporarily or indefinitely disrupting services of a host connected to the Internet 拒绝服务型攻击

12. PDA: A personal digital assistant (PDA), also known as a handheld PC, is a variety mobile device which functions as a personal information manager. 掌上电脑

13. big data: data sets so large and complex that traditional data processing and application software cannot adequately handle them 大数据

14. AI: artificial intelligence 人工智能

 **Word Bank**

| | |
|---|---|
| electromagnetic [ɪˌlektrəʊmægˈnetɪk] | *adj.* 电磁的 |
| infrared [ˌɪnfrəˈred] | *adj.* 红外线的 |
| neutralize [ˈnjuːtrəlaɪz] | *v.* 使无效 |
| decoy [dɪˈkɔɪ] | *n.* 诱饵 |
| massed [mæst] | *adj.* 聚集的；联合的 |
| jammer [ˈdʒæmə] | *n.* 干扰机 |
| blip-enhancer [blɪpɪnˈhɑːnsə] | *n.* 尖头信号增强器；光电增大器 |
| chaff [tʃɑːf] | *n.* 干扰物；金属反射体（用于干扰敌人雷达） |
| cyberspace [ˈsaɪbəspeɪs] | *n.* 网络空间 |
| hack [hæk] | *v.* 非法侵入(他人计算机系统) |
| espionage [ˈespɪənɑːʒ] | *n.* 间谍活动 |
| deface [dɪˈfeɪs] | *v.* 损伤……外貌；丑化 |
| infrastructure [ˈɪnfrəstrʌktʃə(r)] | *n.* 基础设施 |
| counterfeit [ˈkaʊntəfɪt] | *adj.* 伪造的 |
| interoperable [ˌɪntərˈɒpərəbl] | *adj.* 互相操作的；配合动作的；互用的 |
| AI-powered [ˌeɪˈaɪˈpaʊəd] | *adj.* 人工智能赋能的 |
| electronic attack (EA) | [军] 电子攻击 |
| electronic protection (EP) | [军] 电子防护 |
| electronic warfare support (ES) | [军] 电子战支援 |
| deception device | 诱骗装置 |

| deception transponder | 诱骗应答机（应答器） |
| radar-reflecting decoy | 雷达反射假目标 |
| strike group | [军] 攻击群，战斗群 |
| web vandalism | [军] 网络破坏 |
| real time | 实时 |

 **Exercises**

## I. Comprehension

**Part A   Questions**

*Answer the following questions in accordance with the text.*

1. What are the three categories of electronic warfare?

2. What are the definitions of EA, EP and ES respectively?

3. What are the responsibilities of an information operations warfare commander?

4. What is a cyber warrior? What are the major skills of a cyber warrior?

5. What are the common tactics of attack in cyber warfare?

**Part B   Multiple Choices**

*Choose the most appropriate answer from the given choices below each question in accordance with the text.*

1. Devices whose functions depend upon the EMS are used for the following purposes except _____.

    A. positioning, navigation, and timing

    B. command and control

    C. data interception

    D. information storage and processing

2. Which of the following is NOT an EA activity?

    A. Employing self-propelled decoys.

    B. Jamming an enemy's radar or C2 systems.

    C. Using anti-radiation missiles to suppress an adversary's air defenses.

    D. Synchronizing and integrating the planning and operational use of sensors.

3. Which of the following descriptions of ES is NOT true?

    A. ES prepares the commander to perform operational missions.

B. ES data can be used to produce signal intelligence.

C. ES is the actions taken to protect personnel, facilities, and equipment from any effects of friendly, neutral or enemy use of the EMS.

D. ES provides targets for electronic or destructive attack.

4. Which of the following descriptions of cyber warfare is true?

A. Approximately 140 countries have been developing ways to use the Internet as a weapon.

B. It is the use of computers and the Internet in conducting warfare in cyberspace.

C. Attacking critical infrastructure and using compromised counterfeit hardware are not tactics in cyber war.

D. Cyber and Electronic warfare are not related.

5. Which of the following is NOT included as the driving force for the next phase development of EW and cyber warfare?

A. Big data.

B. Machine-to-machine communications.

C. Cloud computing.

D. AI-powered algorithms.

## II. Translation

### Part A Terms & Phrases

*Translate the following terms or phrases from Chinese into English and vice versa.*

1. 电磁的
2. 电子攻击
3. 电子防护
4. 电子战支援
5. 传感器
6. 攻击群
7. 网络战
8. 非法侵入计算机
9. 间谍活动
10. 拒绝服务型攻击
11. positioning, navigation and timing
12. command and control
13. directed energy
14. intelligence, surveillance and reconnaissance
15. airborne optical sensors
16. signal intelligence
17. information operations warfare commander
18. cyber warrior
19. computer forensic
20. web vandalism

**Part B    Paragraph**

*Translate the following paragraph from English into Chinese.*

Devices whose functions depend upon EMS are used by the military for intelligence, communication, positioning, navigation and timing (PNT), sensing, command and control (C2), attack, ranging, data transmission, and information storage and processing. EW is essential for maritime forces to achieve offensive and defensive purposes.

## III. Reading Report

What have you learned after reading the text? Have you obtained a better understanding of EW and cyber warfare? Now create your reading report in no more than 150 words to generalize your achievement in text study.

## Text B
## Radar

### What is Radar?

Radar is short for radio detection and ranging. It is a system for detecting the presence, position or movement of solid objects within its range by sending out electromagnetic waves or short radio waves which they reflect.That is to say, radar transmit electromagnetic waves to the objects and receive their reflected waves or echoes, thereby determining the objects' size, position, direction, height, distance and speed. More specifically, radar illuminates target with the radio frequency (RF)[1] pulse and then pick up its return wave or echo. Since the RF pulse propagates at the speed of light, the time for the echo to return is proportional to the distance from the target. This, of course, applies to a primary radar[2], one that relies on reflected energy bouncing back off the target. A secondary radar[3], retransmitting the signal back from a transponder[4], has an additional delay. The radiated RF signals are "bounced" off a target and picked up by the receiver. Thus, the characteristics of the echo can be identified. Most often, low duty-cycle[5] pulses are used. Although the technology has greatly developed, the basic concept of radar has not yet changed. At the same time, the accuracy and resolution of radar as well as its applications have dramatically increased over time.

### Radar Applications

Radar has a lot of military applications. Ground-based radar is used for long-range threat detection and air traffic control. Ship-based radar provides surface-to-surface and surface-to-air observation. Airborne radar is utilized for threat detection, surveillance, mapping and altitude determination. Missile radar is used for tracking and guidance. Radar has also many applications in commercial aviation, such as air traffic control, long-range surveillance, terminal air traffic monitoring, surface movement tracking and weather surveillance. Additionally, short-range radar is increasingly being used in automotive applications for collision avoidance, driver assistance and autonomous driving. Specialized radars are used for specific purposes. For example, in recent years, large radars have been used to investigate the nature of the upper atmosphere and study ionospheric and auroral phenomena. They have also been used to observe the large numbers of meteors entering the earth's atmosphere from outer space.

Radar has played a vital role in tracking earth satellites and in making important measurements of their orbit paths. Radar is also making contributions in astronomy, and radar returns have been obtained from the Moon, Venus, and the Sun. By these means, it is possible to make studies of radio propagation in space and investigate such features as the surface roughness of the Moon and its liberation motion.

## Continuous Wave Radar

Radar that can transmit continuous wave signals is called continuous wave (CW) radar. CW radar applications include simple unmodulated Doppler[6] speed sensing systems, for example, those used by police and sports related radars, or employing modulation to sense range and speed. Modulated CW radar has many specialized and military applications such as maritime observation and communication, missile homing[7], and target altitude measurement. The detection range of CW radar is relatively short because it is constrained by continuous RF power. As there is no limit to its minimum detection range, so CW radar can be made to be particularly useful for tracking close-in targets.

## Pulse Radar

Pulse radar is a kind of radar that can transmit shorter high-frequency pulse signals which are then picked up by the receiver via the antenna. Pulse radar is used for ranging, especially suitable for determining the distances from multiple targets at the same time. So it is more commonly used now. Pulse radar falls into two categories: moving target indication (MTI) radar[8] and pulsed-Doppler radar. MTI radar is a long-range, low pulse repetition frequency (PRF)[9] radar used to detect and track small moving targets at long distances (up to 30 km) by eliminating ground clutter[10]. It is useful when velocity is not a big concern (i.e. "just tell me if something is moving"). Pulsed-Doppler radar, in contrast, utilizes a high PRF to avoid "blind speeds". Therefore, it has the ability to measure a shorter "unambiguous" range (up to 15 km) and high resolution. It can provide detailed velocity data. It is used for airborne missile tracking, air traffic control and medical care (e.g. blood flow monitoring).

According to the pulse characteristics, it is possible to obtain valuable information about which type the radar signals belongs to and where it is located — maybe sailboat, battleship, passenger plane, bomber, missile, etc.

### SPY-6V1 Radar

SPY-6V1 radar, which was designed by US company Raytheon, is different from the air and missile defense radar in that it is built on the gallium nitride technology and modular design. SPY-6V1 radar, with its prominent performance, can play an important role in air defense and missile defense. Its performance characteristics are also prominent.

The basic building block of SPY-6 is called a "radar modular assembly." It is a self-contained radar in a two-foot cube that can be easily connected with other cubes to form an array of some size. The more cubes, the larger the power. The US Navy's latest version of the multi-mission Arleigh Burke-class destroyer[11] will have four arrays for 360-degree protection, each containing 37 cubes.

Because the gallium nitride technology is superior to the previous technologies in power density, the resulting array is 100 times more sensitive than the SPY-1 radar currently used for air defense on US Navy destroyers. This array is of vital importance to tracking fast-moving targets such as ballistic missiles.Thus, the destroyers have time to be prepared to intercept or destroy the targets.

The US Navy thinks highly of SPY-6 radar and it plans to install them onto its destroyers, aircraft carriers, amphibious warships and a new frigate. SPY-6V1 radar has broad prospects for application for its characteristic of long-distance detection, high target discrimination, accurate target tracking and location.

### Meter-wave Active Phased Array Radar (APAR)

The meter-wave APAR is China's latest generation of radar, with new advances in technology such as active phased array and digital processing. Its technological features give it advantages over the conventional meter-wave radar in detection probability, ranging accuracy, sensitivity and reliability.

In addition, the meter-wave APAR has better anti-stealth performance and strong anti-interference ability, so it is not easily attacked by anti-radiation missiles. With an increase in the number of stealth aircraft and warships, electronic warfare (EW) is becoming intenser. It is believed that the meter-wave APAR can play a more important role in EW in the future.

The PLA Navy's Type 054AE frigate is the first to be equipped with this kind of radar. It can be used for the long-range active detection of incoming targets in naval battles. When the position of a target is predicted in advance, the radar can quickly locate the target, providing the target indication and relay guidance for HQ16 ship-to-air missile[12]. Moreover, the meter-

wave APAR can obtain information about air activity through data link and send it to the early-warning aircraft and ground air-defense command post[13] to assist fighters in intercepting incoming air targets.

*(1155 words)*

*Sources:*

1. https://www.tek.com/wenjian/application-note/radar-basics

2. https://www.china-arms.com/2019/12/054ae-frigate-meter-wave-radar/

## Notes

1. radio frequency (RF): the frequency of electromagnetic waves used in radio transmission 射频

2. primary radar: a device which sends a high-powered radio frequency from a rotating antenna and uses any reflected signals to determine the distance and speed of objects in the air or on water 一次雷达，初级雷达

3. secondary radar: It needs to be equipped with a transponder. Also, it is different from the primary radar in that it actively emits electromagnetic pulse. 二次雷达

4. transponder: a device that emits a different signal in response immediately after receiving it 应答机；应答器

5. duty-cycle: the ratio between pulse duration and pulse interval 占空比；占空率

6. Doppler: a specialized radar exploiting Doppler effect to provide data about the velocity of an object at a distance 多普勒雷达

7. missile homing: a missile fitted with an electronic device that enables it to find and hit a target 导弹自导引（寻的）

8. moving target indication (MTI) radar: a radar that indicates a moving target 活动目标显示器雷达

9. pulse repetition frequency (PRF): pulse frequency that is repeated 脉冲重复频率

10. ground clutter: unwanted echoes from the ground in electronic systems 地面杂波

11. Arleigh Burke-class destroyer: the US Navy Arleigh Burke-class of guided missile destroyers (DDGs)（美国海军）阿利·伯克级驱逐舰

12. HQ16 ship-to-air missile: the first domestically-produced and medium/short-range air defense missile in the PLA Navy 红旗16防空导弹

13. ground air-defense command post: a command center for ground to air defense 地面防空指挥所

## Word Bank

| | |
|---|---|
| propagate ['prɒpəgeɪt] | v. 传播 |
| resolution [ˌrezə'luːʃn] | n. 分辨率 |
| terminal ['tɜːmɪnl] | n. 航空站 |
| ionospheric [aɪˌɒnə'sferɪk] | adj. 电离层的 |
| auroral [ɔː'rɔːrəl] | adj. 极光的 |
| unmodulated [ʌn'mɒdjʊleɪtɪd] | adj. 未调制的；未调整的 |
| modulation [ˌmɒdjʊ'leɪʃən] | n. 调制 |
| velocity [və'lɒsətɪ] | n. 速度 |
| unambiguous [ˌʌnæm'bɪɡjʊəs] | adj. 清楚的；明确的 |
| modular ['mɒdjələ(r)] | adj. 模块化的 |
| self-contained [ˌself kən'teɪnd] | adj. 独立的；自持的；配套的 |
| array [ə'reɪ] | n. 排列；天线阵 |
| meter-wave ['miːtə(r) weɪv] | n. 米波 |
| anti-stealth ['æntɪstelθ] | n. 反隐身 |
| autonomous driving | 自动驾驶 |
| radar return | 雷达回波；雷达反射信号 |
| continuous wave radar | 连续波雷达 |
| speed sensing system | 速度传感系统 |
| pulse radar | 脉冲雷达 |
| gallium nitride | 氮化镓 |
| relay guidance | 中继制导 |

## Exercises

### I. True or False

*Decide whether the following sentences are true or false in accordance with the text.*

1. Radars illuminate their targets with a radio frequency pulse and then listen for the return echo.

2. Ground-based radar is used for short-range threat detection.

3. Long-range radar is increasingly being used in automotive applications for collision avoidance, driver assistance and autonomous driving.

4. The detection range of continuous wave (CW) radar systems is relatively long.

5. There are two general categories of pulse radar, moving target indication (MTI) radar and pulsed-Doppler radar.

6. Meter-wave radar has better anti-stealth performance and strong anti-interference ability.

## II. Word Match

*Match the words/terms/phrases in the left column with its appropriate correspondents in the right column.*

| | |
|---|---|
| 1. radio frequency | A. 连续波 |
| 2. pulse | B. 反隐身 |
| 3. transponder | C. 脉冲 |
| 4. continuous wave | D. 米波 |
| 5. Doppler | E. 射频 |
| 6. resolution | F. 抗干扰 |
| 7. modulation | G. 应答器 |
| 8. anti-interference | H. 分辨率 |
| 9. anti-stealth | I. 多普勒 |
| 10. meter-wave | J. 调制 |

# Text C
## A Global Network for a Modern Navy

A modern navy needs a global network for effective and secure communication through radio and satellite communication links. With the advent of network-centric warfare, applicable voice-data communication networks are also becoming even more important.

To enable the network to operate securely and efficiently, it is necessary to coordinate the command, control, communication, computer, intelligence, surveillance and reconnaissance systems in peacetime or wartime. The integration of the systems can ensure secure and stable communication. Also, it promotes close cooperation between different operational platforms in different physical environments, such as subsurface, surface, land, air and space, especially between joint or coalition forces. Furthermore, these interoperable systems can be robust enough to deal with a constant rise in the amount of data transmission. Now, they are also available for use in some other weapon platforms such as unmanned aerial vehicles (UAV).

The existing satellite communication networks, owned or rented by the military, are the backbone for connecting and controlling the naval platforms around the world, which rely on different radio frequencies to keep themselves informed of their individual messages. However, according to military experts, whether the present satellite communication networks can meet with the needs for future communication will be a problem to be seriously considered and solved.

### SDR and JTRS

Surface communication links can meet the requirement of future communication. They can offer much higher bandwidth and the ability to work with different equipments in the conditions of joint or multinational operations. They are also secure and jam-resistant. In addition, there are some other different radio systems used for communication, for example, software defined radios (SDR). SDR is a kind of radio communication system, whose function is performed by computer software or embedded system of software instead of the hardware system composed of mixer, filter, modulator, demodulator and detector. SDR is very useful for military purposes because it can provide various radio communication protocols in real time. In view of its functions and advantages, SDR is expected to be a dominant technique in radio communication.

The US Department of Defense intended to use the joint tactical radio system (JTRS)[1] in

battles to come. JTRS is supposed to work with existing military and civilian radios and systems. The airborne and shipborne JTRS reached its initial operating capability in 2014. It will ultimately link more than 100 platforms, including aircraft carriers, cruisers, destroyers, submarines, UAVs, Marine Corps helicopters and fixed-wing aircraft using a secure internet-like tactical network[2]. By connecting all operational platforms to the future US military global information grid (GIG)[3], JTRS will be able to provide non-line-of-sight[4] capability, wide band network service, clear communication, easy upgrade and interoperability.

### Cloud Computing[5]

Modern surface ships and submarines still use different shipborne computer networks. If these different networks can be combined into a commonly-used host computer network for an entire fleet, the communication resources will be fully utilized. For future communication, the network will play a vital role in information gathering and handling, target tracking, monitoring and control, voice communication, and energy and asset management. In short, the host computer network is beneficial for all the operations as mentioned above.

This network can be extended to a larger data acquisition system. Thus, all parts of the system can be monitored, and any fault can be found in time and tackled before it causes the system to go out of service. Nowadays, cloud computing has come into use. It is central to such a network. Governments and military forces of many countries are now considering making schemes for cloud computing.

The US Navy will establish a new cloud computing network to manage data and services on a commonly-used host network accessible to all users in order to bring ships' networks under unified control. The consolidated afloat network enterprise services (CANES)[6] utilize a centralized software architecture for integrating the entire navy networking hardware. The network can free more resources of naval vessels for operations and other uses and provide a more favorable computing environment for the entire fleet.

The CANES programme is a step towards the tactical "cloud computing" network. It will consolidate the networking hardware and centralized software to be accessible to users on the sea and on land. It optimizes the networks on board US warships according to IP[7]. The primary goal of the CANES programme is to build the secure afloat network necessary for naval and joint operations. At the same time, it will integrate servers, workstations and networking systems with the US Navy's shore-based next-generation communication network.

## 5G Network

With the development of Internet technology, 5G network has come into being, opening up a new era of intelligent Internet. Now it is widely used in the field of commercial communication and also begins to enter the field of military communication. By the way, it is useful for addressing the problem of increasingly dense channels. 5G is believed to have great potential for use in military communication because of its advantages of faster communication speed, less time delay, higher frequency spectrum availability, lower energy consumption and larger system capacity. As the next generation of mobile communication, 5G is available for use in the military field, but the biggest single threat it faces is jamming and signal interception. Man-portable radio is considered to be a good solution to that. With its expanded and enhanced spectrum, 5G offers broad prospects for communication throughout the world.

## Competition for Data Supremacy

The competition for data supremacy in the field of communication is gaining momentum. The 5G network developed by Huawei, China's biggest mobile communications and tech company, has taken the lead in this competition. Its communication technology has produced inestimable effects. Just as *South China Morning Post*[8]pointed out, 5G could bring about revolutionary changes in military communications, which would have an extremely important effect on cyber security and network-centric warfare.

The illegal action recently taken by the US against Huawei, and much concern about its influence in Europe show that the US never allows any other country, especially China, to surpass its science and technology levels. Nevertheless, it appears that Huawei will play a central role in the global deployment of the next generation of cellular networking technology despite the American government's efforts to hobble the company.

*(1035 words)*

**Sources:**

https://www.naval-technology.com

## Notes

1. joint tactical radio system (JTRS): JTRS is a single set of software-defined radios with new frequencies and modes added via upload. The US military plans to use it instead of the

existing radios. 联合战术无线电系统

2. tactical network: a communication network which interconnects various communication facilities, control terminals, weapon platforms and sensors according to IP 战术网络

3. global information grid (GIG): an all-encompassing communications project of the United States Department of Defense 全球信息网格

4. non-line-of-sight (NLOS): Non-line-of-sight and near-line-of-sight are radio transmissions across a path that is partially obstructed. 非视距

5. cloud computing: a kind of distributed computation, which means using the network "cloud" to divide enormous data computing and handling program into innumerable subprograms, which are handled by the system consisting of multiple severs and then, the results are given to users 云计算

6. consolidated afloat network enterprise services (CANES): CANES provides for the US army and Navy by use of its integrated network hardware and software. 统一浮动网络体系服务

7. IP: Internet Protocol 互联网协议，网际互联协议

8. *South China Morning Post*: an English newspaper published in Hong Kong 《南华早报》

 **Word Bank**

| | |
|---|---|
| network-centric [ˈnetwɜːkˈsentrɪk] | *adj.* 以网络为中心的 |
| backbone [ˈbækbəʊn] | *n.* 脊柱；支柱；骨干 |
| jam-resistant [dʒæmrɪˈzɪstənt] | *adj.* 抗干扰的 |
| mixer [ˈmɪksə(r)] | *n.* 混频器 |
| filter [ˈfɪltə(r)] | *n.* 滤波器 |
| modulator [ˈmɒdjʊleɪtə] | *n.* 调节器 |
| demodulator [dɪˈmɒdjʊleɪtə] | *n.* 解调器 |
| detector [dɪˈtektə(r)] | *n.* 探测器 |
| supremacy [suːˈpreməsɪ] | *n.* 最高权威；最高地位 |
| hobble [ˈhɒbl] | *n.* 阻止；妨碍 |
| voice-data communication network | 话频和数据（综合）通信网络 |

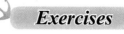

**Exercises**

Based on what you have acquired in this text, you are supposed to conduct an online study to explore further into the relevant sphere. Comb and frame what you have found with an online study report in no less than 200 words. In addition, any assistant image, audio, video, or other first-hand material will be preferred when you present your report in class.

# Unit 12 Weaponry

**Bridge-in**

*Answer the following questions in accordance with the microlesson "Ship-borne weapons".*

1. What are the basic types of ship-borne weapons?

2. How do you define naval guns?

3. What do you think is the key trend for ship-borne weapons development?

## Text A
## Navy Weapons Strategy for Future Maritime Operations

The US naval forces often perform maritime operational training, including combat firing and tactical application, according to their rigorous training programs. All this aims at making better preparations for future maritime operations.

Surface Warfare Advanced Tactical Training (SWATT)[1], which the US Navy officers call "high-velocity learning", focuses on the increase of operational decision-making level and the real-time rapid reaction to any possible changes in combat scenarios, as well as effective ways to cope with hostile high-tech weapons such as ballistic missile, long-range anti-ship missile, sea mine, torpedo and laser weapon.

"We concentrate our attention on the high-end warfare or high-tech modernized war," said Emily Royse, leader of SWATT, in an interview. The emphasis on training refers to a wide range of academic and maritime operational subjects, including briefing and debriefing, which are specially prepared and taught by Warfare Tactics Instructors.

The training focus is on sea control operations. Combat units are presented with a scenario of naval fight to help them make a correct strategic decision and adopt different tactics to deal with what may happen in the scenario.

For surface warfare, making an operational plan of how to get the units' ships through narrow high-risk straits, or how to respond to threats from small boats is also an important subject of training.

The training covers various maritime military drills such as mine countermeasures, antisubmarine warfare, anti craft defense, amphibious operation and surface strike or attack. The purpose of training is to better coordinate the actions of different combat groups and meanwhile to further improve tactics and techniques, thereby adapting to large-scale naval battles in the future.

"With sea control, it is possible to ensure that our warships can move freely on the sea lanes and that they are free from threats or able to counter them," Royce said.

The training courses involve understanding the tactical and technical characteristics of sophisticated weapons — antiship/antisubmarine missile, cruise missile, strategic ballistic missile, high-energy laser weapon, microwave weapon and **electromagnetic rail gun**.

What is worth mentioning is that the Navy's 2016 Surface Force Strategy[2] is a guiding document. The document has also become an important course content. There is a paper titled "Return to Sea Control". Which describes some specific threats from enemy capabilities from the strategic viewpoint. Examples of threats given in the paper include anti-ship ballistic and cruise missiles, integrated and **layered** sensor systems, targeting networks, long range bombers, advanced strike aircraft, submarines, mines, integrated, air-defense systems, electronic warfare, and cyberspace warfare.

The Navy's Distributed Maritime Operations Concept[3] is built on the Navy's much-discussed "distributed **lethality**" strategy. The concept emphasizes the need to arm the fleets with more and better offensive and defensive weapons and enable naval forces to be deployed where they are needed.

The "distributed lethality" strategy refers to the use of cyber weapons, space weapons, and missiles as well as over-the-horizon combat equipment and air launchers in offensive operations. It is particularly important for a fleet to possess the capability of defending itself from long-distance attacks or strikes. If so, the fleet can deploy its warships and use all kinds of weapons and equipments for distributed operations.

As a matter of fact, the Navy's emphasis on offensive operations stems from its established strategic guidelines or principles. The most important part of the strategic principles is to continue maintaining the Navy's open sea or "blue water" combat capability

against its adversary, just as it was carried out during the Cold War. So far, the navy has also applied those useful strategic and tactical principles to anti-terrorism, anti-piracy, protection of international waterways and things like Visit Board Search and Seizure (VBSS) [4].

Of course, these missions are still important. Given that other countries have precision-guided anti-ship missiles able to hit targets at a distance of greater than 900 miles, the Navy thinks it necessary to enhance its offensive "lethality". With advent of cyber and electronic warfare, drone attack technology and other high-end weapons, the combat mode adopted in this modern age is, in some degree, different from previous Cold War strategic paradigms.

The paper "Strategy Concept of the US Navy," published by Naval History and Heritage Command[5] in 1987 stresses the importance of long-range offensive firepower in a geographically dispersed or extensive ocean warfare environment and points out that the very survivability of US Naval Forces and the accomplishment of their missions depend upon offensive firepower. It also states that the naval forces may be separately deployed to different waters, but their command, control and communication systems, sensors and weapons can be well coordinated to provide maximum mutual support and offensive capability.

A document on the Cold War Era Strategic Concepts specifies that the Naval defensive capability is closely related to long-range detection systems such as airborne early warning, quick-reaction support systems, and efficient defensive systems.

Organizations like the Defense Advanced Research Projects Agency (DARPA)[6] and the Office of Naval Research (ONR)[7] have been devoting their efforts to military research on what is mentioned above. The innovation based on the research includes upgrading the existing hardware from the implementation of the US-led F-35 joint strike fighter programme[8] to further improvement in unmanned aerial vehicle (UAV) system and weapons-locating system.

In addition, the US Navy has been researching and developing other high-tech projects, two of which have a major breakthrough in technology. One is the free electron laser; the other is the electromagnetic rail gun. Both of them will greatly contribute to the enhancement of combat capability of a new generation of warships. They mark a milestone in the history of technological development of weapons system.

*(935 words)*

**Sources:**

www.foxnews.com/tech/navy-weapons-strategy-preps-for-future-high-end-fight-massive-ocean-war

*Notes*

1. Surface Warfare Advanced Tactical Training (SWATT): It refers to advanced tactical training exercises organized and led by the Naval Surface and Mine War-fighting Development Center (SMWDC). 水面作战高级战术训练

2. Navy's 2016 Surface Force Strategy：a new surface-force strategy issued by the Navy in 2016 海军2016水面部队战略

3. the Navy's Distributed Maritime Operations Concept: a new operational concept aiming at producing larger combat effects through strengthening the offensive power of individual components of the naval force to gain sea control 海军分布式海上作战概念

4. Visit Board Search and Seizure(VBSS): a term taken by the US military and law enforcement agencies, maritime boarding actions and tactics such as anti-terrorism, anti-piracy, and anti-smuggling operations 查证、登临、搜索和缉捕，通常简称为"临检拿捕"

5. Naval History and Heritage Command: responsible for US naval history and heritage 海军历史和遗产司令部

6. Defense Advanced Research Projects Agency (DARPA): an agency of the US Department of Defense responsible for research project 国防高级研究计划局

7. Office of Naval Research (ONR): an organ attached to the Department of the Navy that coordinates, executes and promotes the science and technology programs of the US Navy and Marine Corps 海军研究处

8. F-35 joint strike fighter programme: program for F-35 joint strike fighters F-35联合攻击战斗机计划

*Word Bank*

| | |
|---|---|
| rigorous [ˈrɪgərəs] | *adj.* 严格的，严厉的；严密的；严酷的 |
| briefing [ˈbriːfɪŋ] | *n.* 简报；简令；（任务的）简要说明 |
| debriefing [ˌdiːˈbriːfɪŋ] | *n.* 情况汇报；汇报（执行任务情况） |
| layered [ˈleɪəd] | *adj.* 分层的；层状的 |
| lethality [lɪˈθælətɪ] | *n.* 杀伤力；致命性；毁坏性 |
| drone [drəʊn] | *n.* 无人机（非正式） |
| paradigm [ˈpærədaɪm] | *n.* 范例 |

electromagnetic rail gun　　　　　电磁轨道炮

## I. Comprehension

**Part A**　Questions

*Answer the following questions in accordance with the text.*

1. What is the focus of Surface Warfare Advanced Tactical Training (SWATT)?

2. What is the significance of sea control according to Royse?

3. What are the examples of threats cited by the Navy's 2016 Surface Force Strategy document?

4. Why does the Navy seek to enhance its offensive "lethality"?

5. What does the Cold War ERA Strategic Concepts specify?

**Part B**　Multiple Choices

*Choose the most appropriate answer from the given choices below each question in accordance with the text.*

1. What does Surface Warfare Advanced Tactical Training (SWATT) include?

　A. Amphibious Ready Groups, Carrier Strike Groups and other elements of surface warfare.

　B. Mine countermeasures, Carrier Strike Groups and other elements of surface warfare.

　C. Mine countermeasures, Amphibious Ready Groups, and other elements of surface warfare.

　D. Mine countermeasures, antisubmarine warfare, anti craft defense, amphibious operation and surface strike or attack.

2. The training courses involves understanding the tactical and technical characteristics of sophisticated weapons—

　A. antiship/antisubmarine missile, cruise missile, strategic ballistic missile, high-energy laser weapon, microwave weapon and electromagnetic rail gun.

　B. cruise missile, strategic ballistic missile, high-energy laser weapon, microwave weapon and electromagnetic rail gun.

　C. antiship/antisubmarine missile, strategic ballistic missile, high-energy laser weapon, microwave weapon and electromagnetic rail gun.

　D. antiship/antisubmarine missile, cruise missile, strategic ballistic missile, high-energy laser weapon, electromagnetic rail gun.

3. What does the Navy's Distributed Maritime Operations Concept build upon?

   A. The training courses.

   B. The Surface Force Strategy.

   C. "Distributed lethality" strategy.

   D. All of the above.

4. What do the survivability of US Naval Forces and the accomplishment of their missions depend upon according to the essay "Strategy Concept of the US Navy"?

   A. Peaceful strategy.

   B. Advanced technology.

   C. Offensive firepower.

   D. Forward deployment.

5. What are the technologies which have a major breakthrough in technology?

   A. The free electron laser and the long-range missiles.

   B. The nuclear-powered submarine and the electromagnetic rail gun.

   C. The long-range missiles and the electromagnetic rail gun.

   D. The free electron laser and the electromagnetic rail gun.

## II. Translation

**Part A** Terms & Phrases

*Translate the following terms or phrases from Chinese into English and vice versa.*

1. 水面作战高级战术训练
2. 反潜战
3. 防空
4. 冷战
5. 无人机
6. 作战指示
7. 任务报告
8. 对策
9. 激光
10. 磁轨炮
11. 远程的
12. 传感器
13. 杀伤力
14. over-the-horizon
15. drone
16. mine countermeasure
17. sea lane
18. microwave weapon
19. electron
20. electromagnetic
21. targeting networks
22. cruise missile
23. cyberspace warfare
24. integrated air-defense systems
25. airborne early warning
26. command, control and communication systems

**Part B　Paragraph**

*Translate the following paragraph from English into Chinese.*

The most important part of the strategic principles is to continue maintaining the Navy's open sea or "blue water" combat capability against its adversary, just as it was carried out during the Cold War. So far, the navy has also applied those useful strategic and tactical principles to anti-terrorism, anti-piracy, protection of international waterways and things like Visit Board Search and Seizure.

## III. Reading Report

What have you learned after reading the text? Have you obtained a better understanding of Navy weapons and its strategy? Now create your reading report in no more than 150 words to generalize your achievement in the text study.

# Text B
## The World's Deadliest Torpedoes

The modern torpedo is a self-propelled weapon with an explosive warhead. It can be fired on the surface or under the water from a boat ship or submarine and explodes when it hits its target.

In 1866, a British engineer, Robert Whitehead succeeded in designing the first real torpedo, which was driven by a compressed cold air engine coupled to a propeller. Since then, torpedoes have evolved into a deadly weapon. The process of evolution refers to different torpedoes appearing in chronological order, such as heat-driven torpedo (or steam and gas torpedo), electrically-driven torpedo with no wake, passive and active acoustic-homing torpedo, rocket-assisted torpedo (also called antisubmarine missile) and microcomputer controlled torpedo.

The torpedo, a long narrow bomb, is like fish in shape, so it is colloquially called "fish". Now there are a number of torpedoes whose designations are related to "fish", for example, Tigerfish, Sting Ray and Sparefish. With great progress in the underwater weapons field, the self-propelled torpedo with a homing device has become a striker beneath the sea. In both surface warfare and anti-submarine warfare, torpedo boats, lighter surface ships, submarines, unmanned submarines, anti-submarine aircraft and lightweight bomber (or torpedo bomber) can launch their self-propelled torpedoes to destroy hostile warships or big armored ships equipped with large-caliber guns, and double-hulled submarines, though sometimes at the risk of being struck by long-range fire.

Modern torpedoes are classified as lightweight and heavyweight. They include straight heading, self-homing and wire-guided torpedoes, which can be launched from a variety of platforms, such as submarines, surface vessels, aircraft and helicopters.

## Black Shark Torpedo

The Black Shark Advanced (BSA)[1], a new-generation multi-role heavyweight torpedo fired from submarines or surface ships, is designed to counter threats from all surface and underwater platforms. The Black Shark is intended to replace the ageing A-184 heavyweight torpedo[2] used by the Italian Navy.

The Black Shark is currently being produced by Whitehead Alenia Sistemi Subacquei

(WASS)[3] for several major naval forces. The Scorpene-class[4], U209[5], U214[6] and U212[7] submarines are armed with this kind of torpedoes.

The wire-guided, self-homing torpedo which is 21 inches in diameter is fitted with an ASTRA[8] [(Advanced Sonar Transmitting and Receiving Architecture)] and loaded with a high-explosive warhead. The propulsion system with Al-AgO battery[9], **contra-rotating** brushless motor and **skew** propeller sensors can operate at a maximum speed of 50 knots.

### F21 Heavyweight Torpedo

The F21 heavyweight torpedo[10] from DCNS[11] is a double-purpose torpedo that can be fired at its targets — submarine and surface ship. It will replace F17 mod2 torpedo[12] aboard the French Navy's submarines.

The 1.3-ton F21 torpedo is available for use in all types of submarines such as **SSBN** and **SSN** as well as **diesel-electric** submarine. In other words, it is a submarine-launched torpedo. It is equipped with a new-type acoustic homing head from Thales Underwater System[13], in addition to an impact/acoustic fuse warhead.

The F21 is driven by electric propulsion based on the silver **oxide-aluminium (AgO-Al)** primary battery. It can operate under the water 10 to 500 meters deep and at a speed of 25 to 50 knots, with an endurance distance of over 50 kilometers.

### Spearfish Heavyweight Torpedo[14]

The advanced heavyweight torpedo Spearfish made by the BAE Systems[15] is very effective in attacking submarines and surface ships in oceanic and coastal waters. The 1.85-ton torpedo has gone into service in the submarine forces of the UK Royal Navy.

The Spearfish which carries **Aluminised PBX** explosive warhead weighing 300 kilograms can home in on its target by the aid of high-capacity wire-guided system and passive and active sonars.

Its power plant is composed of a gas turbine engine using Otto Fuel as liquid **monopropellant**, and **Hydroxyl Ammonium Perchlorate (HAP)** as **oxidant**. The propulsion system allows the Spearfish to move towards a target at low speed within the range of 48 kilometers.

### Torpedo 62 (Torpedo 2000)[16]

The Torpedo 62 (Export designation: Torpedo 2000) produced by Saab[17] company is a double-purpose heavyweight torpedo system, which finds application in the submarine forces of the Royal Swedish Navy[18]. It is a lethal weapon used for destroying various submarines and surface ships.

The Torpedo 62 with a launching weight of 1,450 kilograms is loaded with a high explosive warhead. It can operate at a depth of 500 meters under the guidance of the active/passive homing system.

The torpedo propelled by an advanced pump jet engine can home in on its target within the range of more than 40 kilometers, at a maximum speed of 40 knots.

### DM2A4/SeaHake mod 4[19]

The DM2A4 Seehecht (Export Name: SeaHake mod 4) is the main underwater weapon of the German Navy's Type 212 submarines. The heavyweight torpedo weighing 1.37 tons can be launched from both submarines and surface ships.

The SeaHake mod 4 torpedo with a 255kg warhead, which has been developed by Atlas Elektronik[20], can strike underwater and surface targets by means of fiber optic wire guidance.

Equipped with a high-frequency permanent-magnet motor and a group of silver-zinc batteries, the torpedo can move towards the target at the highest speed of 50 knots within the range of over 50 kilometers.

### Shkval-E[21]

The Shkval-E is a high-speed unguided underwater missile or torpedo produced by "Region" State Research & Production Enterprise of Tactical Missiles Corporation JSC[22]. This kind of torpedo is mounted on surface vessel or submarines. It can be fired from a 30-meter depth of water in Sea State[23] 4.

The underwater weapon weighing 2,700kg has a high-explosive warhead (210-kilogram TNT equivalent) with the impact and proximity fuse.

Its propulsion system consisting of hydro-reactive jet and the solid-fuel rocket booster enables it to move towards the target at a high speed. The torpedo's effective launching range is 7 kilometers and its cruising range is 10 kilometers.

### Mk48 ADCAP Mod 7[24] CBASS

The Mk48 ADCAP Mod 7 is equipped with the Common Broadband Advanced Sonar System (CBASS) developed by Lockheed Martin. The system uses active and/or passive

homing, broadband sonars to detect and track targets in deep and shallow waters so as to take countermeasures against them. It is the most advanced heavyweight torpedo that is widely used by the submarine forces of the US Navy and allied nations.

The torpedo which has a launching weight of 1,676 kilograms and a 292.5 kilograms high explosive warhead is powered by a **piston** engine using Otto Fuel II[25] mono-propellant. Its maximum speed and firing range are over 28 knots and 8 kilometers respectively.

### MU90/Impact

The MU90/IMPACT is a kind of advanced lightweight anti-submarine torpedo developed by EuroTorp[26]. It is jointly manufactured by Italian WASS, French DCNS International and Thales mainly used to attack deep-sea submarines equipped with advanced counter measure devices. Its launching platforms include surface ships, fixed-wing aircraft, helicopters, and rocket-launchers.

With its superior performance characteristics such as lightweight (360 kilograms) higher speed, longer firing range, ideal submergence depth (more than 1,000 meters) and good maneuverability, this 3rd generation torpedo is capable of fulfilling the anti-submarine warfare requirement of the 21st century. Now it has been purchased by the naval forces of France, Italy, Germany, Denmark, Poland and Australia, which intend to improve their combat capability or operational efficiency.

*(1185 words)*

**Sources:**

www.naval-technology.com/features/featurethe-worlds-deadliest-torpedoes-4286162/

*Notes*

1. Black Shark Advanced (BSA): a heavyweight torpedo produced by WASS （由意大利 WASS公司生产的）黑鲨高级重型鱼雷

2. A-184 heavyweight torpedo: a wire-guided heavy torpedo produced in Italy A184重型 鱼雷

3. Whitehead Alenia Sistemi Subacquei (WASS): one of the main companies manufacturing Advanced Underwater Systems 意大利白头·艾尔尼亚系统公司

4. Scorpene-class: a class of diesel-electric attack submarines jointly developed by the French Direction des Constructions Navales (DCN) and the Spanish company Navantia 鲉鱼级

潜艇

5. U209 submarines: a class of diesel-electric attack submarine developed exclusively for export by Howaldtswerke-Deutsche Werft of Germany 209型潜艇

6. U214 submarines: a diesel-electric submarine evolved from the Type 212. 214型潜艇

7. U212 submarines: also Italian Todaro class, non-nuclear submarines developed by Howaldtswerke-Deutsche Werft AG (HDW) for the German and Italian navies 212型潜艇

8. ASTRA: Advanced Sonar Transmitting and Receiving Architecture 先进声纳发射暨接收结构

9. Al-AgO battery: a primary battery made of aluminum and silver oxide Al-AgO电池

10. F21 heavyweight torpedo: a heavy torpedo developed by French DCNS F21型重型鱼雷

11. DCNS: a French industrial group specialized in building warships 法国舰艇制造局

12. F17 mod2 torpedo: a torpedo developed by French DCNS F17-2型鱼雷

13. Thales Underwater System: a French company engaged in the design and manufacture of sonar systems for submarines, surface warships, and aircraft 泰利斯水下系统公司

14. Spearfish Heavyweight Torpedo: a primary anti-ship and anti-submarine weapon of Royal Navy submarines 旗鱼重型鱼雷

15. the BAE Systems: a global defense, aerospace and security company, whose products and services cover air, land and naval forces, as well as advanced electronics, security, information technology, and support services 英国宇航系统公司

16. Torpedo 62 (Torpedo 2000): a kind of dual-purpose heavyweight torpedo used by the submarine forces of the Royal Swedish Navy 62 重型鱼雷

17. Saab: a Swedish aerospace and defense company, founded in 1937 萨博公司（瑞典）

18. Royal Swedish Navy: the naval branch of the Swedish Armed Forces 瑞典皇家海军

19. DM2A4/SeaHake mod 4: the latest heavyweight torpedo developed by Atlas Elektronik for the German Navy 德国DM2A4重型鱼雷

20. Atlas Elektronik: a naval/marine electronics and systems business based in Bremen, Germany, which designs and manufactures integrated sonar systems for submarines and heavyweight torpedoes 德国阿特拉斯电子公司

21. Shkval-E: a nuclear-capable underwater anti-ship missile designed for use by nuclear-powered submarines against large surface ships such as aircraft carriers （风暴）高速超空炮反舰水下导弹

22. "Region" State Research & Production Enterprise of Tactical Missiles Corporation JSC：a company which develops and supplies aerial bombs for front aviation "区域"俄罗斯战

术导弹公司

23. Sea State: the degree of turbulence at sea, generally measured on a scale of zero to nine according to average wave height 海况，4级海况指中浪

24. Mk48 ADCAP Mod 7: the most advanced US Navy heavyweight torpedo. MK48 Mod 7重型鱼雷

25. Otto Fuel II: a distinct-smelling, reddish-orange, oily liquid that the US Navy uses as a fuel for torpedoes and other weapon systems 单节火箭推进

26. EuroTorp: a European Economic Interest Group, based in southern France, comprising WASS, DCNS and Thales.; the world leader in the field of Light Weight Torpedoes and associated systems 欧洲鱼雷公司

## Word Bank

| | |
|---|---|
| warhead [ˈwɔːhed] | *n.* 弹头 |
| colloquially [kəˈləʊkwɪəlɪ] | *adv.* 口语地；用通俗语 |
| designation [dezɪgˈneɪʃ(ə)n] | *n.* 指定；名称；指示；选派 |
| caliber [ˈkælɪbər] | *n.* [军] 口径 |
| contra-rotating [ˈkɒntrə rəʊˈteɪtɪŋ] | *adj.* 反向旋转的；向对转的 |
| skew [skjuː] | *adj.* 斜的；不轴的；不对称的 |
| diesel-electric [ˈdiːzl ɪˈlektrɪk] | *adj.* 柴（油）电（力）的 |
| oxide-aluminium (AgO-Al): [ˈɒksaɪd ˌæljəˈmɪnɪəm] | |
| | *n.* 铝氧化物 |
| monopropellant [ˌmɒnəʊprəˈpelənt] | *n.* 单元燃料；单元（一元）推进剂 |
| oxidant [ˈɒksɪdənt] | *n.* 氧化剂 |
| piston [ˈpɪstən] | *n.* 活塞 |
| SSBN | 核动力弹道导弹潜艇 |
| SSN | 核动力潜艇 |
| Aluminised PBX | 铝化高聚物粘结炸药 |
| Hydroxyl Ammonium Perchlorate (HAP) | 高氯酸羟铵 |
| pump jet engine | 泵式喷气发动机 |
| fibre optic wire guidance | 光纤有线制导 |

# Exercises

## I. True or False

*Decide whether the following sentences are true or false in accordance with the text.*

1. Today's torpedoes can be divided into lightweight and heavyweight classes; and into straight-running and wire-guided. They can be launched from a variety of platforms.

2. The process of evolution refers to different torpedoes appearing in chronological order.

3. The Black Shark is intended to replace the ageing A-184 heavyweight torpedo used by the US Navy.

4. The F21 is driven by nuclear power based on the silver oxide-aluminium (AgO-Al) primary battery.

5. The advanced heavyweight torpedo Spearfish made by the BAE Systems is very effective in attacking submarines and surface ships in oceanic and coastal waters.

6. The propulsion system allows the Spearfish to move towards a target at low speed within the range of 48 kilometers.

7. The Torpedo 62 (Export designation: Torpedo 2000) produced by Saab Company is a double-purpose lightweight torpedo system.

8. The SeaHake mod 4 heavyweight torpedo, weighing 1.37 tons, can be launched from both submarines and surface ships.

## II. Word Match

*Match the words/terms/phrases in the left column with its appropriate correspondents in the right column.*

| | |
|---|---|
| 1. SSBN | A. 声学的 |
| 2. diameter | B. 英国皇家海军 |
| 3. piston | C. 海况 |
| 4. Black Shark Advanced (BSA) | D. 推进力 |
| 5. propeller | E. 直径 |
| 6. UK Royal Navy | F. 核动力弹道导弹潜艇 |
| 7. SSN | G. 活塞 |
| 8. acoustic | H. 黑鲨高级重型鱼雷 |
| 9. propulsion | I. 核动力潜艇 |
| 10. Sea State | J. 螺旋桨 |

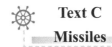

### Text C
### Missiles

A missile is a self-propelled precision guided weapon directed at a target by remote control. It is generally composed of four parts: body structure, control system, power plant and warhead. The body structure means a supporting structure to connect a missile's individual components. The control system is a guidance system controlling a missile's flight direction, attitude, altitude and speed. The missile can be guided in different ways, which include inertial, homing, remote-control, wireless or wire guidance. The power plant often uses a solid or liquid rocket engine, or a jet engine as a source of power for missile flight. The warhead which is a specialized device for destroying a target consists of shell case, combat-loading, explosive and security devices. Different types of missiles suitable for different purposes encompass surface-to-surface, surface-to-underwater, surface-to-air, air to surface, air to air, anti-submarine and anti-satellite missiles.

Missiles are generally categorized according to their launch platforms and intended targets. In a broad sense, they are used for surface or air warfare. Many missile weapons are designed to be launched from both the surface and the air, and a few are designed to attack either surface or air targets (such as the ADATS[1] missile). In order to be launched from the air or surface, most weapons require some modification, for example, adding boosters to the surface-launched version. Below is a description of some principal missiles.

#### Surface-to-Surface/Air-to-Surface

● **Ballistic missile.** Under the action of the rocket-engine thrust, a ballistic missile follows the preset program, that is to say, it only can keep its predetermined course without deviation. Its flight trajectory is commonly divided into active phase and passive phase. The active phase refers to power flight or boost phase. The passive phase involves free flight and reentry.

Ballistic missiles are largely used to attack land targets. A ballistic missile can deliver a warhead to a target city with no possibility of interception. However, in the early period of development, its accuracy was fairly poor. In the post-war period, the upgraded design concept led to much improvement on its inertial guidance system, so that the system could be applied to an intercontinental ballistic missile (ICBM), which is a long-range ballistic missile with its firing distance more than 8000 kilometers. Today, the ICBM serves the function of strategic deterrence. However, some ballistic missiles are used for special purposes, such as the Russian

Iskander[2] — tactical surface-to-surface missile and the Chinese DF-21D anti-ship ballistic missile[3]. Ballistic missiles are usually launched from mobile launchers, **silos**, surface ships or submarines, with the exception of the Skybolt[4] missile, which is likely to be launched from the air.

- **Cruise missile**. Cruise missiles are not only used for ground attack, but also for anti-shipping operations. They are primarily launched from air, sea or submarine platforms, in addition to land-based launchers available for use.

- **Anti-ship missile**. The anti-ship-class missile was one of the major German missile development projects during the World War II. It was intended to stop the British ships from cross-channel invasion. However, the British were able to render its system ineffective by radio jamming, and Germany failed to get its wire-guided missiles ready by D-day[5]. After the War, the anti-ship class slowly developed and became a major missile weapon in the 1960s with the introduction of the low-flying jet-propelled or rocket-powered cruise missiles known as "sea-skimmers". These played a significant role during the Falklands War[6], when an Argentine Exocet missile sank a Royal Navy destroyer.

Now there are missiles specially used for attacking submarines, or torpedo and anti-submarine missiles, in addition to depth charge.

- **Anti-tank missile**. By the end of WWII, unguided rockets loaded with **high-explosive** anti-tank warheads were widely used as main anti-tank weapons (see Panzerfaust, Bazooka). However, their effective firing range were limited to 100 meters or so. The German army sought to extend the firing range by use of a wire guidance missile. In the late 1950s, this kind of missiles became a major design project and began its production. By the 1960s, it had developed into a practical anti-tank weapon. As for wire guidance, it is one of the remote-control guidance modes. An instruction is transmitted to an anti-tank missile via wire to control its flying path for the purpose of hitting its target. Anti-tank missiles can be launched from aircraft and vehicles. Especially they can be used conveniently by ground troops in land combat.

**Surface-to-air**

- **Anti-aircraft**. The anti-aircraft missile is a weapon which can be launched from land, ship or submarine to intercept an air target. Before World War II, it was researched and developed in some countries, including Germany. In order to defeat the German aggressors, the US and British air forces started to send huge air fleets over the occupied Europe in 1944. On the Luftwaffe day[7] the **night fighter forces** were dispatched there for attack.

The Germans tried to get their ground-based anti-aircraft missiles into operation, but they could not display operational efficiency. Even some anti-aircraft weapons systems were underdevelopment before the end of the war. Now anti-aircraft weapons can be fired from various launch platforms such as Shipboard launcher, surface launcher and man-portable air defense system. Take the example of the S-300 (missile)[8], S-400 (missile)[9], Advanced Air Defense and MIM-104 Patriot[10] with explosive warheads, they are all air defense missiles used for destroying air targets.

### Air-to-air

The air-to-air missile is a weapon launched from aircraft to attack its air targets. It has experienced a long process of development. During World War II, the Germans felt it quite difficult to destroy large aircraft. Therefore, they made considerable efforts to develop their air-to-air missile systems. In the post-war period, the R4M served as the pattern for a number of similar systems, used by almost all interceptor aircraft during the 1940s and 1950s. Lacking guidance systems, such rocket projectiles had to be carefully aimed at a target at a relatively close range before hitting it accurately. The US Navy and Air Force began deploying guided missiles in the early 1950s, including well-known AIM-9 Sidewinder and AIM-4 Falcon. Improvement on the missile system is still in progress. So to speak, modern air warfare can not do without missiles.

### Anti-satellite

The anti-satellite missile is a kind of missile used for destroying satellites or other space vehicles. As early as the 1950s and 1960s, Soviet designers started to develop an anti-satellite weapon, called the Istrebitel Sputnik, which literally means "interceptor of satellites" or "destroyer of satellites". From 1963 to 1982, it was tested for 20 times, and what's more, it succeeded in destroying several satellites on the orbit. In order to compete with the former Soviet Union for superiority in the field of space weapons, the United States started testing their own systems. For example, its Brilliant Pebbles Defense System is an intelligent and miniaturized space-based defense system, which can intercept hostile space weapons. Anti-satellite missiles can explode their nuclear or conventional warheads to hit targets and may also use their warheads to directly collide against targets. They can be launched from land, air or space.

*(1162 words)*

*Sources:*

https://encyclopedia.thefreedictionary.com/missile

## Notes

1. ADATS: air-defense anti-tank system 防空防坦克系统

2. Russian Iskander: a ballistic missile system used by the Russian armed forces since 2006 俄罗斯伊斯坎德尔弹道导弹系统

3. Chinese DF-21D anti-ship ballistic missile: an anti-ship ballistic missile 东风21D反舰弹道导弹

4. Skybolt: an air-launched ballistic missile 空中弩箭导弹

5. D-day: a day (6 June, 1944) on which the Allied forces landed in North France during the Second World War 第二次世界大战盟军在法国北部的登陆日（1944年6月6日）

6. Falklands War: a war fought between Argentina and Great Britain in 1982 over control of the Falkland Islands (Islas Malvinas) 马岛战争

7. Luftwaffe day: the Establishment day of the Nazi German Air Force 纳粹德国空军日

8. S-300 (missile): a long-range surface-to-air missile produced by NPO Almaz, based on the initial S-300P version S-300导弹

9. S-400 (missile): an air defense missile developed by Almaz Central Design Bureau of Russia, replacing the S-300P and S-200 air defense systems S-400导弹

10. MIM-104 Patriot: a long-range, all-altitude, all-weather air defense system to counter tactical ballistic missiles, cruise missiles and advanced aircraft MIM-104爱国者导弹

## Word Bank

| | |
|---|---|
| booster [ˈbuːstər] | *n.* 升压机；支持者；扩爆器 |
| inertial [ɪˈnɜːʃl] | *adj.* 惯性的 |
| silo [ˈsaɪləʊ] | *n.* （核武器的）发射井；（危险物品的）地下贮藏库；筒仓 |
| high-explosive [haɪ ɪkˈspləʊsɪv] | *n.* 烈性炸药；高爆炸药；猛炸药 |
| night fighter force | 夜间战斗机部队 |

Based on what you have acquired in this text, you are supposed to conduct an online study to explore further into the relevant sphere. Comb and frame what you have found with an online study report in no less than 200 words. In addition, any assistant image, audio, video, or other first-hand material will be preferred when you present your report in class.

# Unit 13  Coastal Defense Force

**Bridge-in**

*Answer the following questions in accordance with the video "the Coastal Defense Force".*

1. What typical missions have been mentioned in the video?
2. What is your understanding of the function of the coastal defense force?

## Text A
## The PLAN Coast Defense Force

The coastal defense force, as one of the arms of the PLAN, is primarily composed of coastal artillery units and coastal missile units, which are deployed in the key sectors along the Chinese coast. Its missions include defending naval bases, ports and key coastal areas against attacks from enemy ships and Marine amphibious troops, destroying enemy ships, blocking sea lanes, supporting ships operating in the coastal waters, and assisting the forces garrisoned on the islands and in the coastal fortress areas in operations. Armed with state-of-the-art weapons, such as shore-to-ship missiles, the Chinese Coast Defense force has developed into a mighty long-range strike force.

### History of PLAN Coast Defense Force

After the founding of the People's Republic of China, the PLA reorganized the 6th artillery division of the Northeast Military Command and the 10th artillery regiment of the Southwest Military Command into a naval coastal artillery school (later renamed the PLA Navy Artillery School) in August, 1950. In October of the same year, the first coastal artillery battalion was established. In 1951, more than ten coastal artillery regiments were set up.

In 1952, the Navy Artillery Department was founded and later renamed the Coastal Defense Artillery Department. In 1955, the Navy established mobile coastal artillery regiments and independent battalions. In the early 1960s, shore-to-ship missiles began to be distributed to the forces. In the middle 1970s, the naval shore-to-missile units experienced rapid development, so that they became a relatively modern coast defense force on a certain scale. In the 1980s, the Navy coastal defense units were armed with improved extended-range missiles and more advanced equipment like anti-jamming terminal-guidance[1] radar to enhance their combat capability. In 2004, the PLAN established a new shore-to-missile regiment for the purpose of expanding the scale of the coast defense arm and further improving its comprehensive combat efficiency.

Since its founding, the PLAN coast defense force has taken part in over 400 combats alone or in coordination with other arms, sinking and damaging more than 70 enemy ships, and shooting down and damaging over 40 enemy planes, and has played an increasingly important role in consolidating China's coastal defense and safeguarding its maritime interests.

With the continuous development of information technology, weapons and equipment, the PLAN coast defense force will make further improvement on the weapon performance, extended-range firing and precision guidance. And it will make greater efforts to raise the level of command and control, perfect its coastal defense systems, enhance the capability of coastal defense and strike, and strengthen the ability to coordinate with other services and arms.

### Organizational Structure

The PLAN coast defense force is an important branch of China's naval forces, which is capable of defending against amphibious and air attacks. Usually, the coast defense force includes coastal missile troops and coastal artillery troops mostly composed of regiments and battalions, which are equipped with antiaircraft artillery or AA guns and shore-to-ship missiles, such as HY-2[2], YJ-82[3], C-602[4] and YJ-18[5]. These regiments and battalions are separately subordinate to naval bases and naval districts. Now the coast defense force is deemed to be the backbone of naval coastal defense because it is able to make full use of advanced weapons as well as favorable island and coastal conditions for protracted operations.

### Training

The PLAN coastal defense troops conduct four types of training: technical specialty training, firing training, tactical training and common training.

Technical specialty training focuses on expertise. The trainees are required not only to learn theoretical knowledge and skills but also to understand the know-how about the principles, structure, operational performance and management of weapons, technical equipment and other relevant systems.

Firing training focuses on the use of weapon systems by individuals or by an entire company. The contents of firing training refer to the principles of firing guns or missiles at moving maritime targets.

Tactical training focuses on tactical principles, tactical operations and operational methods. It includes single-branch and combined-arms tactical training.

Single-branch tactical training involves studying artillery and missile tactics as well as principles of combat, command and support. It also includes learning how to defend firing or launch sites and conduct mobile operations.

Combined-arms tactical training aims to make the trainees understand combined-arms principles: coordination between the artillery and missile units, and requirements of combat in coordination with surface forces and naval aviation.

Common training focuses on naval common-sense education as well as fundamental knowledge about **camouflage**, concealment, and defense against winds and floods.

According to the OMTE[6]5,Personnel Training, Basic Technical and Tactical Training and Combined-arms Training will have to be fulfilled in three phases.

Cadets usually receive their basic training at a PLAN academy. Enlisted persons receive their technical training at an academy or a training base. The purpose of their training is to learn the professional theory and master basic knowledge about effective control and command of weapon systems and equipment.

After the cadets and enlisted persons are assigned to coast-defense companies or battalions, they will apply theoretical knowledge to and apply their expert knowledge or skill to practical activities, which include deploying, controlling and launching the weapon systems as well as concealing and defending everything at the firing sites.

When the basic technical and tactical training has been completed at the company and battalion levels, regiments and brigades will organize a lot of coordinated training on a larger scale.

The training gradually expands from the coordination of artillery and missile battalions to that of several missile battalions. On this basis, these units begin carrying out larger coordinated training tasks in operational or tactical-level exercises with the surface forces and naval aviation under the leadership of the naval base.

Summary

In recent years, PLAN coast defense force has been committed to deepening its military reform, optimizing its command and control systems, further improving the operational performance of its weapons and equipment, and enhancing its integrated combat capability. There is no denying that the Chinese Naval Coast Arm is an essential defense force capable of anti-ship and anti-aircraft operations which cannot be replaced by any other arms in defense of China's coastal areas and territorial seas. What is worth mentioning is that its advanced weapons and equipment can be brought into full play in air defense operations, for instance, shooting down enemy aircraft and intercepting cruise missiles.

Over the past 70 years, the Chinese navy has experienced countless trials and hardships and covered the process from small to large and from weak to strong. Today, the PLA Navy is growing into a "Blue-Water" naval force, which ventures into the blue waters of the high seas. To be sure, the Navy will always perform its sacred mission and will certainly make greater contributions to defending China's territorial sovereignty, maintaining the maritime interests of the nation and safeguarding the world peace.

*(1119 words)*

*Sources:*

1. http://en.people.cn/90001/90776/90785/6776526.html（2020年9月12日访问）

2. https://www.globalsecurity.org/military/world/china/plan-cdf.htm

*Notes*

1. terminal-guidance: any guidance system that is primarily or solely active during the "terminal phase", just before the weapon impacts its target 末制导

2. HY-2: a type of anti-ship missile, version of HY-1, launched from the land 海鹰-2 反舰导弹

3. YJ-82: a Chinese subsonic anti-ship cruise missile, launched from submarines 鹰击-82反舰导弹

4. C-602: a Chinese subsonic anti-ship cruise missile with a range of 280 km, a 300 kg (660 lb) semi-armour-piercing warhead, and GPS guidance 鹰击-602反舰导弹

5. YJ-18: a missile with a subsonic cruise mode and a supersonic terminal attack 鹰击-18反舰导弹

6. OMTE: the Outline of Military Training and Evaluation 军事训练与考核大纲

## Word Bank

| | |
|---|---|
| state-of-the-art | *adj.* 最先进的，最新的 |
| battalion [bəˈtælɪən] | *n.* 营 |
| regiment [ˈredʒɪmənt] | *n.* 团 |
| camouflage [ˈkæməflɑːʒ] | *n.* 伪装；掩饰 |
| anti-jamming terminal-guidance radar | 抗干扰末端制导雷达 |

## Exercises

### I. Comprehension

**Part A  Questions**

*Answer the following questions in accordance with the text.*

1. What branches are the Coast Defense Force composed of?

2. When was the Navy Artillery Department founded?

3. What does tactical training focus on?

4. What is the purpose of enlisted personnel's technical training?

5. What does the PLAN highlight in training?

**Part B  Multiple Choices**

*Choose the most appropriate answer from the given choices below each question in accordance with the text.*

1. Which of the following statement is right in terms of the mission of the coastal defense force?

   A. To defend naval bases, ports and key coastal areas.

   B. Destroy enemy ships, block sea lanes.

   C. Support ships operating and assist the garrison forces.

   D. All of the above.

2. When were the C series of coastal defense missiles developed?

   A. In the end of 1955.

   B. In August, 1985.

   C. In the 1980s.

D. In the summer of 1987.

3. Which of the following is not the subject of common training?

A. Naval common-sense education.

B. The use of weapon systems.

C. Camouflage, concealment.

D. Defense against winds and floods.

4. Which statement concerning the coastal defense forces' training is not true?

A. The training is divided into four phases.

B. Enlisted persons receive the technical training at an academy or a training base.

C. The coastal defense forces conduct individual training and unit training at the company and battalion levels.

D. The coordinated trainings are conducted with the surface forces and naval aviation.

5. What has PLAN coastal defense force been committed to in recent years?

A. Deepening military reform.

B. Optimizing the command and control systems.

C. Improving the weapons and equipment.

D. All of the above.

## II. Translation

**Part A** Terms & Phrases

*Translate the following terms or phrases from Chinese into English and vice versa.*

1. 东海舰队
2. 南海舰队
3. 北海舰队
4. 联合作战能力
5. 潜艇部队
6. 水面舰艇部队
7. 陆战队
8. 钢铁长城
9. 先进武器
10. 通讯站
11. coastal defense force
12. naval base
13. fishery security
14. cruise missile
15. navigation
16. fire coverage
17. AAA
18. combat capability
19. the aviation force
20. maritime target

**Part B** Paragraph

*Translate the following paragraph from English into Chinese.*

Over the past 70 years, the Chinese navy has experienced countless trials and hardships and covered the process from small to large and from weak to strong. Today, the PLA Navy is growing into a "Blue-Water" naval force, which ventures into the blue waters of the high seas. To be sure, the Navy will always perform its sacred mission and will certainly make greater contributions to defending China's territorial sovereignty, maintaining the maritime interests of the nation and safeguarding the world peace.

## III. Reading Report

What have you learned after reading the text? Have you obtained a better command of PLAN Coastal Defense Force? Now create your reading report in no more than 150 words to generalize your achievement in text study.

# Text B
## The United States Coast Guard

The Coast Guard is charged with the mission of maritime security, safety, and personal management. While the Coast Guard is led by the Department of Homeland Security[1] during peacetime, it will be under the command of the Department of the Navy during wartime, as it was in WWI and WWII.

The Coast Guard is comprised of approximately 40,000 active duty personnel as well as additional 7,000 reservists.

US Coast Guard boat-helicopter-port

### Coast Guard History

The Coast Guard's official history dates back to August 4, 1790, when the first Congress authorized the construction of ten vessels to be used for preventing and supporting maritime smuggling in accordance with the federal tariff and trade laws. The Coast Guard, known as the Revenue Marine and the Revenue Cutter Service[2] in the 19th and the early 20th century, expanded in size and took on more responsibilities as the nation grew in strength.

The service was officially termed the Coast Guard in 1915 under an Act of Congress of merging the Revenue Cutter Service with the Life-Saving Service.Thus, the United States would own a special maritime force dedicated to enforcing its maritime laws and maintaining maritime safety. The Coast Guard began to take control of navigational facilities, including lighthouses, when President Franklin Roosevelt ordered the Lighthouse Service be turned over to the Coast Guard in 1939.

In 1946, the US Congress approved the permanent transfer of the Commerce Department's

**Bureau of Marine Inspection and Navigation** to the Coast Guard. As a result, merchant marine licensing and merchant vessel safety belonged to the **purview** of its administration.

The Coast Guard adopted the stripe design in 1967, as a result of the recommendation made to President John F. Kennedy in the spring of 1963 by the industrial design firm of Raymond Loewy[3]/William Snaith, Inc.

The Coast Guard is one of the oldest organizations of the Administration. It served as the nation's only maritime armed force until Congress approved the establishment of the Navy Department in 1798. The Coast Guard performed its duty of defending the nation in its long course of history, participating bravely innumerous fights or combats and succeeding in coping with various conflicts. Today, safeguarding national defense remains its most important responsibility or duty.

Since 2003, the Coast Guard has been subordinate to the Department of Homeland Security. As the nation's front-line agency, the Coast Guard has been carrying out its missions, for instance, enforcing the nation's maritime laws, protecting the marine environment and the nation's vast coastline and ports, and providing rescue and assistance. In times of war, the Coast Guard is to be commanded by the Navy Department according to the directive from the president.

### Coast Guard Training

The Coast Guard is the only service that does not send most recruits straight to job training after they finish their basic training, but send them on their first duty assignment.

For the first duty assignment, they will each act as a non-rated seaman (SN), or fireman (FN), which means they have no specific rating (job) and are assigned to do a lot of jobs on ships, such as painting, machine operation, maintenance and repair of equipment, systems safety management, refueling operation and dish washing.

After completing their first duty assignment, the recruits will be allowed to take on-the-job-training for a specific rating (Coast Guard job). If they want to apply for higher ratings, they will have to receive more formal training at a training center, known as "A" school[4].

NOTE: If they wish to gain knowledge or skill about Coast Guard aircraft and related systems, they must first be assigned to an air station as an airman (AN) to complete the basic aviation training before going to "A" school.

Once they finish their training or "A" school training they will get designation and, in most cases, they will be promoted to **3rd Class Petty Officer**.

This system has its advantages. On the other hand, the recruits may be required to select a job in advance, based on what they have read about it in an official recruiting job description. The job description is intended to arouse the recruits' great interest in any job. In the Coast Guard, it takes a couple of years for enlisted persons to be competent for their jobs.

### Joining the Coast Guard

If a person joins the Coast Guard, he will become a guardsman on active duty. Active Duty means full-time service in the armed forces. The term of service is from two to six years. The enlisted persons who have ratings must do their duty in their units.

### Enlisted Coast Guardsmen

The enlisted coast guardsmen are the backbone of the Coast Guard. They play an important role in their units because they have experienced various specialized training. Directed by Coast Guard officers, the enlisted guardsmen make efforts to fulfill different missions by use of know-how and expertise.

### Approaches to Developing Officers

There are three approaches needed for a person to become a Coast Guard officer. The Coast Guard does not offer a ROTC[5] program.

Direct Commission — Direct commission provides civilians in professional fields like law, medicine and religion the opportunity to become Coast Guard officers. On completing the officer training program, they will be commissioned as corresponding military ranks.

Officer Candidate School — Officer Candidate School aims at training office candidates to gain the required expert knowledge and skills. After finishing their schooling, they will serve as officers in the Coast Guard through classroom instruction and training exercises.

US Military Academy — The Coast Guard Academy provides full scholarships and four-year Bachelor of Science degree programs. It is the smallest among the academies of the five US armed forces. Every year roughly 200 students graduate there and are commissioned as Ensign.

Service in the Coast Guard Reserve is different from that in the Coast Guard in that it is not full-time. Reserve-duty personnel can live where they want or stay close to their own families, doing their civilian jobs. They can also enjoy many of the benefits of active-duty Coast Guardsmen, while the time spent on duty is much less. In the Reserve, the recruits usually spend one weekend a month in training and two weeks a year attending a Field Training Exercise[6] (FTX). The term of service in the Coast Guard Reserve may be from three to six years, depending on the needs of work.

*(1056 words)*

*Sources:*

1. https://www.military.com/

2. https://www.military.com/coast-guard-birthday/coast-guard-history.html

3. https://www.military.com/join-armed-forces/coast-guard-training.html

4. https://www.military.com/join-armed-forces/joining-the-coast-guard-overview.html

## Notes

1. Department of Homeland Security: Its duty is to safeguard the homeland security of the United States. Its missions include guarding customs border, enforcing immigration laws and making emergency response to natural and manmade disasters, countering terrorists and maintaining cybersecurity. 国土安全部

2. the Revenue Marine and the Revenue Cutter Service: The United States Revenue Cutter Service, officially the Division of Revenue Cutter Service, was established in 1790 as the Revenue-Marine by then-Secretary of the Treasury Alexander Hamilton, to serve as an armed maritime law enforcement force. It operated as the Revenue-Marine until July 1894, when it was renamed as the Revenue Cutter Service. 水陆关税队和海关缉私船队（美国早期历史并没有专责海上事务的组织，后来考量有关机关间权责不清，导致无法有效执行联邦任务，有五个联邦机关合并组成：缉私船队(Revenue Cutter Service)、水上救生队（Life Saving Service）、航务局（Bureau of Navigation）、轮船监察局（Steamboat Inspection Service）及灯塔局（Lighthouse Service））

3. Raymond Loewy: His full name was Raymond Fernand Loewy, who was born on November 5, 1893, in Paris, France and died on July 14, 1986, Monaco. He was one of the most famous American industrial designers. 雷蒙德·洛维（20世纪最著名的美国工业设计师之一）

4. "A" school: commonly known as recruit training school, where recruits receive technical training in their selected MOS field 专业技术训练（新兵接受完入伍训练之后接受的专业技术方面的训练）

5. ROTC: Reserve Officers' Training Corps. It provides a four-year program that helps cadets learn leadership skills while in college. After graduation, they will become officers in the United States Armed Forces. 美国后备役军官训练团

6. Field Training Exercise: Training exercises are conducted according to actual field combat requirements and in simulated field conditions. 实战训练演习

## Word Bank

| | |
|---|---|
| reservist [rɪˈzɜːrvɪst] | *n.* 预备役军人 |
| smuggling [ˈsmʌɡlɪŋ] | *n.* 走私 |
| merge [mɜːrdʒ] | *v.* 合并，融合 |
| lighthouse [ˈlaɪthaʊs] | 灯塔 |
| purview [ˈpɜːvjuː] | *n.* 范围，有限…… |
| Bureau of Marine Inspection and Navigation | 海军检验与航行局 |
| 3rd Class Petty Officer | 三级下士 |

## Exercises

### I. True or False

*Decide whether the following sentences are true or false in accordance with the text.*

1. The Coast Guard is under the Department of Homeland Security during times of war.

2. The Coast Guard officially got its present name in 1967.

3. At the direction of the President or in times of war, the Coast Guard serves the Navy Department.

4. The Coast guard is one of the services that automatically sent most recruits straight to job training after basic training.

5. At the first duty assignment, recruits have a specific rating.

6. In the Coast Guard, recruits can scope out the various jobs before making any choices.

7. The length of service for active duty service members may range from two to five years.

8. The Coast Guard reservists will spend one week a year attending a Field Training Exercise.

## II. Word Match

*Match the words/terms/phrases/in the left column with its appropriate correspondents in the right column.*

| | |
|---|---|
| 1. active duty personnel | A. 加油 |
| 2. marine environment | B. 直接任命 |
| 3. fueling operation | C. 海员 |
| 4. aviation training | D. 现役人员 |
| 5. direct commission | E. 海洋环境 |
| 6. bachelor of science | F. 服役时长 |
| 7. ensign | G. 航行训练 |
| 8. seaman | H. 理学学士 |
| 9. length of service | I. 少尉 |

# Text C

## Coast Guard College Student
## Pre-Commissioning Initiative (CSPI)

Many people wonder if the Coast Guard has a ROTC program, as do the other military branches. The answer is no. The Coast Guard has an Officer Candidate School（OCS）[1], and an Academy, as do the other services, but no ROTC program. Instead, it has its own College Student Pre-Commissioning Initiative, or CSPI[2].

Under this program, the enrolled sophomores can receive active duty pay at the rate of E-3[3], as well as a scholarship for their junior and senior year. Upon graduation, candidates will have to attend a 17-week training course at the Coast Guard OCS. After they are commissioned as an ensign, they must be on service in the Coast Guard for at least three years.

### An Overview of CSPI

The CSPI is actually a Coast Guard scholarship program for college sophomores. The program provides a monthly salary, full tuition, some fees, and the cost of some books for the students in their third and fourth year. According to CSPI, students must take part in military drill and various Coast Guard training exercises throughout the period of study. When they are juniors, the students will be sent to study at the Officer Indoctrination School[4]of the Coast Guard Academy or take on-the-job training at various Coast Guard operational units. Upon graduation, they are offered an opportunity to attend Coast Guard OCS. After finishing their schooling at OCS, they will be commissioned as an ensign and serve at least three years in the Coast Guard.

### Qualifications and Requirements for Applicants:

- Scoring 1000 in the SAT[5], 1100 in the SAT I, 23 in the ACT[6], or ASVAB[7] GT of 109 or higher.
- Aged 19 to 27, that is, only people in the age-bracket 19-27 can apply.
- Required to be a sophomore or junior (with at least 60 credits earned before taking a degree).
- Enrolled in a four-year degree program at an approved institution with a minimum 25% minority population.
- Required to complete credential education within 24 months to get a bachelor's degree.

- Never being a **conscientious** objector[8].

- Meeting all physical requirements for a Coast Guard Commissioned officer.

- Achieving a GPA[9] of 2.5 or better.

- American citizenship.

- Needing to obtain qualifications for security clearance[10].

- Dependency — As a single person, he has no **custody of dependents**. As a married person, his camp family only includes his spouse, regardless of military status, not including his other dependents.

- Finances — Performing all financial obligations, without the ratio of debt to income exceeding 30% at the applicant's accession level (i.e. at the E-3level).

**Welfare:**

- Monthly salary of E-3 pay

- Medical coverage and Servicemen Group Life Insurance

- An annual 30-day paid leave (vacation)

**Sources of Students**

College/University: Applicants must be the second-or-third-year undergraduate students who study for a bachelor's degree at one of the **accredited** colleges or universities as following:

- Historically Black Colleges and Universities[11] (HBCU)

- Hispanic-Serving Institutions[12] (HSI)

- Tribal Colleges and Universities[13] (TCU)

- The following colleges and universities located in Guam, Hawaii, and Alaska:

    — University of Guam

    — The University of Hawaii at Manoa, Hilo, and West Oahu

    — Argosy University – Hawaii

    — Institute of American Indian and Alaska Native Culture

Online Degrees: Online degrees are not included in CSPI. However, individuals may apply for their undergraduate degree if they are admitted into a four-year program and can succeed in finishing the online required courses.

Foreign Degrees: An applicant on whom an associate degree[14] has been **conferred** by a foreign school is required to include in his application the accomplishment evaluation of each course from an organization such as Education Credential Evaluation, in addition to the

translation of his degree (from another language into English).

Service Obligation. In order to enroll in CSPI, students must enlist as servicemen in the Coast Guard, acting on a four-year active-duty contract, and taking on a four-year reserve duty obligation. The term of obligated military service is eight years altogether. Sometimes, it will take an individual a longer or shorter time to be on active duty than on reserve duty, but it is obligatory for him to fulfill his 8-year service. For example, if one spends two years in training according to the program, and then serves three years as a commissioned officer, he will have to continue serving in the Ready Reserve[15] for the remaining three years. Of course, during this period, he will be recalled to active duty at any time in the event of a war or conflict.

Enlistment. As mentioned above, students must serve in the Coast Guard and attend Coast Guard enlisted basic training. If one fails to fulfill the training subjects specified in the program and attain a GPA of 2.5, or drops out, he may (and probably will) be reassigned to serve in a Coast Guard operational unit according to the enlistment contract. If he cannot complete his enlistment obligation, he may be required to reimburse the Coast Guard for the expenses of his college education in accordance with United States Code[16], Title 10, Section 2005.

Duty Requirements. During the training based on the program, students must wear the Coast Guard uniform while attending college classes. As the Coast Guard officer candidates, they must control their weight, maintain their fitness, and be attentive to their appearance. Additionally, they must be enrolled in a minimum of 12-credit-hours course, attend all scheduled classes and work at least three hours per week at the local Coast Guard district (performing the duties assigned to them).

UCMJ[17]. The students enrolled in CSPI personnel are on active duty. As members of the military, they are subject to the provisions of the Uniform Code of Military Justice (UCMJ). If one violates discipline, he will be given disciplinary punishment or administrative sanctions. For example, if one skips a class to see the latest movie, or feels like sleeping in, he will be punished for "Failure to Go," which is a violation of Article 86 of the UCMJ. If one is found to smoke a cigarette on the weekend, he will be punished for a violation of Article 112a... In addition to such punishments, a student who has violated the related provision of UCMJ, is very likely to be removed from the program and required to perform his active duty as an enlisted man in the remaining years. And what's more, if one commits a military offense, i.e. illegal act or crime, he will face a court martial.

*(1083 words)*

*Sources:*

https://www.thebalancecareers.com/coast-guard-college-pre-commissioning-initiative-3345174（2020年6月17日访问）

## Notes

1. Officer Candidate School(OCS): an instruction that trains candidates to be officers serving in the Coast Guard 预备军官学校

2. CSPI: an abbreviation for College Student Pre-Commissioning Initiative 大学生任命前培训计划

3. E-3: one of pay grades, for seamen 一项薪资等级，主要是针对海员一级的

4. Officer Indoctrination School (OIS): a school responsible for indoctrinating officers with a particular set of benefits 军官教导学校

5. SAT: Scholastic Aptitude Test, a test prepared and supervised by the College Entrance Examination Board to test the general intelligence and academic aptitude of a prospective applicant to a college 学习能力考试

6. ACT: American College Test, also an entrance examination 美国大学入学考试

7. ASVAB: Armed Services Vocational Aptitude Battery, a multiple-aptitude battery that measures developed abilities and helps predict future academic and occupational success in the military 军队职业倾向测验

8. conscientious objector: person who refuses to serve in the armed forces because he thinks it is morally wrong （因觉不合道义）拒服兵役者

9. GPA: Grade Point Average, which represents the average value of the accumulated final grades earned in courses. In other words, a student's grade point average is a measure of his academic achievement, based on an average of the total number of grade earned in all the course 平均学分绩点

10. security clearance: granting somebody permission to read secret documents 接触保密材料许可（证）

11. Historically Black Colleges and Universities (HBCU): institutions that were established prior to 1964 with the principal mission of educating Black Americans, such as Wiley College, Spelman College, Morehouse College, University of Maryland Eastern Shore, Florida Agricultural and Mechanical University, Fisk University, Tuskegee University 传统黑人大学

12. Hispanic-Serving Institutions (HSI): institutions of higher education that are designated for an enrollment of eligible students for full-time undergraduate study students who account for at least 25 percent of Hispanic high school graduates, such as California College San Diego, California Lutheran University 拉美裔服务机构

13. Tribal Colleges and Universities (TCU): higher education institutions that provide an opportunity for the American Indian students and a vital pathway to the future, such as Maskwachees Cultural University, Old Sun Community College and Rea Crow Community College 部族学院和大学

14. associate degree: a degree that is given to a student who has completed two years of study at a junior college, college, or university in the US 副学士学位，准学士学位

15. Ready Reserve: An organization associated with the reserve components of the United States military. Members are former service personnel who continue to perform their remaining obligation in reserve-duty units according to their contracts, without serving in the military as active-duty members. 第一类预备役

16. United States Code: a set of laws or rules arranged in a system in the US 美国法典

17. UCMJ: Uniform Code of Military Justice, a federal law enacted by Congress. The UCMJ defines the military justice system and lists criminal offenses under military law 统一军事司法法典

## *Word Bank*

| | |
|---|---|
| sophomore [ˈsɑːfəmɔːr] | *n.* 大二学生 |
| junior [ˈdʒuːnɪər] | *n.* 大三学生 |
| senior [ˈsiːnɪər] | *n.* 大四学生 |
| conscientious [ˌkɑːnʃɪˈenʃəs] | *adj.* 道义的 |
| accredit [əˈkredɪt] | *v.* 委派，认可 |
| confer [kənˈfɜːr] | *v.* 授予 |
| reimburse [ˌriːɪmˈbɜːrs] | *v.* 偿还 |
| custody of dependents | 家属监护权 |
| court martial | 军事话语，军事审判 |

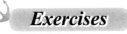

## *Exercises*

Based on what you have acquired in this text, you are supposed to conduct an online study to explore further into the relevant sphere. Comb and frame what you have found with an online study report in no less than 200 words. In addition, any assistant image, audio, video, or other first-hand material will be preferred when you present your report in class.

# Unit 14　The Law of the Sea

**Bridge-in**

*Answer the following questions in accordance with the microlesson "Define Our Position in the South China Sea.".*

1. What historical facts do you know about the South China Sea?

2. What is the legal basis for our rights and interests in the South China Sea?

3. How should we react to other countries' close-in reconnaissance or illegal entry to the South China Sea?

## Text A
## An Overview of United Nations Convention on the
## Law of the Sea

The United Nations Convention on the Law of the Sea[1] aims at maintaining law and order in the world's oceans and seas and utilizing the seas and their resources by law. To be more exact, the Convention has far-reaching implications for peace and security, distribution of natural resources, navigation, transport, marine research and environment.

The Convention was signed on December 10,1982 in Montego Bay[2], Jamaica[3]. It took nearly 14 years to produce the Convention. In those years, more than 150 sovereign States with different legal, political, economical and social systems in all regions of the world participated in the marathon negotiations that culminated in the adoption of the Convention. The successful **culmination** demonstrated that Governments can accomplish what they want when turning from their traditional narrow national interests to making greater efforts to strengthen international cooperation. The Convention specified in one **instrument** the traditional rules for the exploitation of oceans and seas and meanwhile introduced new legal concepts and rules to address some issues concerned. The Convention also provided the framework for further development of specific provision of the Law of the Sea.

The Convention came into force on November 16,1994 in accordance with its article 308. Today, it is commonly recognized that the 1982 Convention on the Law of the Sea has provided the legal basis of dealing with matters relating to the seas and their resources.

The Convention contains 320 articles and nine annexes, which encompass all aspects of ocean space, such as legal divisions of the oceans, environmental control, marine research and exploration, trade and commerce, technical development and technology transfer and the settlement of disputes over the issue of marine jurisdiction.

Some of the key points of the Convention are as following:

● Coastal countries exercise sovereignty over their territorial seas, each with its territorial sea claim up to a maximum breadth of 12 nautical miles. Foreign vessels, however, are allowed "innocent passage[4]" through those waters.

● Ships and aircraft of all countries are allowed "transit passage[5]" through straits used for international navigation; countries bordering the straits can regulate navigational routes for passage.

● Archipelagic Nations, each being constituted wholly one or more groups of islands, usually draw straight archipelagic baselines by joining the outermost points of their islands. The waters enclosed within the archipelagic baselines are called archipelagic waters. In those waters archipelagic nations may designate their sea lanes and air routes suitable for continuous and expeditious passage of ships and aircraft and also for archipelagic passage[6] of other nations.

● In addition to the enforcement of related laws within their territorial seas, coastal countries have certain maritime rights to deal with what may happen in an area beyond the territorial sea. This area is known as a contiguous zone, which extends 24 nautical miles from the baselines used to measure the territorial sea. In the contiguous zone, a coasted or island nation may exercise the control necessary to prevent or publish infringement of its customs, fiscal, immigration, and sanitary laws and regulations that occur within its territory or territorial sea.

● Coastal nations have the sovereign rights to prescribe and enforce their laws in a 200-nautical mile exclusive economic zone (EEZ) for the purposes of exploration, exploitation, management and conservation of the natural resources of the waters, seabed, and subsoil, as well as for the production of energy from the water, currents and winds. The nations

may exercise jurisdiction in the zone over the establishment and use of artificial islands, installations and structures having economic purposes, over marine scientific research, and over some aspects of marine environmental protection.

- All other nations have freedom of navigation and overflight in the EEZ and of laying submarine cables and pipelines.

- Land-locked countries enjoy the right to participate on an equitable basis in exploitation of an appropriate part of the surplus of the living resources in the EEZs of the coastal nations, which give special protection to highly migratory species of fish and marine mammals.

- Coastal nations exercise sovereign rights over the continental shelf for purposes of exploring and exploiting its natural resources. The juridical continental shelf of a coasted or island nation consists of the seabed and subsoil of the submarine areas that extend to a distance of 200 nautical miles from the baseline used to measure the territorial sea where the continental margins do not extend to that distance. All nations have the right to lay submarine cables and pipelines on the continental shelf.

- Coastal nations share with the international community part of the resources exploited from any part of their shelf beyond 200 nautical miles.

- The Commission on the Limits of the Continental Shelf shall make recommendations to States on the shelf's outer boundaries when the shelf extends to a distance beyond 200 nautical miles.

- All States enjoy the traditional freedoms of navigation, overflight, scientific research and fishing on the high seas. They are obliged to take measures to manage and conserve marine resources.

- The limits of the territorial sea, the exclusive economic zone and continental shelf of islands are determined in accordance with rules applicable to land territory. As rocks are islands which cannot sustain human habitation or economic life of their own, they have no economic zone or continental shelf.

- Coastal or island countries are required to closely cooperate in protecting marine environment, conserving resources, and conducting marine scientific resources.

- Land-locked countries have the right to get in and out of the sea and enjoy freedom of passing through the territory of coastal countries.

- States must protect the marine environment from pollution, which is one of their international obligations.

● A country's request for marine scientific research in the EEZ and on the continental shelf is subject to the consent of the coastal nation. In most cases, the coasted nation will consent to it if the research is to be conducted for peaceful purposes in accordance with specified criteria.

● States should promote the development and transfer of marine technology "on fair and reasonable terms and conditions", with due regard for all legitimate interests.

● All parties concerned are obliged to settle their disputes over the interpretation or application of the Convention through peaceful negotiations and consultations.

● Disputes can be submitted to the International **Tribunal** for the Law of the Sea established under the Convention, to the International Court of Justice, or to **arbitration**. The Tribunal has exclusive jurisdiction over deep seabed mining disputes. **Conciliation** is also available and, in certain circumstances, submission to it would be compulsory.

The implementation of the Convention and the exercise of extended jurisdiction can better guarantee appropriate marine activities and reasonable uses, but it will confront all States with a lot of major challenges. In order to meet these challenges, each state should implement the new **provisions** to the letter, keep its national legislation consistent with the spirit of the Law of the Sea, and perform its obligations according to the Convention.

The United Nations has been playing a major role in the supervision of the implementation of the 1982 Convention by every country and remains responsible for informing all countries and related international marine affair organs about marine activities, including exploitation and exploration of oceans and seas, as well as the progress made in the implementation of the Convention on the Law of the Sea.

*(1207 words)*

**Sources:**

1. https://www.un.org/Depts/los/convention_agreements/convention_overview_convention. htm

2. https://www.un.org/Depts/los/convention_agreements/convention_historical_perspective. htm#Historical Perspective

 Notes

1. The United Nations Convention on the Law of the Sea: UNCLOS for short, also called the

Law of the Sea Convention or the Law of the Sea treaty, is the international agreement that resulted from the Third United Nations Conference on the Law of the Sea.《联合国海洋法公约》。

2. Montego Bay: the capital of the parish of St. James in Jamaica 蒙特哥湾

3. Jamaica: an island country in the Caribbean 牙买加（加勒比岛国）

4. innocent passage: the right of a foreign ship to enter and pass through a coastal state's territorial waters under the prerequisites of not damaging the peace, good order or security of the coastal state 无害通过

5. transit passage: It means that a vessel or aircraft enjoys the freedom of navigation or overflight solely for the purpose of continuous and expeditious transit of a strait between one part of the high seas or exclusive economic zone and another part in accordance with the UNCLOS. 过境通行

6. archipelagic passage: It means the right of continuous and expeditious transit, or navigation through and overflight over archipelagic waters in a normal mode according to the rules of the UNCLOS. 群岛海道通过权

## Word Bank

| | |
|---|---|
| culmination [ˌkʌlmɪˈneɪʃn] | *n.* 顶点，极点；高潮；极盛期；完成，成就 |
| instrument [ˈɪnstrəmənt] | *n.* 正式的文件，文书 |
| annex [ˈæneks] | *n.* （文件）附录 |
| outermost [ˈaʊtəməʊst] | *adj.* 最外面的；最远的 |
| contiguous [kənˈtɪɡjuəs] | *adj.* 连续的；邻近的；接触的 |
| jurisdiction [ˌdʒʊərɪsˈdɪkʃn] | *n.* 司法权，审判权，管辖权；权限，权力 |
| equitable [ˈekwɪtəbl] | *adj.* 公平的，公正的；平衡法的 |
| surplus [ˈsɜːpləs] | *n.* 剩余；[贸易] 顺差；盈余；过剩 |
| mammal [ˈmæml] | *n.* [脊椎] 哺乳动物 |
| conserve [kənˈsɜːv] | *v.* 保存；保护；使守恒 |
| habitation [ˌhæbɪˈteɪʃn] | *n.* 居住；住所 |
| tribunal [traɪˈbjuːnl] | *n.* 法庭；裁决；法官席 |
| arbitration [ˌɑːbɪˈtreɪʃn] | *n.* 公断，仲裁 |
| conciliation [kənˌsɪlɪˈeɪʃn] | *n.* 调解；安抚；说服 |
| provision [prəˈvɪʒn] | *n.* 规定；条款 |

 **Exercises**

## I. Comprehension

### Part A Questions

*Answer the following questions in accordance with the text.*

1. What is the United Nations Convention on the Law of Sea about?

2. What countries can be regarded as "archipelagic States" and which part is the archipelagic waters?

3. What rights do the coastal States enjoy in the contiguous zone?

4. What rights do the coastal States and other States enjoy in the exclusive economic zone?

5. What are the rights and obligations of all the states concerning the high seas?

### Part B Multiple Choices

*Choose the most appropriate answer from the given choices below each question in accordance with the text.*

1. Which of the following is NOT included as the content of the United Nations Convention on the Law of the Sea?

   A. Traditional rules for the uses of the oceans

   B. New legal concepts and regimes and new concerns for the uses of the oceans

   C. Legal rights of more than 150 countries representing all regions of the world

   D. The framework for further development of specific areas of the law of the sea

2. When did the Convention go into effect?

   A. In 1968.

   B. In 1982.

   C. In 1993.

   D. In 1994.

3. What is the breadth of a coastal state's territorial sea?

   A. 12 miles.

   B. 24 miles.

   C. 12 nautical miles.

   D. 24 nautical miles.

4. Which of the following statements about the continental shelf is Not True?

   A. Coastal States have sovereign rights over the continental shelf for exploring and exploiting it.

   B. Coastal States can get all the revenue derived from exploiting resources from any part of their shelf beyond 200 nautical miles.

   C. When the State's continental shelf extends beyond 200 nautical miles, the State shall follow the recommendations given by the Commission on the Limits of the Continental Shelf on the shelf's outer boundaries.

   D. The continental shelf can extend at least 200 nautical miles from the shore, and more under specified circumstances.

5. Which of the following organizations does not deal with the problems of ocean space?

   A. International Maritime Organization

   B. International Tribunal for the Law of the Sea

   C. International Court of Justice

   D. The Permanent Court of Arbitration

## II. Translation

**Part A** Terms & Phrases

*Translate the following terms or phrases from Chinese into English and vice versa.*

1. 内水
2. 领海
3. 毗邻区
4. 专属经济区
5. 公海
6. 大陆架
7. 内陆国家
8. 联合国海洋公约
9. 沿海国
10. 群岛国
11. 实施管辖权
12. 无害通过
13. 自然资源
14. 海洋研究
15. 过境通行
16. enter into force
17. international navigation
18. sovereign rights
19. marine pollution
20. international obligations
21. archipelagic passage
22. exploration and exploitation of the resources
23. consent of the coastal State
24. settlement of disputes
25. natural resources
26. international community
27. lay submarine cables and pipelines
28. sea lanes

29. enclosed and semi-enclosed seas  30. the interpretation or application of the Convention

## Part B  Paragraph

*Translate the following paragraph from English into Chinese.*

The limits of the territorial sea, the exclusive economic zone and continental shelf of islands are determined in accordance with rules applicable to land territory, but rocks which could not sustain human habitation or economic life of their own would have no economic zone or continental shelf.

## III. Reading Report

What have you learned after reading the text? Have you obtained a better command of United Nations Convention on the Law of Sea, its contents, and application? Now create your reading report in no more than 150 words to generalize your achievement in the text study.

## Text B
## US Provocation in South China Sea—Acting in Defiance of
## the International Law

### US Breach of Freedom of Navigation in South China Sea

The warship, USS William P. Lawrence[1], illegally entered China's waters near the islands without the permission of the Chinese government.

Washington has long claimed that the US Navy has the freedom of navigation [2] to sail on the world's seas for the purpose of safeguarding public access to waters and airspace according to the international law.

However, such a statement of the seemingly lofty purpose cannot absolutely cover up the fact that the US Navy maneuvers in the South China Sea have threatened China's sovereignty and security, disturbed the regional peace and stability, and violated the international law.

Washington has always boasted about how to act on the international law in excuse of its arbitrary moves, but, ironically, it has so far not accepted the United Nations Convention on the Law of the Sea, which establishes legal order and regulations on international waters.

The real intention behind such moves is crystal clear: The United States is unwilling to bind itself to the Law of the Sea, which it claims as severely flawed, because it is the sole superpower pursuing hegemony. Now, it has already controlled huge maritime resources and seabed minerals such as oil and gas.

Also, it seems ironic that Uncle Sam speaks of its provocation in the South China Sea as the maintaining of freedom of navigation based on the international law, but it in fact acts on the norm unilaterally defined by itself, which is not generally recognized.

In a document issued in 2015 regarding the so-called program for freedom of navigation, the US government said the foremost target of the US action is "excessive maritime claims that are defined by the US side." The document reveals that Washington attempts to substitute its own standard for the international law in order to unilaterally impose it upon the other countries.

Moreover, the US so-called freedom of navigation under the banner of international law is actually a contravention of the principles of international law.

The Law of the Sea stipulates that any resort to threats or arms to intrigue upon other coastal countries' sovereignty, territorial integrity or political independence, and to violate the aim of the UN Charter, is regarded as a breach of the peace, stability and security in coastal nations.

Since the recovery of the islands in the South China Sea after the end of World War II, it has never been heard that the freedom of navigation in the South China Sea is a problem. China reiterates that each country will enjoy the freedom of navigation in the South China Sea so long as it acts upon the international law. Now, China has established the cooperation mechanism with many countries to ensure the security of navigation on the sea lanes there.

China once suggested that the United States, when talking about "freedom of navigation," make a distinction between commercial ships and warships. As known to all, freedom of navigation for commercial vessels has never been obstructed in the South China Sea, said Foreign Ministry spokesman Lu Kang at a daily press briefing.

US assistant secretary of state for East Asia and the Pacific, Daniel Russel said in Vietnam that freedom of navigation was important to smaller nations. "If the world's most powerful navy cannot sail where the international law permits, then what happens to naval ships of smaller countries?" Russel told reporters.

Lu refuted Denial Russel's advocacy of freedom of navigation for military vessels in the South China Sea, and pointed out that such an argument was full of hegemonism, absurd, and against international law.

According to the UN Convention on the Law of the Sea (UNCLOS), foreign merchant vessels can enjoy the right of innocent passage through territorial seas, but military vessels cannot, said Lu.

The fact that the United States repeatedly sends its warships to the South China Sea under the guise of the so-called freedom of navigation reveals its hegemonism of abusing the freedom of navigation and disregarding the national interests and sovereignty of other countries.

The United States should abandon its selfish motives, observe the international law and act as a responsible power, but not stir up trouble in the South China Sea and then put the blame on others.

### The So-called International Airspace Claimed by the US

The Pentagon released a statement accusing China of conducting "unsafe" interception of a US spy plane in the "international airspace" over the South China Sea. This accusation immediately reminds people of the 2001 EP-3 collision incident between China Navy and US

Navy[3], which led to the death of a Chinese pilot. Both incidents were related to the US EP-3 spy planes, which were conducting intelligence-gathering activities over the same area of the South China Sea.

This raises concern about the possibility of another looming confrontation in the airspace of the South China Sea, and also a question of who should be to blame. The answer to this question may necessitate a full analysis of the lawfulness of the US reconnaissance activities in the airspace of foreign exclusive economic zones (EEZs).

Under the 1982 United Nations Convention on the Law of the Sea (UNCLOS), the world oceans are divided into various jurisdictional zones, where different legal rules concerning navigational rights must be observed. These legal rules enforced in various jurisdictional zones serve as a benchmark to judge whether conducts of relevant parties are legal or not, for example, the US reconnaissance activities.

The US has always claimed that the Chinese naval aircraft intercepted the reconnaissance plane in the international airspace. As a matter of fact, the term "international airspace" cannot be found in the UNCLOS at all. However, it is ridiculous that the US stance demonstrated in its public statement was based on the interpretation of "international space" in US Navy Commander's Operational Handbook. The term is defined as the airspace of the maritime areas beyond territorial waters, which may include airspace of both the EEZs and the High Seas. This is a typical American unilateral understanding of the international law of the sea. In the strict sense, each maritime area and its airspace should be named exactly according to the relevant stipulations in the UNCLOS, for instance, territorial sea, territorial sky, EEZ, etc.

Notwithstanding the fact that the US is not a party to the UNCLOS but habitually takes advantage of some articles of UNCLOS for its own interest, the coined term in the Handbook does lead to a serious conflict in the understanding of the law regarding the legal status of each maritime area and its airspace, in particular within EEZs.

While the international community which follows the UNCLOS takes the EEZ as a particular maritime zone regulated by a specific legal system with equal rights and obligations any coastal or island nation should implement, the US, which is not a signatory to the UNCLOS, insists that the freedom of navigation and overflights exercised within and beyond EEZs " should be much the same as the traditional high seas freedoms recognized by the international law." As a result, such a different understanding of the law makes it possible for a military confrontation to occur at sea.

*(1193 words)*

*Sources:*

1. www.ecns.cn/2016/05-12/210074.shtml

2. http://www.ecns.cn/voices/2016/02-01/197738.shtml

3. www.globaltimes.cn/content/984174.shtml

# Notes

1. USS William P. Lawrence: US Navy's 60th Arleigh Burke-class guided-missile destroyer (DDG 110), which was named after Vice Adm. William P. Lawrence. He was a fighter pilot and was taken prisoner during the Vietnam War, and later acted as US Third Fleet commander, Chief of Naval Personnel, and Superintendent of the US Naval Academy. 威廉·劳伦斯号（DDG 110）是美国海军第60艘阿利·伯克级导弹驱逐舰。该船以美国海军中将威廉·劳伦斯（William P.Lawrence）的名字命名，他是战斗机飞行员，越战俘虏，美国第三舰队司令，海军人事主管和美国海军学院院长。

2. freedom of navigation: Freedom of navigation (FON) is a principle of the customary international law. According to the principle, ships flying the national flag of any sovereign state should not be subjected to interference from other states, apart from the exceptions provided for in international law. In terms of international law, FON is defined as "freedom of movement for vessels, freedom to enter ports and utilize plants and docks, to load and unload goods and to transport goods and passengers." 航行自由（FON）是习惯国际法的一项原则，除国际法规定的例外情况外，悬挂任何主权国家国旗的船舶不得受到其他国家的干扰。在国际法范围内，它被定义为"船舶的通行自由，进入港口和利用工厂和码头的自由，装卸货物以及运输货物和乘客的自由"。

3. 2001 EP-3 collision incident between China Navy and US Navy: On April 1, 2001, a major incident between a US Navy EP-3E ARIES II electronic reconnaissance aircraft and a PLA Navy J-8II interceptor fighter jet happened over the South China Sea, which caused an international dispute between the US and China. 2001年4月1日，美国海军EP-3E ARIES II电子侦察机与中国海军（PLAN）J-8II拦截战斗机在空中相撞，导致中美两国之间发生国际争端。

# Word Bank

lofty ['lɒftɪ]          *adj.* 高的；崇高的；高级的；高傲的

| | |
|---|---|
| flawed [flɔːd] | *adj.* 有缺陷的；有瑕疵的；有裂纹的 |
| unilaterally [ˌjuːnɪˈlætrəlɪ] | *adv.* 单方面地 |
| stipulate [ˈstɪpjʊleɪt] | *v.* 规定；保证 |
| obstruct [əbˈstrʌkt] | *v.* 妨碍；阻塞 |
| accusation [ˌækjʊˈzeɪʃn] | *n.* 控告，指控；谴责 |
| looming [ˈluːmɪŋ] | *adj.* （不希望或不愉快的事情）逼近的 |
| necessitate [nəˈsesɪteɪt] | *v.* 使成为必需，需要；迫使 |
| jurisdictional [ˌdʒʊərɪsˈdɪkʃənl] | *adj.* 管辖权的；司法的；司法权的；裁判权的 |
| benchmark [ˈbentʃmɑːk] | *n.* 基准 |
| notwithstanding [ˌnɒtwɪðˈstændɪŋ] | *prep.* 尽管，虽然 |
| regulate [ˈregjəleɪt] | *v.* （尤指使按照某种方式运作而）控制，管理，调节，调整 |

## Exercises

### I. True or False

*Decide whether the following sentences are true or false in accordance with the text.*

1. The United Nations Convention on the Law of the Sea establishes legal order and regulations on international waters.

2. The United States conducts its freedom of navigation in South China Sea on the legal basis of international law.

3. With the joint efforts of China and the relevant countries, the freedom of navigation in the South China Sea has never been a problem.

4. Military vessels enjoy the freedom of navigation in the South China Sea.

5. Military vessels enjoy the right of innocent passage through territorial seas.

6. The US reconnaissance activities in the airspace over foreign Exclusive Economic Zones (EEZs) are lawful.

7. The US is a party to the United Nations Convention on the Law of the Sea (UNCLOS).

8. The US always makes use of some articles of UNCLOS to fulfill its own purposes.

## II. Word Match

*Match the words/terms/phrases in the left column with its appropriate correspondents in the right column.*

| | | | |
|---|---|---|---|
| 1. intelligence-gathering activities | | A. 沿海国主权 | |
| 2. freedom of navigation | | B. 侦察活动 | |
| 3. shared resolve | | C. 石油和天然气储量 | |
| 4. legal status | | D. 军舰 | |
| 5. territorial integrity | | E. 商船 | |
| 6. commercial vessels | | F. 情报收集活动 | |
| 7. reconnaissance activities | | G. 共同决心 | |
| 8. oil and gas deposits | | H. 领土完整 | |
| 9. coastal sovereignty | | I. 法律地位 | |
| 10. military vessels | | J. 航行自由 | |

 **Text C**

## The Hague Arbitration on the China-Philippines Sea Dispute

The Permanent Court of Arbitration（PCA）[1], an international judicial organ based in The Hague, the Netherlands, is set to release its award in the Philippines-initiated case involving the territory in the South China Sea which both Manila and Beijing claim. China has repeatedly denied the legitimacy of the case filed unilaterally by the Philippines, saying it will not participate in or accept the result of the case.

Chinese marine guards patrol the Nansha Islands on February 9, 2016. (Photo: CFP)

### Permanent Organization

The PCA was established in 1899 at the first Hague Peace Conference in The Hague, the Netherlands. It is the oldest international organ for arbitration of conflicts in the world.

If necessary, it will set up temporary tribunals to deal with disputes among states, intergovernmental organizations or private parties.

According to the PCA website, the International Bureau has made a list of PCA judges who are nominated by the Member States. Its function is to select some judges from the list as arbitrators of PCA-administered proceedings and special panels to resolve environmental disputes and space-related disputes. However, the Secretary-General and parties in PCA proceedings are not obliged to select arbitrators from this list but can use their discretion in selecting the individuals best suited to the case at hand.

### Illegitimate Arbitration

The crux of the China-Philippines dispute in the South China Sea is the Philippines' occupation of some islands and reefs in the Nansha Islands, or Nansha Archipelago which China regards as its own territory. China argues that the Philippines' illegal act is in violation of the UN Charter and the basic norms of international relations. As opinions are divided on the new rules of the law of the sea, disputes over the question of maritime delimitation disputes have arisen.

On January 22, 2013, the Republic of the Philippines instituted arbitral proceedings against the People's Republic of China under Annex VII to the United Nations Convention on the Law of the Sea (UNCLOS) "with respect to the dispute with China over the maritime jurisdiction of the Philippines in the West Philippine Sea." Philippine president Benigno Aquino III issued an administrative order to rename the South China Sea the "West Philippine Sea" in September 2012.

An article published by the US-based Center for Strategic and International Studies pointed out that the Philippines "is seeking a ruling that the claim to the South China Sea should conform with the UNCLOS, in an attempt to invalidate China's nine-dash line by defining what China holds as rocks, low tide elevations, or submerged banks, but not islands, and to have the right to operate inside of its EEZ (exclusive economic zone) and continental shelf as outlined by the UNCLOS without any interference from China."

On February 19, 2013, China presented to the Philippines a document which reiterated "the position of China on the South China Sea issues," rejected the arbitration and urged the Philippines to resolve the disputes through bilateral negotiations. China argues that the Arbitral Tribunal lacks jurisdiction in the case.

Experts made comments on the arbitration unilaterally initiated by the Philippines on January 22, 2013, criticizing the Philippines for violating the agreements which had been reached with China and breaking a promise of the settlement of disputes through negotiations and consultations. They also pointed out that the Philippines violated the provisions of the UNCLOS, abused its procedures of settling disputes and infringed upon China's maritime rights. China is of the opinion that such an act done by the Philippines is illegal and null and void. Furthermore, these submissions are related to more complicated territorial sovereignty issues, over which the court has no jurisdiction.

"Strictly speaking, the arbitration to be made by the PCA should be agreed upon by the both sides in the dispute. Because the Philippines unilaterally initiated the arbitration, China rejected it flatly. On the principle of arbitration, such an event should never have taken place," Tao Duanfang, an independent commentator, wrote in a commentary published on Baidu's

online opinion platform Baijia.

In February, the US and the EU asked China to respect the ruling, but China would never accept it because the PCA had no powers of enforcement.

### Joint Exploitation

China maintains its sovereignty over the reefs and islands based on its ample historical evidence in support of its territorial claims. Therefore, the Philippines' denial of the irrefutable facts recorded in the historical documents is of no avail.

The U-shaped, nine-dash line indicates that most of the South China Sea belongs to China's territory. It was first marked on a map drawn by the Kuomintang's Republic of China government in 1947 and then inherited by the People's Republic of China in 1949.

No official dispute on China's sovereignty over the South China Sea happened until the 1960s. People there have been engaged in productive activities such as fishing around the islands and reefs since ancient times. During World War II, the Japanese aggressors took control of the islands. The occupied islands were returned to the bosom of China after Japan had to agree to surrender unconditionally according to "Potsdam Proclamation"[2] which stipulated that the terms of "Cairo Declaration"[3] be put into effect in July 1945. In the following decades, no country questioned China's right to control the area. The US always recognized China's sovereignty over the South China Sea islands, for example, informing the Chinese government of its flybys over the islands in advance.

The territory of the Philippines did not include the Nansha Islands or Huangyan Island according to various territory treaties signed by the US from 1898 to 1930.

Disputes over the Nansha Islands appeared in the late 1960s when massive reserves of oil and natural gas were discovered in the South China Sea. After then, the Philippines and several other countries bordering the South China Sea began encroaching upon the reefs and islands. They claimed ownership of the islands, completely ignoring China's sovereignty.

China has not been a trouble-maker in this matter, but a victim, said Guo Jiping, a political commentator. As for the maritime territory dispute, China has exhibited great patience and sincerity, hoping for the peaceful settlement of the dispute without escalating it. And what is more, China is the first country to propose the "joint exploitation" of the South China Sea in the interests of the countries bordering the Sea.

*(1067 words)*

*Sources:*

http://www.globaltimes.cn/content/993588.shtml（2022年6月15日访问）

## Notes

1. The Permanent Court of Arbitration (PCA): It is an international disputes arbitration organ according to the treaty which was put into effect in 1910. 海牙常设仲裁法院，也称海牙仲裁法院，是依据1910年条约生效时建立的国际争端仲裁机构。

2. "Potsdam Proclamation": The Proclamation was announced on July 26, 1945. Heads of states of the Soviet Union, the United States and Britain held a meeting in Potsdam on the outskirts of Berlin in July 17, 1949. At the meeting, an ultimation was issued to Japan. 《波茨坦公告》发于1945年7月26日，苏美英三国首脑于1945年7月17日在柏林近郊波茨坦举行会议，会议期间发表对日最后通牒式公告。

3. "Cairo Declaration": After winning the decisive victory of World War II, heads of states of China, Britain and the United States held a conference in Cairo, Egypt on November 22–26, 1943, discussing the military issues of cooperation in fighting against Japan and the political issues of punishment after the War. The conference was historically known as "Cairo Conference". As for China's territorial sovereignty, both China and the US agreed that the provinces in Northeast China, Taiwan and Penghu Islands which were occupied by Japan must be returned to China after the War. The "Cairo Declaration" was drafted according to what had been discussed at the conference. 开罗宣言，第二次世界大战取得决定性胜利后，中、美、英三国首脑于1943年11月22至26日在开罗举行会议，讨论如何协调对日作战的共同军事问题和战后如何处置日本等政治问题，史称"开罗会议"。其中，关于中国的领土主权问题，中美双方同意：日本用武力从中国夺去的东北各省、台湾和澎湖列岛，战后必须归还中国。

## Word Bank

| | |
|---|---|
| legitimacy [lɪˈdʒɪtɪməsɪ] | *n.* 合法；合理；正统 |
| arbitrator [ˈɑːbɪtreɪtə(r)] | *n.* 公断人，仲裁人（或机构） |
| proceeding [prəˈsiːdɪŋ] | *n.* 进行；程序；诉讼；事项 |
| discretion [dɪˈskreʃn] | *n.* 自行决断的自由，自行决定，行动判断等的自由 |
| crux [krʌks] | *n.* 关键，症结；难题 |

| | |
|---|---|
| reef [ri:f] | *n.* 暗礁 |
| arbitral [ˈɑːbɪtr(ə)l] | *adj.* 仲裁的；仲裁人的 |
| ruling [ˈruːlɪŋ] | *n.* （尤指法庭的）裁定 |
| invalidate [ɪnˈvælɪdeɪt] | *v.* 使无效；使无价值 |
| elevation [ˌelɪˈveɪʃn] | *n.* 高地；海拔 |
| consultation [ˌkɒnslˈteɪʃn] | *n.* 咨询；磋商 |
| infringe [ɪnˈfrɪndʒ] | *v.* 侵犯；违反；破坏 |
| submission [səbˈmɪʃn] | *n.* 提交（物）；（向法官提出的）意见 |
| flyby [ˈflaɪbaɪ] | *n.* 飞越；飞近探测；在低空飞过指定地点 |
| encroach [ɪnˈkrəʊtʃ] | *v.* 蚕食，侵占 |
| escalate [ˈeskəleɪt] | *v.* 使逐步上升；升级，（使）恶化 |
| null and void | 无效的 |

 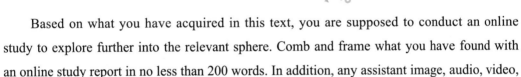

## Exercises

Based on what you have acquired in this text, you are supposed to conduct an online study to explore further into the relevant sphere. Comb and frame what you have found with an online study report in no less than 200 words. In addition, any assistant image, audio, video, or other first-hand material will be preferred when you present your report in class.

# Unit 15  Naval Academy

**Bridge-in**

*Answer the following questions in accordance with the microlesson "Things you should know about Chinese Military Academies".*

1. How many types of military academies are there in China? What are the characteristics of them?

2. What are the qualifications required in the enrollment of Chinese military academies?

3. What are the differences between military academies and civilian colleges?

## Text A
## Famous Chinese Naval Academies

Every naval cadet begins his military career with basic training at an academy. The academy education aims to train cadets to be officers. They must take strict training and make **strenuous** efforts to **remould** and **temper** themselves and act upon the military codes of conduct and moral norms so that they can become servicemen with lofty ideals, high educational level, strong **physique** and **willpower**. The rigorous basic military training can enable naval cadets to have a deep understanding of what they are trained for, to be more exact, understanding of their duty, responsibility and mission in the military. Only through such training can they understand how to become a qualified serviceman or an excellent officer, who is supposed to remain calm and firm and to make right decisions rapidly in unexpected conditions.

During the 4-year study in a Chinese naval academy, cadets learn basic and compulsory courses, and master scientific knowledge and military skills. Besides, they must learn how

to follow and how to lead. Midshipmen, as a rule, work as squad and platoon leaders. Only a few can be appointed as part-time leaders of cadet battalions. In addition, some of the Party members among the students are elected to be members of the Party's branches or committees, and some members of the Communist Youth League to be members of the League branches. In their jobs of leadership, they can display their talents and initiative. In the senior year, some of the midshipmen have a chance to be appointed as **provisioned** leaders to be responsible for freshmen's military training. In this process, they can fully exhibit their skills of leadership and work style.

Acting according to the requirements of PLA's military reform, the PLAN has carried out several reforms in its educational system by creating comprehensive universities and expanding the curriculum and special fields of study. Now, the PLAN has eight institutions of higher learning in total (Naval University of Engineering, Dalian Naval Academy, Naval Command College, Naval Aeronautical University, Naval Logistical Academy, Naval Submarine Academy, Naval Medical University, Bengbu Naval Petty Officer Academy). They implement Naval Officer Training programs, which aim at preparing students for careers as officers in the Chinese Navy.

Below is a brief account of the two typical PLA naval schools.

### Naval University of Engineering

The Naval University of Engineering (NUE), established on November 22, 1949 and now situated in Wuhan, Hubei province, is listed as the army "2110 project" that gives priority to the development of education. It is a state key university in engineering, highlighting the harmonious **multidisciplinary** development of four major fields, namely, military science, science, engineering and management. The university adheres to the guiding principle of placing equal weight on personnel training and scientific research, which are necessary to undergraduates and postgraduates and linking **credential** education and on-the-job training.

In addition to offering 34 undergraduate specialties[1], NUE has five authorized agencies for granting level-1 discipline Master Degree[2] and 21 for level-2 discipline Master Degree, and five for level-1 discipline Doctorate Degree and 28 for level-2 discipline Doctorate Degree[3] as well as seven mobile centers for **post-doctoral** research[4].

Led by the Central Military Commission and the Party Committee of PLA Navy, and acting upon its school motto of "rigorous, truth-seeking, **enterprising** and innovative"[5], NUE has turned out tens of thousands of high-quality military and engineering personnel for the

Navy in the past 70 years. Therefore, it is praised as "a cradle of naval officers"[6]. As one of the vital bases for talents cultivation and scientific research in military, NUE has won one special award of State Teaching Achievements[7] and three first class awards of State Scientific and Technologic Progress[8] as well as other state awards in recent years, outranking the other military universities and academies both in the grade of awards and in number.

NUE boasts a teaching staff which is not only reasonable in age structure and the distribution of professional titles but also high in political and professional quality. Currently, the university has 500-plus professors and associate professors who have made valuable achievements in teaching and research, including Prof. Ma Weiming and Prof. He Lin, academicians of the Chinese Academy of Engineering[9]; Wang Dong, Distinguished Professor of Changjiang Scholars Program[10]; Xiao Fei, winner of China Youth May Fourth Medal, and also a great many prominent teachers and middle-aged and young leaders of different academic fields of the navy, the whole army and the country.

The NUE library has a collection of 600,000 books, 13,000-plus Chinese and foreign electronic periodicals or journals. In addition, there are two fields for track and field events, a gymnasium, a service center and other facilities. All those can meet the demands of campus life like culture, physical education and recreation.

### Dalian Naval Academy

PLA Dalian Naval Academy (DNA), a military institution under the command of the navy headquarters, offers regular education to bachelor, master and Ph.D. candidates, mainly training them as commanding officers onboard surface vessels, naval political commanding officers and technical officers of marine survey engineering. The academy is famous for strictness and regularity in managing its education. For over half a century, with the motto "Dedication, Strictness, Strenuousness and Truthfulness", the academy has turned out over 50,000 officers for the navy.

PLA Dalian Naval Academy, established on November 22nd, 1949, is the earliest regular military school ever founded in the navy. The academy has been awarded many times as Model Unit in education[11], ideological and political construction as well as Model Unit in management evaluations throughout the armed forces and all over the country. As one belonging to the army "211 project", the academy is the only "Double A-class" training unit of international hydrography and chart cartography worldwide[12]. The naval cadets from the academy have participated in all the national dress parades[13] in front of Tian'anmen Square as

the Navy Formation[14] so far.

As one of the earliest military schools opening to the outside world, the academy has trained over 200 overseas students for 11 countries. In addition, the academy has received over 200 delegations, about a hundred foreign military experts and scholars from more than 70 countries on official visits and academic exchanges. The ocean-going training ship Zhenghe, Dengshichang and Qijiguang have paid visits to over 20 countries during the long voyage training. The academy has established friendly and cooperative relations with the naval colleges of Turkey, Britain and France and sent more than 100 officers and professors to study and lecture in other countries.

Now the academy offers seven disciplines for bachelor degrees: Seamanship, Communication Engineering, Electronic Information Engineering, Weapons System and Engineering, Detective Guidance and Control Technique, Survey Engineering and Military Oceanography. It has five authorized agencies for granting level-1 discipline Master Degree and six for level-2 discipline Master Degree, and two for level-2 discipline Doctorate Degree as well as five mobile centers for post-doctoral research. Recently, it has established a comprehensive training system covering military science, engineering, sciences, laws and educational science in order to train students at different levels, such as doctoral students, postgraduates, undergraduates, 3-year college students as well as students pursuing continued programs.

In addition to programs offered to undergraduates, the academy also offers career programs to cadets and active officers. Faced with the challenges of new military transformation all over the world, PLA Dalian Naval Academy, with many years of rich experience in training, will continue to follow the trend of the times and make greater efforts to rank among the most famous military schools in the world.

*(1257 words)*

**Sources:**

1. http://www.81.cn/201311jxjjh/2019-05/30/content_9518448.htm

2. http://www.81.cn/hj/2019-05/23/content_9511943.htm

3. http://www.nue.edu.cn/index.aspx?lanmuid=89&sublanmuid=719（2020年6月访问）

# Notes

1. **undergraduate specialties**: subjects learnt in a university or college where students study for their first degree 本科专业

2. **five authorized agencies for granting level-1 discipline Master Degree**: formal or legal permission to give a student the master degree, which is a further university degree that you study for after a first degree 5个一级学科硕士授权点

3. **28 for level-2 discipline Doctorate Degree**: formal or legal permission to give a student the doctorate degree, which is a further university degree that you study for after a master degree 28个二级学科博士授权点

4. **seven mobile centers for post-doctoral research**: a place where a postdoctoral student has completed his or her doctorate and is doing further study or research 7个博士后科研流动站

5. **rigorous, truth-seeking, enterprising and innovative**: do anything carefully and with a lot of attention to detail, seek for truth, show the ability to think of new projects or new ways of doing things and make them successful, introduce or use new ideas, ways of doing sth. 严谨、求实、拼搏、创新

6. **a cradle of naval officers**: a place where naval officers are cultivated 海军军官的摇篮

7. **one special award of State Teaching Achievements**: an important award for achievements in teaching nationwide 一项国家级优秀教学成果特等奖

8. **three first class awards of State Scientific and Technologic Progress**: award at highest level for advancements and achievements in science and technology nationwide 三次国家科技进步一等奖

9. **academician of the Chinese Academy of Engineering**: An academician is a member of an academy, usually one that has been formed to improve or maintain standards in a particular field. 中国工程院院士

10. **Distinguished Professor of Changjiang Scholars Program**: an honorary title given to professors in particular fields in Changjiang Scholars Program 长江学者特聘教授

11. **Model Unit in education**: a teaching unit which has played great exemplary role in education 教育示范单位

12. **"Double A-class" training unit of international hydrography and chart cartography worldwide**: A-level training unit in both hydrographer and chart cartographer all over the world 国际海道测量师、海图制图师"双A级"培训单位

13. national dress parades: military parades (in which a formation of soldiers whose movement is restricted by close-order maneuvering known as drilling or marching) aiming to observe the founding of PRC. 国庆阅兵

14. Navy Formation: a military parade formation which consists of naval soldiers 海军方阵

## Word Bank

| | |
|---|---|
| strenuous [ˈstrenjʊəs] | *adj.* 奋发的；艰辛发奋的 |
| remould [ˌriːˈməʊld] | *v.* 改造，改铸；重新塑造 |
| temper [ˈtempə(r)] | *v.* 使回火；锻炼；调和；使缓和 |
| physique [fɪˈziːk] | *n.* 体格；体形 |
| willpower [ˈwɪlpaʊə(r)] | *n.* 意志力；毅力 |
| provision [ prəˈvɪʒn] | *v.* 为……提供所需物品 |
| multidisciplinary [ˌmʌltɪˈdɪsəplənerɪ] | *adj.* 包括各种学科的 |
| credential [krəˈdenʃl] | *n.* 证书；资质 |
| post-doctoral [ˌpəʊstˈdɒktərəl ] | *adj.* 博士后的 |
| enterprising [ˈentəpraɪzɪŋ] | *adj.* 有事业心的；有进取心的 |
| academician [əˌkædəˈmɪʃn] | *n.* 学会会员；院士；学者 |
| periodical [ˌpɪərɪˈɒdɪkl] | *n.* 期刊；杂志 |
| hydrography [haɪˈdrɒgrəfɪ] | *n.* 水文（地理学）；水道学，海道测量术 |
| cartography [kɑːˈtɒgrəfəɪ] | *n.* 制图学，（地图）绘制法 |
| oceanography [ˌəʊʃəˈnɒgrəfɪ] | *n.* 海洋学 |

## I. Comprehension

**Part A** Questions

*Answer the following questions in accordance with the text.*

1. Why does NUE enjoy the priority in development?

2. How many disciplines fields does NUE possess? And which one is the primary one?

3. Why has NUE been praised as "a cradle of naval officers"?

4. What is NUE proud of in terms of its faculty?

5. By citing the example of the midshipmen's participation in all the national dress parades in front of Tian'anmen Square as the Navy Formation, what does the author intend to prove?

### Part B  Multiple Choices

*Choose the most appropriate answer from the given choices below each question in accordance with the text.*

1. Which of the following is NOT included in undergraduate subjects of PLA Dalian Naval Academy?

   A. Detective Guidance and Control Technique

   B. Electronic Communication Engineering

   C. Survey Engineering

   D. Military Oceanography

2. Which of the following descriptions about NUE is NOT true?

   A. NUE was established on November 22nd, 1949, so did DNA.

   B. NUE is a state key university which belongs to one of the five comprehensive universities.

   C. NUE specializes in engineering and is known as Model Unit in management evaluations all over the country.

   D. NUE attaches equal importance to personnel training and scientific research and links credential education and on-job training education.

3. What will the midshipman learn from initial military training?

   A. To have a correct conception about what they can do and acquire in the military.

   B. To be aware of requirement and morality that a serviceman should have.

   C. To grasp the shortcut to become an excellent officer.

   D. To get rid of panic and turn to commanders in stressful conditions.

4. Which of the following statements about Chinese naval academies is true?

   A. NUE is the earliest regular military school established in the navy.

   B. DNA is one of the earliest military schools opening to the outside world and has established friendly relationships with a wide range of foreign naval colleges.

   C. NUE has established a comprehensive training system covering military science, engineering, sciences, laws and educational science with a combination of different training levels.

D. DNA offers 34 disciplines for undergraduates including Seamanship, Communication Engineering, Electronic Information Engineering and so on.

5. How do the midshipmen acquire leadership skills?

A. Every midshipman can make a choice to be a part-time leader in the military committee or the Youth Leagues when entering senior year.

B. Every midshipman can work dependently to exercise leadership over others.

C. Every midshipman has chances to be part-time leaders of freshmen squadrons during the 4-year study in the academy.

D. Every midshipman can display their talents and initiative, skills of leadership as well as work style during practices to be part-time leaders, party secretary and other roles during the 4-year study in the academy.

## II. Translation

**Part A**   Terms & Phrases

*Translate the following terms or phrases from Chinese into English and vice versa.*

1. 海军航空大学

2. 海军潜艇学院

3. 海军指挥学院

4. 海军军医大学

5. 海军勤务学院

6. 海军蚌埠士官学校

7. 基础部

8. 动力工程学院

9. 电子工程学院

10. 电气工程学院

11. 兵器工程学院

12. 舰船与海洋学院

13. 核科学技术学院

14. 信息安全系

15. 管理工程与装备经济系

16. state key university

17. military science

18. bachelor degree

19. Seamanship

20. Weapons System and Engineering

21. Electronic Information Engineering

22. Communication Engineering

23. Military Oceanography

24. Survey Engineering

25. Detective Guidance and Control Technique

26. credential education

27. on-job training education

28. military drills

29. part-time roles of leaders

30. party secretary

*Translate the following paragraph from English into Chinese and vice versa.*

The Naval University of Engineering (NUE), established on November 22, 1949 and now is situated in Wuhan, Hubei province, is listed as the army "211 project" that gives priority to the development of education. It is a state key university in engineering, highlighting the harmonious multidisciplinary development of four discipline fields, namely, military science, science, engineering and management.

## III. Reading Report

What have you learned after reading the text? Have you obtained a better command of Naval University of Engineering and Dalian Naval Academy? Now create your reading report in no more than 150 words to generalize your achievement in the text study.

# Text B
# United States Naval Academy

The United States Naval Academy (also known as Annapolis Naval Academy) located in Annapolis, Maryland, was established in 1845. Its campus covers 338 acres (137 hectares), being a National Historic Landmark[1] and home to many historic sites, buildings and monuments. The academy is the second oldest of the US five service academies[2]. It is listed among the top fifty universities in the United States in academic excellence and among the top three in engineering. Its purpose is to train regular officers for the Navy and Marine Corps. After four years of intensive study and training, midshipmen are commissioned Ensign, Regular Navy, with a six- to eight-year obligation, depending upon the welfare specialty chosen.

Candidates for admission generally need to directly apply to the academy and get a recommendation from a congressman as a rule. After admission into the academy, the midshipmen's tuition is fully funded by the Navy. Midshipmen must take formal professional courses with academic credit. Approximately 1,300 "plebes" have to receive rigorous training each summer, but only about 1,100 midshipmen can graduate. Graduates are usually commissioned as Ensign in the Navy or Second Lieutenant in the Marine Corps, and occasionally as officers in the US Air Force, US Army, and US Coast Guard.

According to the academic program[3], a midshipman must complete 140 credit hours with a cumulative quality-point[4] rating of 2.0 (C average). All eight bachelor of science degrees awarded lean heavily toward engineering, although eighteen credit hours, exclusive of required English courses, must be devoted to humanities and social sciences. In addition, every midshipman takes training in military leadership ability and participates in competitive athletics. They are required to adhere to the Academy's Honor Concept[5].

With the heavy emphasis on engineering, it is not generally possible for the average Academy graduate to attain the level of liberal arts education a naval officer should ideally have. In 2020, US News & World Report ranked the Naval Academy as No. 17 in the National Liberal Arts category in the 2020 edition of its Best Colleges ranking report. In addition, according to the Rankings of National Liberal Arts Colleges, the Naval Academy was ranked No. 4 on the list of Best Undergraduate Engineering Programs in 2020. In the same year Forbes.com ranked the Naval Academy as No. 24 in its report "America's Best Colleges

2019".

As midshipmen actually serve in the United States Navy, starting from the moment that they swear an oath of enlistment at the school-opening ceremony, they are subject to the Uniform Code of Military Justice, of which USNA regulations are a part, and to all executive policies and orders formulated by the Department of the Navy. For personal development, part of the threefold objective of the Academy is to give midshipmen a moral education. The Academy has an excellent honor system, conceived and administered by the midshipmen and monitored by the administration. Midshipmen agree not to lie, cheat, or steal and not to tolerate anyone who does. Only in the first year will occasional minor indiscretions sometimes be tolerated and corrected, under the theory that this is a learning experience for fourth class and a teaching experience for the upper classes. After graduation, midshipmen will serve as officers in the US Navy, and foreign midshipmen will be in the service in the armed forces of their native countries. Since 1959, the policy on exchange of graduates has been carried out. According to the policy, a small number of graduates, as commissioned officers, are assigned to the Coast Guard and also to the Air Force or Army every year, with their Military Rank equal to that of other academy graduates in the units where they serve.

### Rank Structure

The organization in charge of students is known as the Brigade of Midshipmen. Midshipmen at the Academy wear service uniforms the same as those of US Navy officers, with the shoulder board and sleeve insignia of rank.

Midshipmen are classified not as freshmen, sophomores, juniors, and seniors, but as fourth class, third class, second class, and first class.

A member who enters the class—the Fourth Class, the lowest rank of midshipman—is also called "plebe" (word of Latin origin, or "plebeius"). Because the first year at the Academy is an important school year of transformation from a civilian into a military officer, plebes must observe a number of rules and regulations, which are different from those for their seniors—the upper three classes of midshipmen—to follow. They also must take on additional tasks and responsibilities until their promotion to midshipman Third Class.

Third-Class midshipmen of the Brigade, who are relatively well treated due to their advancement, are commonly called "Youngsters". Because of their promotions in rank or status, they are allowed such privileges as watching television, listening to music, watching movies, taking a nap, etc.

Second-Class midshipmen are charged with plebes' training. They report directly to and obey orders from the first class, which outranks in the cadet command chain. By the way, they are allowed to drive their own cars (no parking on campus) and to enter or leave the Yard (campus) in civilian clothes (weekends only).

First-Class midshipmen enjoy more liberties, but need to shoulder the most challenging responsibilities. While maintaining their academic performance and participating in mandatory athletic sports, they must bear the responsibility of managing the other classes in the Brigade. On the other hand, they are a little different from second-class midshipmen in that they can park their cars on campus and have greater liberty to enter and leave. So, they are generally called "Firsties".

The Brigade is composed of two regiments, each with three battalions. Each battalion includes five companies. The number of companies adds up to 30. The midshipmen command chain is headed by a first-class midshipman chosen for outstanding leadership performance. He or she is responsible for much of the brigade's day-to-day activities as well as midshipmen's professional training. All brigade activities are under the supervision of the Commandant of Midshipmen, an active-duty Navy Captain or Marine Corps Colonel. To aid the Commandant in work, experienced Navy and Marine Corps officers are needed to act as leaders of companies and battalions.

Faculty

The academy has a teaching staff of 600 or so, consisting of civilian professors and military instructors. The civilian professors who all have a Ph.D. are usually granted tenure, after promotion from Assistant Professor to Associate Professor. Fewer of the military instructors have a Ph.D. but almost all have a Master's degree. Most of them are assigned to the Academy for only two or three years. Additionally, some Adjunct Professors are hired to fill temporary shortages in various disciplines in time of need. The Adjunct Professors are not eligible for tenure.

A small number of officers at the Academy are designated as Permanent Military Professors (PMP), initially from the academic rank of Assistant Professor. All PMPs have PhDs, and remain at the Academy until statutory retirement. Most once acted as commanders in the Navy and a few as captains. Like civilian professors, they seek promotion to the academic rank of Associate Professor and Professor. However, they are not eligible for tenure.

*(1186 words)*

**Sources:**

1. https://www.forwardpathway.com/21232

2. https://www.usnews.com/best-colleges/united-states-naval-academy-2101

3. https://www.usnews.com/best-colleges/united-states-naval-academy-2101/overall-rankings

# Notes

1. National Historic Landmark: A landmark is a building or a place that is very important because of its history, and that should be preserved. 国家历史地标。美国政府官方承认的有历史意义的建筑、遗址或区域。

2. service academies: institutions for the cultivation of soldiers 美国军校

3. academic program: a program of education in liberal arts and sciences (usually in preparation for higher education) 学历教育大纲

4. quality-point: grade point 积分点（美国以此计算学生的学业成绩，每门学科的学分数乘以该科成绩的积点，即可得出这门学科的积分点）

5. Honor Concept: The Honor Concept and Honor Treatise are parts of the United States Naval Academy's Honor Program. Similar to the Cadet Honor Codes of the United States Military Academy and United States Air Force Academy, the Concept formalizes the requirement for midshipmen to demonstrate integrity while refusing to lie, cheat or steal. 荣誉观念（海军学院学员要求做到正直、率真、处事公正，从不说谎、偷窃。）

# Word Bank

| | |
|---|---|
| commissioned [kəˈmɪʃənd] | *adj.* 服役的，现役的 |
| congressman [ˈkɒŋɡrəsmən] | *n.* 国会议员；众议院议员 |
| plebe [pliːb] | *n.* （美国军校）一年级学生；新生 |
| adhere [ədˈhɪə(r)] | *v.* 粘附；坚持 |
| oath [əʊθ] | *n.* 誓言；宣誓 |
| enlistment [ɪnˈlɪstmənt] | *n.* 征募，应征入伍；服兵役期限 |
| indiscretion [ˌɪndɪˈskreʃn] | *n.* 不慎的言行；（尤指道德上）不检点的言行 |
| mandatory [mændətərɪ; mænˈdeɪtərɪ] | *adj.* 强制的；法定的；义务的 |

| | |
|---|---|
| supervision [ˌsuːpəˈvɪʒn; ˌsjuːpəˈvɪʒn] | *n.* 监督，管理 |
| company [ˈkʌmpənɪ] | *n.* （军）连；连队；（学员）队 |
| tenure [ˈtenjə(r)] | *n.* （官职等的）保有；任期 |
| adjunct [ˈædʒʌŋkt] | *n.* 附属物；附加物 |
| eligible [ˈelɪdʒəbl] | *adj.* 适任的；合格的 |

## I. True or False

*Decide whether the following sentences are true or false in accordance with the text.*

1. The USNA is the second oldest of the US service academies and boasts a historically famous campus.

2. Graduates from the USNA are commissioned as Ensigns in the Navy, Marine Corps and Coast Guard.

3. The Navy Academy ranks high in various reports and gets funded from the *Forbes.com* in 2019.

4. Midshipmen are of the line of the US Navy from their school-opening ceremony, regardless of gender.

5. The rules and regulations for midshipmen vary according to their years of serving in the academy.

6. Midshipmen are forbidden to wear civilian clothes and leave the yard except the first-class midshipmen.

7. Both civilian professors and military professors can be promoted academically.

8. All PMPS must have PhDs, and those who are outstanding can be awarded tenure, though the chance is slim.

## II. Word Match

*Match the words/terms/phrases in the left column with its appropriate correspondents in the right column.*

1. physical fitness test

2. school-opening ceremony

3. officers-in-training

A. 臂章

B. 获得推荐

C. 在职培训军官

4. shoulder board

5. sleeve insignia

6. statutory retirement

7. receive a recommendation

8. active-duty

9. midshipman

10. civilian clothes

D. 海军学校学员

E. 现役

F. 体能测试

G. 肩章

H. 开学典礼

I. 便服

J. 法定退休

## Text C
## The Reform of Military Education: Twenty-Five Years Later

It has been 25 years since the landmark Goldwater-Nichols Act[1] for reforming US national defense was passed in 1986. Part of the important legislation refer to specific mandated guidelines for military education, with intent to open the military culture, encourage military personnel and civilians in academic cooperation and promote military exchange among the services. Twenty-five years after the Act was adopted, the US military is still faced with, perhaps, the most complex environment in which it has ever operated. Then, does it indicate that the Goldwater-Nichols mandate was unsuccessful in the improvement on military education? If so, what might be done?

### Training versus Education

War colleges are part of the Professional Military Education (PME)[2] system, a large complex of institutions including the Army War College[3] in Carlisle, PA; the Naval War College[4] in Newport, RI, the Air War College[5] in Montgomery, AL, and so on. Every institution has distinct features and different strengths and weaknesses, but all are, in varying degrees, confronted with overriding institutional and cultural issues that hinder the educational goals set in the Goldwater-Nichols Act approved by the Congress. The frustrations due to the inertia of the PME system, however, are understandable.

Neither the Joint Staff responsible for PME, nor the individual military services, have well tackled what education for intellectual agility, as opposed to training, would entail. This is not surprising, because few of those in charge of PME (individually or collectively) have spent much time thinking about the difference between education and training. Not many have reflected on what it means "to educate" or "to be educated." Unfortunately, training and education are regarded by the military bureaucracy as almost synonymous. The Navy and the Air Force even group the two words together to name their respective commands: the Naval Education and Training Command (NETC)[6] and the Air Education and Training Command (AETC)[7]. Education actually requires thinking and reflection, which takes time. Training means the process or being prepared for a job, while education means the training and instruction of young people in colleges for them to acquire knowledge and develop skills. However, the confusion of the definitions of "training" and "education" is the issue that initially led to some kind of reform intended by the Goldwater-Nichols over two decades ago, and represents a clash of cultures to some extent. Culture issues are always the most difficult to deal with in hybrid organizations, including the military and academic cultures in PME. Those issues persist today.

### Different Cultures

In PME, these cultural differences arise from work habits, definitions of productivity, and views on what constitutes education. For the military faculty, daily productivity may be displayed through office work, meetings, **communal** class preparation, and consultations. Academic indicators of productivity cover a wide range of activities: meeting with students during the scheduled hours, individual class preparation, developing research projects, preparation for new lectures, attending academic conferences, planning publications, and expectation of peer critiques. Academics plan their work in year or longer blocks, and advocate a broader, open-ended, **cumulative** educational model. Conversely, the views on education by active-duty and retired military instructors lean towards a training-oriented model.

### The Faculty: Military Officers verses Civilian Academics

Considering the faculty is an important part of an academy, it is necessary to understand its components. Although the PME faculty is composed of military and civilian personnel, it is somewhat difficult to distinguish between both the groups. A careful look at the roster of the civilian members engaged in PME would find that many of them are actually retired military officers who go out in uniform on Friday and come back in civilian clothes on Monday. This is because military officers can retire ahead of time, draw a full pension immediately and return to their posts as reemployed personnel, who are on the government payroll. That questionable and expensive practice becomes the target of criticism by former Secretary of Defense Robert Gates[8].

As for the civil-military equality of opportunity in an academy, steps need to be taken to reform the system of recruiting and retaining civilian academic personnel, because the best and brightest civilian scholars will rarely consider working at an academy if it cannot satisfy their demands as follows: (1) academic freedom; (2) an ideal path to advancement in career; (3) abundant time for individual research on professional subjects or engineering projects in their field. The Naval War College has taken the lead in this area because its presidents and

the Navy itself have maintained a fine tradition of academic freedom and innovation. Other PME academies have lagged a little behind in this area, thereby failing to establish the same academic standing as the NWC.

### Recommendations

First and foremost, the teaching purpose of the US war colleges must be kept in mind. The purpose is to train students as trustworthy defenders of the United States of America and its national interests and its allies around the world. Toward that goal, the following recommendations are put forward for further discussion:

- Considering priority over other things in college education, considerable time and resources should be invested in educating the students to make them the equals to the best of their civilian counterparts in the field of national defense, as Admiral Turner said forty years ago.
- Active-duty military officers who can play a crucial role in the PME mission should be first chosen as teachers of operational warfare, while former officers short of current experience should not be.
- Employing active-duty military instructors as civilian personnel upon retirement is a good approach to augmenting the teaching staff.
- A tenure system or something like that for civilian faculty needs to be in place to stimulate efficient academic competition among the peers and prevent the teaching staff from becoming "a stagnant pool of water". Thus, those who are qualified for tenure can better work for PME on a long-term contract.
- Academic freedom for the faculty should be a fundamental principle of each war college in order to ensure that students can develop their ability and become talented persons under the PME system.

To sum up, if education is essential to the development of intellectual agility, then what is important for educators at PME academies to do is to help students get over their predilection for a seemingly simple way to solve "black and white" problems easily so as to get high grades. What's more, professors should use better and more appropriate methods for teaching so that students can make great progress in their academic performance and their ability to analyze and solve problems as well as in other aspects. In short, the US war colleges play an extremely important part in professional military education.

*(1115 words)*

*Sources:*

Extracted and edited from *Orbis* published by Elsevier. Inc, Volume 56, Issue 1, 2010, Pages 135-153：

## Notes

1. Goldwater-Nichols Act: The bill named after Senator Barry Goldwater (R-Arizona) and Representative William Flynt "Bill" Nichols (D-Alabama) was signed into law by President Reagan on October 1, 1986. It has thoroughly reorganized the United States Department of Defense since the department was established according to the 1947 National Security Act. Under the Goldwater-Nichols Act the US military command chain has also been restructured. The chain is commanded by President through the Secretary of Defense who directly leads joint combat commanders, bypassing chiefs of all the services, who only play advisory roies. 戈德华特–尼科尔法案

2. Professional Military Education: It focuses on leadership, management theory and practice, military history and operational doctrine, national defense policy, planning and decision-making, legal responsibilities, and professional ethics. 职业军事教育

3. the Army War College（AWC）: Founded in 1901 by Elihu Root, the AWC aims to prepare selected military, civilian, and international leaders for the responsibilities of strategic leadership, educate current and future leaders on the deployment and command of land forces in a multinational joint operational environment, conduct research on national security and military strategy, and engage in activities in support of the Army strategic communication efforts. 美国陆军军事学院

4. the Naval War College（NWC）: The US NWC was established in 1884 on Coasters Harbor Island, Newport, Rhode Island. It offers naval officers various courses of maritime strategy and policy study, national security strategic policy-making, and joint operations. 美国海军军事学院

5. the Air War College（AWC）: The AWC established in 1947 is the highest institution of learning for American Air Force officers' further study, which refers to deployment of air forces, strategy and tactics of joint operations, and defense of national security. 美国空军军事学院

6. the Naval Education and Training Command (NETC): NETC is a major command of the United States Navy responsible for training. The Commander of NETC directs over

22,000 personnel and oversees various training activities of USN and USMC officers and enlisted personnel. Headquartered at Naval Air Station Pensacola, Florida, NETC holds responsibility for numerous subordinate commands across the United States. 海军教育训练司令部

7. the Air Education and Training Command (AETC): Established on July 1st, 1993, AETC is one of the US Air Force's ten major commands led by the US Air Force Headquarters. AETC is headquartered at Randolph Air Force Base, Texas. It has more than 48,000 active - duty and Air Reserve Component members and 14,000 civilian personnel. Its duty is to recruit, train and educate airmen to devote themselves to the development of American air power. 空军教育训练司令部

8. Robert Gates（1943—　）: Dr. Robert M. Gates served as Director of Central Intelligence from 1991 until 1993 and US Secretary of Defense from December 2006 to July 2011. He was the only Secretary of Defense in US history to be asked to remain in that office by President Barack Obama, the eighth president he served. 罗伯特·盖茨（美国职业特工，资深情报分析专家，历任中央情报局局长和国防部长）

## Word Bank

| | |
|---|---|
| mandate ['mændeɪt] | *v.* 授权；命令 |
| overriding [ˌəʊvəˈraɪdɪŋ] | *adj.* 首要的 |
| inertia [ɪˈnɜːʃə] | *n.* 缺乏活力；惰性；保守；惯性 |
| entail [ɪnˈteɪl] | *v.* 牵涉；需要；使必要 |
| bureaucracy [bjʊəˈrɒkrəsɪ] | *n.* 官僚主义；官僚作风；官僚体制 |
| synonymous [sɪˈnɒnɪməs] | *adj.* 同义的 |
| communal [kəˈmjuːnl; ˈkɒmjənl] | *adj.*（集体中）不同群体的，各团体的；共享的，共有的 |
| cumulative [ˈkjuːmjələtɪv] | *adj.*（力量或重要性）聚积的，积累的；渐增的；累计的 |
| counterpart [ˈkaʊntəpɑːt] | *n.* 职位（或作用）相当的人；对应的事物 |
| augment [ɔːgˈment] | *v.* 增加；提高；扩大 |
| predilection [ˌpriːdɪˈlekʃn] | *n.* 喜爱；偏爱；钟爱 |
| intellectual agility | 智慧敏捷性 |

## Exercises

Based on what you have acquired in this text, you are supposed to conduct an online study to explore further into the relevant sphere. Comb and frame what you have found with an online study report in no less than 200 words. In addition, any assistant image, audio, video, or other first-hand material will be preferred when you present your report in class.

# Unit 16 Port Visit and Escort Mission

**Bridge-in**

*Answer the following questions in accordance with the microlesson "PLAN's Escort Missions in the Gulf of Aden".*

1. Why did China dispatch escort task forces to the Gulf of Aden and off the coast of Somalia?

2. Can you give a brief introduction to China's first escort task force?

3. What is the significance of China's escort missions in the Gulf of Aden?

## Text A
### China Takes to the Sea

On December 26, 2008, a three-ship fleet of the Chinese navy set sail from a port in Sanya for its first overseas deployment. The fleet joined in the multinational patrols of the Gulf of Aden and waters off the coast of Somalia. The Navy's DDG-171 Haikou destroyer, together with another destroyer, DDG-169 Wuhan, achieved many breakthroughs and firsts.

The three-ship fleet marked the beginning of many escort missions which have been carried out by the Chinese navy over the past 10 years. It was the first time for China Navy to deploy its naval ships to protect its sea routes, fulfill its **humanitarian** obligations and safeguard its national interests.

Official data shows that China's naval ships succeeded in completing a series of major tasks on the high seas in those years. As of December 24, 2018, the Chinese navy has sent 31 groups of ships, 100 ships altogether, 67 ship-based helicopters and more than 26,000 officers and soldiers to escort more than 6,600 Chinese and foreign merchant ships over the past decade. They successfully rescued and assisted more than 70 Chinese and foreign merchant vessels in distress and prevented pirate boats from hijackings.

### Deployment of Escorting Forces

The size and scale of China Navy escort forces has been constantly adjusted over the past decade. Between December 2008 and February 2012, the East China Sea Fleet and South China Sea Fleet took turns in carrying out escort missions. The North China Sea Fleet did not join in escort actions until February 2012.

In the early stage of escort missions, a couple of warships in formation had to make two voyages at short intervals. The 530 Xuzhou[1] was among them. The then captain told that such a quick turn to perform an escort task reflected a shortage of ships available for this purpose. One replenishment ship had to be at sea for two times in succession to serve the warships carrying out escort missions during that period. "The PLA Navy had a limited number of destroyers and missile frigates capable of conducting escort missions on the high seas. To fill up the shortage of the number, the Navy sent an amphibious transport ship in support of the destroyers and frigates in 2010. That was then an expedient measure to alleviate the pressure on escort," said Zhang Junshe, a senior research fellow at the PLAN Military Studies Research Institute. He also spoke of some problems arising in the first years, such as ships' failure to adapt to various complicated sea states as well as weather conditions, for instance, high temperature, high humidity and high salinity.

### Logistic Support Base

The PLAN support base was established in Djibouti on July 11, 2017. It is China's first overseas support base, attracting wide attention internationally.

The long-term voyage of the first escort group without berthing at any port for a rest set a new record in endurance time and distance. Given the feedback report on its first escort mission, the Chinese navy started to explore a more efficient way of overseas logistic support during the execution of long-term escort mission.

At the beginning, escort fleets mainly relied on an accompanying supply ship for logistic support. Later, they could gradually get logistic support mainly from foreign ports along the way, which greatly reduced their dependence on their own supply ships. An insider said that commercial docks rented for storage are often allowed to resupplying the escorting warships only in a limited time. As soon as a ship is replenished, it will have to leave the harbor. Thus, the sailors cannot have sufficient time for rest. For this reason, China PLAN needs to build its

own logistic support bases at ports of call². For example, Djibouti Logistic Support Base can ensure that the Chinese naval ships get more efficient and timely replenishment, maintain their equipment and allow the crew to have a good rest.

### Anti-piracy Overseas

One day in 2010, the 530 Xuzhou was ordered to beat back a pirate attack on M/V Tai An Kou³ flying the Chinese flag. After a fierce fighting, the special force succeeded in rescuing all the 21 crew members from the attacked ship. Besides, the 530 Xuzhou successfully fulfilled an **arduous** task in the Gulf of Aden to help evacuate Chinese nationals from Libya⁴, though it faced many unknown risks at that time. It is the first time that the Chinese navy has gone abroad to participate in the evacuation of overseas Chinese. It marks a new milestone for China's non-war military operations. Due to its success in many major tasks, the 530 Xuzhou was awarded the first-class merit by the Central Military Commission.

At each ceremony of **devolving** the escort mission to the relief escort fleet, the commander of the previous **convoy** ship group gives a full account of the current maritime situation as well as activities of pirates in the target waters. During the execution of escort missions, each escort fleet must cope with what suddenly happens at sea by use of effective tactics and countermeasures.

In the past ten years, the Chinese Navy escorting forces have stood various severe tests and accumulated a wealth of experience, thereby improving their escort and anti-piracy capabilities and being able to perform the international obligations better, said Zhang Junshe. Escort ships are able to carry out anti-piracy missions better and faster now than in the past decade. Shipborne helicopters are able to conduct a **scramble** mission more rapidly, and special operations personnel are able to be more quickly deployed when they are needed.

### Mutual Communication and Visits

More than 40 escort warships from about 20 countries are carrying out escort missions in the Gulf of Aden. Taking a more open-minded attitude, the Chinese navy actively communicates with other navies and informs them about the Chinese vessels. During its first convoy, the Chinese escort fleet communicated with foreign groups of ships, exchanging the information about escort operations and discussing other related matters, including mutual visits and joint training and exercises. When performing escort missions in the Gulf of Aden, the Chinese naval ships set many new records, such as the first joint escort, joint training and joint exercises with foreign naval ships.

What is worth mentioning is that mutual visits are often paid to the Chinese vessels and vessels from NATO, the EU and the US on the sea. Some of the foreign naval personnel may board Chinese vessels by boat after **authorization**. Even a foreign helicopter can be allowed to land on the deck of a Chinese warship. Such a mutual visit can not only promote friendship but also serve as an open window through which foreign militaries may have a better understanding of the Chinese PLA.

Zhang Junshe believes that escort missions, joint training and exercises, and mutual visits have led to a broadening in the Chinese sailors' horizons and an overall improvement in their ability over the past decade.

*(1152 words)*

**Sources:**

Extracted and edited from *Chinese navy sees broadened horizon, enhanced ability through 10-year escort missions* by Global Times, December 31, 2018. http://www.globaltimes.cn/content/1134066.shtml (2020年6月13日访问)

## Notes

1. 530 Xuzhou: Xuzhou Frigate 徐州号护卫舰
2. port of call: a port where a ship stops during a journey（航行途中的）停靠港，停泊港
3. M/V Tai An Kou: M/V short for merchant vessel 泰安口号商船
4. Libya: a military dictatorship in northern Africa on the Mediterranean 利比亚

## Word Bank

| | |
|---|---|
| humanitarian [hjuːˌmænɪˈteərɪən] | *adj.* 人道主义的（主张减轻人类苦难、改善人类生活）；慈善的 |
| pirate [ˈpaɪrət] | *n.* 海盗 |
| frigate [ˈfrɪgət] | *n.* [军] 护卫舰 |
| expedient [ɪksˈpiːdjənt] | *n.* 权宜之计；应急办法 |
| humidity [hjuːˈmɪdətɪ] | *n.*（空气中的）湿度 |
| salinity [səˈlɪnətɪ] | *n.* 盐度 |

| | |
|---|---|
| arduous [ˈɑːdjʊəs] | *adj.* 困难的；险峻的；辛勤的 |
| devolve [dɪˈvɒlv] | *v.* （将职责、责任、权力等）移交，转交，委任 |
| convoy [ˈkɒnvɔɪ] | *n.* 护航，护卫；（被护送的）船队 |
| scramble [ˈskræmbl] | *n.* 紧急起飞 |
| authorization [ˌɔːθəraɪˈzeɪʃn] | *n.* 批准；授权 |
| replenishment ship | [军] 补给舰 |
| endurance time and distance | [军] 续航时间和距离 |

 **Exercises**

## I. Comprehension

**Part A**　Questions

*Answer the following questions in accordance with the text.*

1. When was Chinese Navy's first overseas deployment?

2. Which fleets of PLAN participated in escort missions?

3. What was China's first overseas support base? When was it established?

4. What is the effect of mutual visits between the Chinese navy and foreign navies?

5. What have Chinese sailors learned during escort missions over the past decade?

**Part B**　Multiple Choices

*Choose the most appropriate answer from the given choices below each question in accordance with the text.*

1. Which of the following is NOT included as the great achievements of the Chinese navy on the high seas?

　A. The Chinese navy has sent 31 groups of ships, 100 ships, and 67 ship-based helicopters.

　B. The Chinese navy has sent more than 26,000 soldiers and soldiers to escort more than 6,600 Chinese and foreign merchant ships over the past decade.

　C. The Chinese navy successfully rescued and assisted more than 70 Chinese and foreign merchant vessels.

　D. The Chinese navy captured four pirates.

2. Which of the following is NOT listed as problems in early stages of the escort missions?

    A. Warships in formation making two voyages at short intervals.

    B. A shortage of ships available for escort tasks.

    C. Ships' failure to adapt to various complicated sea states as well as weather conditions, such as high temperature, low humidity and low salinity.

    D. Limited number of destroyers and missile frigates capable of conducting escort missions.

3. Which of the following descriptions concerning logistic support is true?

    A. At the beginning, escort fleets mainly relied on foreign ports for logistic support.

    B. Commercial docks rented for storage are often allowed to resupplying the escorting warships in an unlimited time.

    C. The Djibouti Logistic Support Base proves to be a more efficient way of overseas logistic support.

    D. Getting logistic support from foreign ports greatly increased escort fleets' dependence on their own supply ship.

4. Which of the following descriptions concerning anti-piracy missions is true?

    A. Evacuating Chinese nationals from Libya is the first time that the Chinese navy has gone abroad to participate in the evacuation of overseas Chinese.

    B. Shipborne helicopters are able to conduct a scramble mission more rapidly so that special operations personnel don't need to be more quickly deployed.

    C. The 530 Xuzhou was awarded the second-class merit by the Central Military Commission.

    D. The special force didn't succeed in rescuing all the 21 crew members from the attacked ship.

5. Concerning performing escort missions in the Gulf of Aden, which of the following statement is NOT true?

    A. More than 40 escort warships from about 20 countries are carrying out escort missions in the Gulf of Aden.

    B. The Chinese navy actively communicates with other navies and informs them about the Chinese vessels.

    C. The Chinese naval ships set many new records.

    D. A foreign helicopter cannot be allowed to land on the deck of a Chinese warship.

## II. Translation

*Translate the following terms or phrases from Chinese into English and vice versa.*

1. 舰队编队              2. 导弹护卫舰

3. 伴随补给舰            4. 两栖运输船

5. 商船                  6. 非战争军事行动

7. 一等功                8. 舰载直升机

9. 互访                  10. 巡逻区

11. 分区合作            12. escort mission

13. escort fleet        14. logistic support base

15. supply ship         16. special force

17. commercial dock     18. special operations personnel

19. escort forces       20. escort operation

21. joint exercises     22. replenishment ship

Part B   Paragraph

*Translate the following paragraph from English into Chinese.*

The three-ship fleet marked the beginning of many escort missions which have been carried out by the Chinese navy over the past 10 years. It was the first time for China Navy to deploy its naval ships to protect its sea routes, fulfill its humanitarian obligations and safeguard its national interests.

## III. Reading Report

What have you learned after reading the text? Have you had a clearer understanding of China's escort missions, logistic support bases, and anti-piracy operations? Now create your reading report in no more than 150 words to generalize your achievement in the text study.

# Text B
# Port Visit

Take a look at any of the world's major ports these days and you will probably find a Chinese naval ship berthing for a port visit. Between 1985 and 2013, warships of the People's Liberation Army Navy (PLAN) made 127 appearances at foreign ports, such as Inchon[1], Portsmouth[2] and Valparaiso[3].

### Port Visit Activities

A port visit means a ship or a group of ships of one country pays a visit to a port of another country, which is an event scheduled by both the visiting and host countries. Port visit activities mainly include military diplomatic and cultural exchanges, friendly and recreational activities, local tour, and shopping. Besides, ships need logistics supply, refueling, and maintenance or repair at the port of call.

### Significance of Port Visit

In early November, 2015, three Chinese ships docked on the east coast of the US. At the port of call both navies had friendly contacts or exchanges in which the two sides tried to avoid the dispute over the problems of the South China Sea and the world's maritime rights in a spirit of seeking common ground while reserving differences.

Overseas Chinese also took pride in the rapid development and powerful strength of China Navy when they saw these ships sail round the world after carrying out their escort tasks and operating in the dangerous waters off the coast of Somalia to deal Somali pirates head-on blows.

The PLAN warships which can succeed in fulfilling their escort missions in the Gulf of Aden and other tasks in international waters are indicative of China's ability to build a world-class navy that can maintain the maritime safety, international order and world peace.

Port visits provide a good opportunity for a country's naval vessels to conduct a series of activities, including replenishment, maintenance, and military diplomatic exchanges. All this can help promote friendship and cooperative relationship between countries. With China Navy's influence expanding in the world, the frequency of visits to foreign ports has been gradually increased. From 2008 on, the PLAN began a military operation in the Gulf of Aden

where Somali pirates often attacked and robbed merchant vessels. In that year, an **escort task force (ETF)** was sent there to escort vessels and combat piracy. After completing its escort mission, the ETF paid visits to ports of the countries on the Indo-Pacific[4] and even to ports of some European countries.

However, in 2003, China Navy only made four port visits. In 2017, that number increased to 45 but dropped to 31 a year later. Now there has been a big increase in the number of port visits made by the Chinese escort task forces. By 2008 the ETFs and other naval vessels had made numerous port visits. For example, the *Peace Ark* hospital ship - the largest ship with the advanced modern medical equipment in China Navy - often pay friendly port visits and provide medical service for the local people. According to China's 2019 defense white paper[5], the *Peace Ark* has visited a total of 43 countries and treated over 230,000 patients. In 2018, *Peace Ark* traveled to 11 countries, including Papua New Guinea[6], Vanuatu[7], Fiji[8], Tonga[9], Venezuela[10] and Ecuador[11], to provide free medical service, a move that demonstrates China's spirit of goodwill in international relations.

In short, port visits can play a very important role in the promotion of friendship, mutual cooperation and military exchanges among the navies.

### Other Types of Visits

● Formal Visit. A formal visit of **courtesy** is officially made only for a special occasion like a national or international celebration. In addition to **honors** and ceremonies, formal procedures, or **formalities** are prescribed by US Navy Regulations.

● Informal Visit. An informal visit is made primarily in the interest of emotion, **goodwill**, and friendly relations. It needs no special formalities used for an official visit. An informal visit also may reach the goal of a routine visit to a certain extent.

● Routine (Operational) Visit. A routine visit means one during which to get logistic support, repairs, liberty, and recreation, or perhaps it is in connection with an operational task. No **protocol** is required other than that prescribed by local practice and the regional commander's guidance.

The following description is about port clearance requirements and procedures applicable to foreign naval vessels.

### Standard Clearance Procedures for Visits of Foreign Naval Vessels to All United States Ports

Standard clearance procedures for a foreign ship's visit refer to two separate requests needed to be made by the country's embassy in the US. One must be submitted to the Department of State, Office of International Security Operations, in order to get authorization to enter the US territorial waters. The other is submitted to the Department of the Navy to obtain clearance for a foreign warship to visit a particular US port.

As for diplomatic procedures, the embassy concerned must submit a request to the Department of State, Office of International Security Operations via the Diplomatic Clearance Application System (DCAS)[12]. Filling in an application form includes the following contents:

- Name(s) and type(s) of vessel(s)
- Name of port(s) to be visited
- Type of visit (formal, informal or routine)
- Date of arrival and departure at each port
- Name and rank of commanding officer
- Number of officers and enlisted personnel aboard
- Civilians/passengers on board
- Name of any civilian or military officer on board who is higher in rank than the commanding officer
- Names and nationalities of other foreign nationals on board who belong to different nationalities
- Whether or not ship-based aircraft will be embarked
- Ship's data: length, draft, beam, cargo, and other related data
- Cargo/supplies to be loaded/off-loaded (including explosives/ordnance)
- Communication frequencies needed for transmission while in territorial waters or in port, and maximum power output (in watts) of navigation radars and communication systems aboard

As for the US Navy procedures for ships' visit to any US port, the Naval Attaché of the country concerned should submit a request to US Navy Foreign Liaison (N2L)[13] at least 30 days ahead of schedule. A copy of request may also be sent by e-mail or fax via the State Department DCAS.

*(1039 words)*

### Sources:

1. Extracted and edited from *What Crunching the Data Tells Us About China's Naval Port Visits* https://warisboring.com/what-crunching-the-data-tells-us-about-china-s-naval-port-visits/

2. Extracted and edited from http://eng.chinamil.com.cn/view/2019-08/15/content_9590442. htm

3. Extracted and edited from https://www.secnav.navy.mil/doni/Directives/03000%20 Naval%20Operations%20and%20Readiness/03-100%20Naval%20Operations%20 Support/3128.10G.pdf（2020年6月13日访问）

4. Extracted and edited from *Why the Chinese navy's port visit to the US is important* https:// america.cgtn.com/2015/11/04/why-the-chinese-navys-port-visit-to-the-us-is-important

5. Extracted and edited from *How is China Bolstering its Military Diplomatic Relations?* https://chinapower.csis.org/china-military-diplomacy/（2020年7月25日访问）

## Notes

1. Inchon: a port city in western South Korea on the Yellow Sea 仁川

2. Portsmouth: a port city in southern England on the English Channel 朴次茅斯

3. Valparaiso: the chief port and second largest city of Chile; located on a wide harbor in central Chile 瓦尔帕莱索

4. Indo-Pacific: of or relating to the region of the Indian and West Pacific Oceans off the coast of Southeast Asia 印太地区的

5. defense white paper: an authoritative report or guide that informs the defense situation of a country 国防白皮书

6. Papua New Guinea: a parliamentary democracy on the eastern half of the island of New Guinea 巴布亚新几内亚

7. Vanuatu: a volcanic island republic in Melanesia 瓦努阿图（西南太平洋岛国）

8. Fiji: an independent state within the British Commonwealth located on the Fiji Islands 斐济（太平洋西南部的岛国）

9. Tonga: a monarchy on a Polynesian archipelago in the South Pacific 汤加（南太平洋岛国）

10. Venezuela: a republic in northern South America on the Caribbean 委内瑞拉

11. Ecuador: a republic in northwestern South America 厄瓜多尔

12. Diplomatic Clearance Application System (DCAS): an application system for diplomatic customs clearance 外交通关申请系统

13. US Navy Foreign Liaison (N2L): an office that deals with contacts between U. S. navy and other navies 美国海军对外联络处

## Word Bank

| | |
|---|---|
| dock [dɒk] | v.（使船）进港，停靠码头，进入船坞 |
| courtesy [ˈkɜːtəsɪ] | n. 礼貌；礼仪 |
| honor [ˈɒnə(r)] | n. 礼仪（向访问军事设施的军官或贵宾所表示的敬意） |
| formality [fɔːˈmælətɪ] | n. 正式手续，正规程序 |
| goodwill [ˌɡʊdˈwɪl] | n. 友好，好意 |
| protocol [ˈprəʊtəkɒl] | n. 礼仪；外交礼节 |
| beam [biːm] | n. 梁；船宽 |
| watt [wɒt] | n. 瓦，瓦特（电功率单位） |
| escort task force | 护航编队 |
| Naval Attaché | 海军武官 |

## Exercises

### I. True or False

*Decide whether the following sentences are true or false in accordance with the text.*

1. Between 1985 and 2013, warships from the PLAN made 127 appearances at foreign ports.

2. There are altogether four types of port visits.

3. Formal procedures, or formalities of a formal visit are prescribed by US Department of Defense.

4. An informal visit needs no special formalities used for an official visit.

5. A special protocol prescribed by US Navy Regulations is required for routine visits.

6. Standard clearance procedures for a foreign ship's visit refer to two separate requests: a request via the Diplomatic Clearance Application System (DCAS) and a ship visit request.

7. Chinese ships docked on the east coast of the US in 2014.

8. Port visits can help promote friendship and cooperative relationship between countries.

## II. Word Match

*Match the words/terms/phrases in the left column with its appropriate correspondents in the right column.*

1. port call

2. commanding officer

3. foreign national

4. clearance procedures

5. maritime safety

6. communication frequency

7. military diplomatic exchanges

8. maximum power output

9. navigation radar

10. routine visit

A. 例行访问

B. 最大输出功率

C. 清关手续

D. 沿途到港停靠

E. 导航雷达

F. 海上安全

G. 军事外交交流

H. 通信频率

I. 外国公民

J. 指挥官

# Text C
# Naval Customs and Courtesies

A custom is a usual, generally accepted and long-established way of behaving or doing things. Courtesy means polite behavior or good manners. Navy life is different from civilian life in that it has the particular customs and courtesies. Such behavior is a way of showing politeness and respect and also mirrors the standardization and orderliness of navy life.

### Saluting

The salute, a kind of military courtesy, is an action performed to show respect, which is symbolic of comradeship among service personnel. The most common forms of salute are the hand salute, rifle salute and gun salute.

While rendering hand salute, navy personnel salute the anthem, the flag, and officers by gesture as follows:

● Raise the right hand smartly until the tip of the forefingers touches the lower part of the service cap or hat, or the forehead above and slightly to the right of the eye.

● Extend and keep the thumb and the other fingers together.

● Turn the palm slightly inward until the person who is saluting can just see its surface from the corner of the right eye.

● Keep the upper arm parallel to the ground.

● Incline the forearm at a 45° angle; hand and wrist are in a straight line.

● Complete the salute (after it is returned) by dropping the arm to its normal position in one sharp, clean motion.

Rifle salutes include three types. Each type is shown as follows:

● Present arms (Fig. A)

● Rifle salute at order arms (Fig. B)

● Rifle salute at right shoulder arms (Fig. C)

A. PRESENT        B. AT ORDER        C. AT RIGHT
   ARMS              ARMS               SHOULDER
                                        ARMS

BMR10605

**Figure** Rifle salutes
(Source: Chapter 9 Customs and Courtesies Figure 9-5
https://www.globalsecurity.org/military/library/policy/navy/nrtc/12018_ch9.pdf)

Gun salutes are used to honor individuals, nations, and certain national holidays. They are always an odd number, ranging from firing a salute of 5 guns for a vice consul to 21 for the President of the United States or for a visiting head of state. Military officers below the rank of commodore are not entitled to gun salutes. Normally, each gun is fired at 5-second intervals. During the salutes, officers and men on the quarterdeck or ashore render the hand salute. All other personnel in the vicinity (in the open) should stand at attention and, if in uniform, render the hand salute.

### Honors

Honors are salutes rendered to individuals of merit, such as recipients of the Medal of Honor[1], to high-ranking individuals, to ships, and to nations. The type of honors rendered depends upon who or what is being saluted.

Passing honors are the honors rendered on occasions when ships, officials or officers pass in boats, or are passed (flag officers or above) close aboard. "Close aboard" means being near a ship, namely within 600 yards of a ship or 400 yards of a boat. Passing honors between ships, which involve sounding "Attention" and rendering the hand salute by all persons standing on deck and not in ranks, are exchanged between ships of the Navy, and between ships of the Navy and the Coast Guard passing close aboard.

Signals for the actions required to be performed by personnel are as follows:

- One blast - Attention (to starboard)
- Two blasts - Attention (to port)
- One blast - Hand salute
- Two blasts - End salute
- Three blasts - Carry on

Side honors, rendered to officers and officials boarding and departing the ship, are a part of the honors stipulated on the occasion of an official visit. The honors include parading the side boys and piping the side.

Side boys are paraded between 0800 and sunset daily except on Sunday. When the Boatswain's Mate (BM)[2] begins to pipe the call "Over the Side," the side boys will salute in unison until the last note of the call and then drop their hands smartly to their sides.

### Colors[3]

For the Navy shore commands and ships at anchor, the ceremonial hoisting and lowering of the national flag at 0800 and sunset are known as morning and evening colors. Every Navy shore command and every ship berthing in a harbor holds the ceremony of colors twice a day.

You will render honors as follows:

- If you stand in ranks, you will be called to attention or order arms.
- If you are in uniform but not in ranks, face the colors and give the hand salute.
- If you are driving a vehicle, stop and sit at attention but do not salute.
- If you are a passenger in a boat, remain at attention, seated or standing. But the boat officer or coxswain should salute.
- If you are in civilian clothes or athletic uniform, face the colors at attention and salute by placing your right hand above your heart.

### Half-Masting Ceremony

National flags flown at half-mast (or half-staff ashore) are an internationally recognized symbol of mourning. The United States honors its war dead on Memorial Day[4] by half-mast from 0800 until the last gun of a 21-minute-gun salute that begins at noon and ends at 1220.

Normally, the flag is half-masted on receiving information of the death of one of the

officials or officers listed in US Navy Register[5]. Notification may be received through news reports or an official message.

### Boarding and Leaving a Naval Vessel

When you board a ship in uniform and see the national ensign flying, you ought to halt at the gangway, face aft, and salute the ensign, and then turn to the Officer of the Deck (OOD) and salute. When returning to your own ship, you say, "I request permission to come aboard, sir/ma'am." The OOD returns a salute and says, "Come aboard". When boarding a ship other than your own, you should give a reason for that, saying: "I'm going to visit a friend." or "I'm going to the canteen."

When leaving a ship, you should salute the OOD and say, "I request permission to leave the ship, sir/ma'am." After receiving permission, you must face and salute the ensign and then depart. If you are not in uniform, you should state your reason for leaving the ship, for example, going on the pier to check the mooring lines or the like.

### Courtesies and Customs of PLA Navy

Let's see what Chinese sailors do on their daily duty or on important occasions.

#### ● Rendering salute and whistling

Rendering salute is the most common courtesy in the Navy. After the flag is raised and before it is lowered, the naval personnel should stand at attention and render hand salute to the national flag or ensign before leaving the deck or getting onboard. When the commander-in-chief or distinguished foreign guests board a ship, the ship will whistle, and its officers and men will render salute.

#### ● Ship in full dress

A ship in full dress means flying all flags and pennants and illuminating the ship. All flags include the national flag, military banner, naval ensign and oval flags. Ships get fully dressed on public holidays like the National Day, International Labor Day, and Army Day or during Spring Festival. If the commander-in-chief, or foreign guests get on board a ship, or when a ship berths at a foreign port, the ship will also be in full dress, and get illuminated after lowering the flag and before midnight. But when the ship carries inflammable and explosive materials or encounters bad weather, it will not be lit up with colored lights.

#### ● Manning the side[6]

Manning the side means the crew stand alongside the rail for saluting or rendering honors to heads of states or on important days and ceremonies. It is a usual occurrence that the crew man the side when the ship is entering or leaving port.

● **Gun-salute**

The vessel fires a gun-salute for ceremonies and celebration. Firing a salute of 21 guns is the highest-ranking, usually in the name of the country or the Central Military Commission.

The PLAN customs and courtesies are playing an important part in sailors' life. And they will continue to be a part of the Navy's daily routine because they are of much value to a further improvement in polite behavior, mutual respect, and sense of pride and honor of naval personnel.

*(1359 words)*

*Sources:*

1. Extract and edited from https://www.globalsecurity.org/military/library/policy/navy/ nrtc/12018_ch9.pdf（2020年7月25日访问）

2. Dictation from and transcript of https://news.cgtn.com/news/3d3d674e3563544d34457a633 3566d54/index.html

# Notes

1. Medal of Honor: a medal that is given to members of the US armed forces who have shown special courage or bravery in battle（美军）荣誉勋章

2. Boatswain's Mate (BM): a boatswain's deputy or assistant 副水手长

3. colors: a flag, badge, etc. that represents a team, country, ship, etc.（代表团队、国家、船等的）旗帜，徽章

4. Memorial Day: a holiday in the US, usually the last Monday in May, in honor of members of the armed forces who have died in war （美国）阵亡将士纪念日

5. US Navy Register: 美国海军人名录

6. manning the side: a manner of saluting or rendering honors used by naval vessels; the crew stand along the rail and on the superstructure of a ship when honors are rendered 站坡；登舷礼

 **Word Bank**

| | |
|---|---|
| salute [sə'lu:t] | n.（尤指士兵和军官之间的）敬礼；鸣礼炮，鸣炮致敬 |
| comradeship ['kɒmreɪdʃɪp] | n. 友谊；同志关系 |
| anthem ['ænθəm] | n. 国歌；（组织或群体的）社歌，团歌 |
| consul ['kɒnsl] | n. 领事 |
| commodore ['kɒmədɔ:(r)] | n. 海军准将 |
| quarterdeck ['kwɔ:tədek] | n. 上层后甲板区（主要供军官使用） |
| starboard ['stɑ:bəd] | n.（船舶或飞机的）右舷，右侧 |
| port [pɔ:t] | n.（船、飞机等的）左舷 |
| boatswain ['bəʊsn] | n. 水手长 |
| note [nəʊt] | n. 单音；音调；音符 |
| hoist [hɔɪst] | v. 升起 (旗、帆等) |
| coxswain ['kɒksn] | n. 舵手 |
| half-mast [ˌhɑ:f 'mɑ:st] | n. 半旗 v. 下半旗 |
| gangway ['gæŋweɪ] | n.（上下船用的）舷门，舷梯，步桥，跳板 |
| canteen [kæn'ti:n] | n. [军] 舰船上的小卖部；军人服务社 |
| pier [pɪə(r)] | n. 凸式码头 |
| pennant ['penənt] | n.（船上用作信号等的）三角旗 |
| illuminate [ɪ'lu:mɪneɪt] | v. 照亮；用彩灯装饰 |
| inflammable [ɪn'flæməbl] | adj. 易燃的 |
| hand salute | 举手礼 |
| rifle salute | 持枪礼 |
| gun salute | 礼炮 |
| order arms | 立正持枪姿势 |
| passing honors | 相遇敬礼，行进间敬礼 |
| side boys | 舰上仪仗队 |
| pipe the side | 梯口迎送笛；舷侧吹哨致敬 |
| over the side | 在舷外 |
| in unison | 一起，一齐 |
| mooring line | 系缆 |
| full dress | 挂满旗 |

**Exercises**

Based on what you have acquired in this text, you are supposed to conduct an online study to explore further into the relevant sphere. Comb and frame what you have found with an online study report in no less than 200 words. In addition, any assistant image, audio, video, or other first-hand material will be preferred when you present your report in class.

# Appendixes

## 附录1　中国人民解放军军制主要用语
## Main Terms of PLA Organization

| | |
|---|---|
| 中央军事委员会 | Central Military Commission |
| 中央军委办公厅 | General Office |
| 中央军委联合参谋部 | Joint Staff Department |
| 中央军委政治工作部 | Political Work Department |
| 中央军委后勤保障部 | Logistics Support Department |
| 中央军委装备发展部 | Equipment Development Department |
| 中央军委训练管理部 | Training Management Department |
| 中央军委国防动员部 | National Defense Mobilization Department |
| 中央军委纪律检查委员会 | Discipline Inspection Commission |
| 中央军委政法委员会 | Political and Legal Affairs Commission |
| 中央军委科学技术委员会 | Science and Technology Commission |
| 中央军委战略规划办公室 | Strategic Planning Office |
| 中央军委改革和编制办公室 | Reform and Organization Office |
| 中央军委国际军事合作办公室 | International Military Cooperation Office |
| 中央军委审计署 | Audit Bureau |
| 中央军委机关事务管理总局 | Organ Affairs General Management Bureau |
| 东部战区 | Eastern Theater Command |
| 南部战区 | Southern Theater Command |
| 西部战区 | Western Theater Command |

| | |
|---|---|
| 北部战区 | Northern Theater Command |
| 中部战区 | Central Theater Command |
| 中国人民解放军 | The People's Liberation Army |
| 中国人民解放军陆军 | The People's Liberation Army Army |
| 中国人民解放军海军 | The People's Liberation Army Navy |
| 中国人民解放军空军 | The People's Liberation Army Air Force |
| 中国人民解放军火箭军 | The People's Liberation Army Rocket Force |
| 中国人民解放军战略支援部队 | The People's Liberation Army Strategic Support Force |
| 中国人民解放军联勤保障部队 | The People's Liberation Army Joint Logistics Support Force |
| 中国人民武装警察部队 | The People's Armed Police Force |
| 中国人民解放军预备役部队 | The People's Liberation Army Reserve Force |
| 海军司令部 | Naval Headquarters |
| 舰队 | Fleet |
| 北海舰队 | The North China Sea Fleet |
| 东海舰队 | The East China Sea Fleet |
| 南海舰队 | The South China Sea Fleet |
| 海军航空兵部 | Naval Aviation Command |
| 舰队航空兵部 | Fleet Aviation Command |
| 海军航空兵师 | Naval Aviation Division |
| 海军航空兵飞行团 | Naval Aviation Regiment |
| 海军基地 | Naval Base |
| 水警区 | Naval District / Naval Garrison |
| 舰艇支队 | Flotilla |
| （舰艇/飞行）大队 | Group |
| （舰艇/飞行）中队 | Squadron |
| 特混舰队 | Task Force |
| 特混大队 | Task Group |
| 特混小队 | Task Unit |
| 总司令 | Commander-in-Chief |
| 司令 | Commander / Commanding Officer |
| 副司令 | Deputy Commander / Executive Officer |

| | |
|---|---|
| 支队长 | Flotilla Commander |
| 大队长 | Group Commander |
| 参谋长 | Chief of Staff |
| 指挥官、舰（艇）长 | Commanding Officer (CO) |
| 副长 | Executive Officer (XO) |
| 通信军官 | Communications Officer |
| 轮机长 | Chief Engineer |
| 航海军官 | Navigation Officer |
| 枪炮军官 | Gunnery Officer |
| 作战军官 | Operations Officer |
| 雷达军官 | Radar Officer |
| 军需主任 | Quartermaster |
| 军医 | Medical Officer |

## 附录2　中、美、英海军军衔中、英文表达法

| 中国 | | 美国 | | 英国 | |
|---|---|---|---|---|---|
| 列兵 | Seaman | 列兵<br>（即：三等兵） | Seaman Recruit | 新兵 | Junior Seaman |
| 上等兵 | Seaman, First Class | 二等兵 | Seaman Apprentice | 二等兵 | Ordinary Seaman |
| 下士 | Petty Officer, Third Class | 一等兵 | Seaman | 下士 | Petty Officer |
| 中士 | Petty Officer, Second Class | 下士 | Petty Officer 3rd Class | 上士 | Chief Petty Officer |
| 上士 | Petty Officer, First Class | 中士 | Petty Officer 2nd Class | 准尉 | Warrant Officer |
| 四级军士长 | Chief Petty Officer, Fourth Class | 上士 | Petty Officer 1st Class | 学员 | Cadet |
| 三级军士长 | Chief Petty Officer, Third Class | 三级军士长 | Chief Petty Officer | 中尉 | Sub-Lieutenant |
| 二级军士长 | Chief Petty Officer, Second Class | 二级军士长 | Senior Chief Petty Officer | 上尉 | Lieutenant |
| 一级军士长 | Chief Petty Officer, First Class | 一级军士长 | Master Chief Petty Officer | 少校 | Lieutenant Commander |
| 学员 | Midshipman | 总军士长 | Master Chief Petty Officer of the Navy | 中校 | Commander |
| 少尉 | Ensign | 学员 | Midshipman | 上校 | Captain |
| 中尉 | Lieutenant, Junior Grade | 四级准尉 | USN Warrant Officer 1 | 准将 | Commodore |
| 上尉 | Lieutenant | 三级准尉 | USN Chief Warrant Officer 2 | 少将 | Rear Admiral |
| 少校 | Lieutenant Commander | 二级准尉 | USN Chief Warrant Officer 3 | 中将 | Vice Admiral |
| 中校 | Commander | 一级准尉 | USN Chief Warrant Officer 4 | 上将 | Admiral |
| 上校 | Captain | 特级准尉 | USN Chief Warrant Officer 5 | 元帅 | Admiral of the Fleet |

（续表）

| 中国 | | 美国 | | 英国 |
|---|---|---|---|---|
| 大校 | Senior Captain | 少尉 | Ensign | |
| 少将 | Rear Admiral | 中尉 | Lieutenant Junior Grade | |
| 中将 | Vice Admiral | 上尉 | Lieutenant | |
| 上将 | Admiral | 少校 | Lieutenant Commander | |
| | | 中校 | Commander | |
| | | 上校 | Captain | |
| | | 准将 | Commodore | |
| | | 少将 | Rear Admiral | |
| | | 中将 | Vice Admiral | |
| | | 上将 | Admiral | |
| | | 五星上将 | Fleet Admiral | |

# 附录3  海军舰艇主要武器装备列表

| 武器装备名称 | 武器装备英译 |
| --- | --- |
| 100 毫米主炮 | 100mm main gun |
| 37 毫米火炮 | 37mm gun |
| 5 管反潜火箭式深弹发射装置 | 5-tubed anti-submarine rocket-driven depth charge launcher |
| 三人显控台 | three-person display and control console |
| 三联装反舰导弹 | triple-canister surface-to-surface |
| 下扬弹机 | lower hoist |
| 副炮 | auxiliary gun |
| 副炮指挥台 | auxiliary gun control console |
| 炮位 | gun position |
| 内外部通讯操纵台 | console of internal-external communications |
| 双联装 100 毫米高平两用全自动火炮 | fully automatic twin 100mm guns (anti-air and anti-surface) |
| 双联装导弹发射架 | twin missile launcher |
| 双联装舰对舰导弹发射装置 | twin ship-to-ship missile launchers |
| 反潜引导控制台 | anti-submarine warfare guidance console |
| 反潜火箭发射装置 | anti-submarine rocket launcher |
| 反潜作战指挥系统 | anti-submarine warfare command system |
| 反潜系统 | anti-submarine system |
| 反潜综合火控系统 | integrated anti-submarine warfare fire-control system |
| 主机遥控装置 | remote-control device for the main engines |
| 主炮指挥台 | main gun control console |
| 防空作战系统 | air defense combat system |
| 平台罗经 | platform compass |
| 电子计程仪 | electronic log |
| 电子战系统 | EW system |
| 电视监视器 | TV monitor |
| 电瞄系统 | electrical sighting system |
| 电源 | power supply |
| 光电跟踪仪 | photoelectric tracker |
| 推进装置 | propulsion plant |
| 导航显控台 | navigation display and control console |

（续表）

| 武器装备名称 | 武器装备英译 |
| --- | --- |
| 导弹保护罩 | weather-proof housing |
| 导航雷达 | navigation radar |
| 导弹发射架 | missile launcher |
| 导弹平台 | missile platform |
| 导弹系统 | missile system |
| 导弹指挥仪 | missile director |
| 机电集控室 | integrated mechanical and electrical control room |
| 机库 | hangar |
| 作战情报指挥系统 | operation and information command system |
| 声纳 | sonar |
| 抗干扰措施 | anti-jamming measures |
| 拖曳式声纳 | towed sonar |
| 武器状态显示台 | weapon status display console |
| 直升机引导控制台 | helicopter guidance console |
| 飞行甲板 | flight deck |
| 直升机飞行甲板 | flight deck for the helicopter |
| 舰桥 | bridge |
| 鱼雷反潜武器系统 | anti-submarine torpedo system |
| 指挥仪 | director |
| 指挥仪系统 | director system |
| 海图室 | chart room |
| 消极抗干扰装置 | passive jamming launcher |
| 自动驾驶仪 | autopilot device |
| 航行信号灯控制台 | control console for navigation lights |
| 航迹仪 | track plotter |
| 舰空导弹发射装置 | ship-to-air missile launcher |
| 舰载电子战指挥系统 | ship-borne electronic warfare command system |
| 舰载直升机 | ship-borne helicopter |
| 掠海飞行导弹 | sea-skimming missile |
| 深弹发射器 | depth-charge projector |
| 深弹投掷装置 | depth-charge thrower |
| 深弹武器系统 | depth-charge system |

（续表）

| 武器装备名称 | 武器装备英译 |
|---|---|
| 短波通信系统 | short-wave communication system |
| 搜索雷达 | searching radar |
| 跟踪雷达 | tracking radar |
| 火控雷达 | fire-control radar |
| 雷达终端设备 | radar terminal devices |
| 避碰雷达 | collision prevention radar |
| 监视与警戒系统 | surveillance and warning system |
| 全舰武器系统 | overall weapon system |
| 舰空导弹武器系统 | surface to air missile weapon system |
| 舰舰导弹武器系统 | surface to surface missile weapon system |
| 舰炮武器系统 | naval gun weapon system |
| 反潜武器系统 | anti-submarine weapon system |
| 水中兵器 | underwater armament |
| 舰载航空武器 | naval airo-weapon |
| 无源干扰火箭武器 | passive jamming rocket weapon |
| 舰用便携式武器 | naval portable weapon |
| 舰用爆破器材 | shipboard demolition apparatuses and materials |
| 武器配置 | weapon disposition |
| 弹药基数 | allowance of ammunition |
| 初发弹药 | ready service ammunition |
| 初发弹药箱 | ready service ammunition locker |
| 炮口冲击波／爆炸气浪 | muzzle blast wave |
| 炮位 | gun position |
| 压弹部位 | station of pressing ammunition |
| 稳定瞄准部位 | stabilizing tracking sighting station |
| 武器幕位 | zero of weapon |
| 射角图 | firing area drawing |
| 交叉射击 | cross fire |
| 喷焰偏转器 | blast deflector |
| 意外点火 | accidental firing |
| 射频防护 | radio-frequency protection |
| 排流通道 | uptake of exhausting gas and stream |

（续表）

| 武器装备名称 | 武器装备英译 |
| --- | --- |
| 航行防倒装置 | cruise anti-toppling means |
| 运弹小车 | ammunition dolly |
| 雷轨 | mine tracks |
| 雷链条 | mine chain |
| 引信箱 | fuze box |
| 挡弹网 | ammunition safety net |
| 引信装定台 | fuze setting plane |
| 发射箱支承架 | launching container support |
| 导弹装载架 | missile loading rack |
| 导流槽冲洗管路 | wash pipeline for blast groove |
| 梳状板 | comb board |
| 分流罩 | blast cap |
| 鱼雷装载架 | torpedo loading rack |

## 附录4　美国海军编制体制

Administrative Chain of Command of the US Naval Operating Forces

美国海军作战部队行政指挥系统

| PRESIDENT OF THE UNITED STATES |
| SECRETARY OF DEFENSE |
| SECRETARY OF THE NAVY |
| CHIEF OF NAVAL OPERATIONS |
| FLEET COMMANDER IN CHIEF |
| TYPE COMMANDER |
| GROUP COMMANDER |
| SHIP SQUADRON/AIR WING COMMANDER |
| INDIVIDUAL UNIT COMMANDING OFFICER |

| | |
|---|---|
| Secretary of Defense | 国防部长 |
| Secretary of the Navy | 海军部长 |
| Chief of Naval Operations | 海军作战部长 |
| Fleet Commander in Chief | 舰队总司令 |
| Type Commander | 舰种（兵种）司令 |
| Group Commander | 大队司令 |
| Ship Squadron/Air Wing Commander | 舰艇中队/航空联队司令 |
| Individual Unit Commanding Officer | 独立分队指挥官 |

Operational Organization of the US Naval Operating Forces
美国海军作战部队作战指挥系统

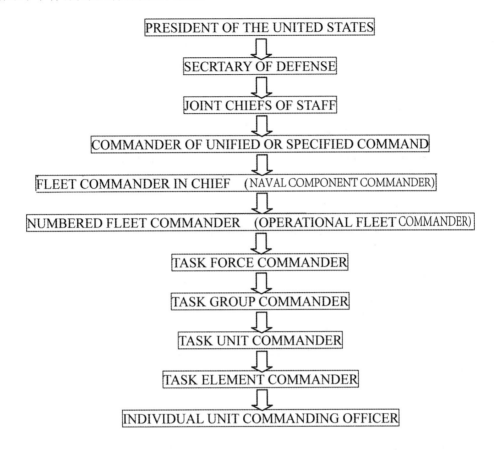

PRESIDENT OF THE UNITED STATES

SECRTARY OF DEFENSE

JOINT CHIEFS OF STAFF

COMMANDER OF UNIFIED OR SPECIFIED COMMAND

FLEET COMMANDER IN CHIEF   (NAVAL COMPONENT COMMANDER)

NUMBERED FLEET COMMANDER   (OPERATIONAL FLEET COMMANDER)

TASK FORCE COMMANDER

TASK GROUP COMMANDER

TASK UNIT COMMANDER

TASK ELEMENT COMMANDER

INDIVIDUAL UNIT COMMANDING OFFICER

| Joint Chief of Staff | 参谋长联席会议 |
| Commander of Unified or Specified Command | 联合司令部或专业司令部司令 |
| Fleet Commander in Chief (Naval Component Commander) | 舰队总司令（海军部队司令） |
| Numbered Fleet Commander (Operational Fleet Commander) | 编号舰队司令（作战舰队司令） |
| Task Force Commander | 特混舰队司令 |
| Task Group Commander | 特混大队司令 |
| Task Unit Commander | 特混小队司令 |
| Task Element Commander | 特混分队司令 |
| Individual Unit Commanding Officer | 独立分队指挥官 |

# 附录5　常用缩略语列表

| | |
|---|---|
| AAA (anti-aircraft artillery) | 高射炮 |
| AC (alternating current) | 交流电 |
| ACE (Aviation Combat Element) | 航空作战单元 |
| ACT (American College Test) | 美国大学入学考试 |
| AETC (the Air Education and Training Command) | 空军教育训练司令部 |
| AEW (Auxiliary Engine Watches) | 辅机值班员 |
| AI (Artificial Intelligence) | 人工智能 |
| ALMDS (Airborne Laser Mine Detection System) | 机载激光水雷探测系统 |
| AMNS-AF (Airborne Mine Neutralisation System-Archerfish) | |
| | 机载反水雷系统——射水鱼 |
| AO (operational availability) | 工作可用性 |
| ARG (amphibious readiness group) | 两栖战备群 |
| ARPA (automatic radar plotting aids) | 自动雷达标绘仪 |
| ASTRA (Advanced Sonar Transmitting and Receiving Architecture) | |
| | 先进声纳发射暨接收结构 |
| ASVAB (Armed Services Vocational Aptitude Battery) | 军队职业倾向测验 |
| ASW (Anti-submarine Warfare) | 反潜战 |
| ATC (air traffic control) | 空中交通管制 |
| AU (The Air University) | 美国空军军事学院 |
| AWC (the Army War College) | 美国陆军军事学院 |
| BALTOPS (Baltic Operations) | 波罗的海演习 |
| BMW (Boatswain Mate of the Watch) | 值班帆缆军士 |
| BSA (Black Shark Advanced) | 黑鲨高级重型鱼雷 |
| C2 (command and control) | 指挥与控制 |
| CACP (Casualty Assistance Calls Program) | 受害者援助电话项目 |
| CANES (consolidated afloat network enterprise services) | 统一浮动网络体系服务 |
| CBASS (Common Broadband Advanced Sonar System) | 普通宽带先进声纳系统 |
| CDO (Command Duty Officer) | 司令部值班军官 |
| CE (Command Element) | 指挥单元 |
| CFIT (Controlled Flight Into Terrain) | 可控飞行撞地 |

| | |
|---|---|
| CIC (Combat Information Center) | 战斗情报中心 |
| CMC (Central Military Commission) | 中央军事委员会 |
| CMC (Commandant of the Marine Corps) | 海军陆战队司令 |
| CNO (Chief of Naval Operations) | [美]海军作战部长 |
| CNS (Chinese Naval Ship) | 中国海军舰艇 |
| CO (Commanding Officer) | 指挥官；舰长 |
| CODAG (combined diesel and gas turbine) | 柴油机与燃气轮机联合（推进）装置 |
| COTS (commercial, off the-shelf) | 商品现货 |
| CPC (the Communist Party of China) | 中国共产党 |
| CSPI (College Student Pre-Commissioning Initiative) | 大学生预选计划 |
| CVN (Nuclear Powered Aircraft Carrier) | 核动力航空母舰 |
| CWO (Communications Watch Officer) | 值班通信军官 |
| DARPA (Defense Advanced Research Projects Agency) | 国防高级研究计划局 |
| DC (direct current) | 直流电 |
| DCAS (Diplomatic Clearance Application System) | 外交通关申请系统 |
| DDG (guided-missile destroyer) | 导弹驱逐舰 |
| DE (directed energy) | 定向能 |
| DMO (Distributed Maritime Operations) | 分布式海上作战 |
| DOD (Department of Defense) | [美]国防部 |
| DOE (Department of Energy) | 能源部 |
| DoS attack (denial-of-service attack) | 拒绝服务型攻击 |
| EEZ (exclusive economic zone) | 专属经济区 |
| EMALS (Electromagnetic Aircraft Launch System) | 电磁飞机弹射系统 |
| EMC (Electromagnetic Compatibility) | 电磁兼容性 |
| EOOW (Engineering Officer of the Watch) | 值班轮机官 |
| EPOW (Engineering Petty Officer of the Watch) | 值班轮机军士 |
| ESG (Expeditionary Strike Group) | 远征打击群 |
| ESGEX (Expeditionary Strike Group Exercise) | 远征打击群演练 |
| ETC (Eastern Theater Command) | 东部战区 |
| ETF (Escort Task Force) | 护航编队 |
| EU (European Union) | 欧盟 |
| EWO (electronic warfare officer) | 电子战军官 |

| | |
|---|---|
| EXO (Executive Officer) | 副舰长；执行官；办公室主任；主任参谋 |
| FAD (Family Advocacy Program) | 家庭宣传项目 |
| FDNF (forward deployed naval force) | 前沿部署海军部队 |
| FFG (Guided Missile Frigate) | 导弹护卫舰 |
| FHCP (Family Home Care Program) | 家庭居家护理项目 |
| FM (frequency modulated) | 调频 |
| FSCs (Family Service Centers) | 家庭服务中心 |
| FTX (Field Training Exercise) | 实战训练演习 |
| FY (Fiscal Year) | 财政年度 |
| FYDP (Future Years Defense Program) | 《未来多年防御计划》 |
| GCE (Ground Combat Element) | 地面战队单元 |
| GIG (global information grid) | 全球信息网格 |
| GPA (grade point average) | 平均学分绩点 |
| HVAC (High Voltage Alternating Current) | 高压交流电 |
| IEEE (Institute of Electrical and Electronics Engineers) | 电气和电子工程师协会 |
| IRR (Individual Ready Reserves) | 个人准备预备役部队 |
| ISO (International Organization for Standardization) | 国际标准化组织 |
| ISR (intelligence, surveillance, and reconnaissance) | 情报、监视与侦察 |
| IWC (information operations warfare commander) | 信息作战指挥官 |
| JOOW (Junior Officer of the Watch) | 副值班官 |
| JTRS (joint tactical radio system) | 联合战术无线电系统 |
| KHz (kilohertz) | 千赫 |
| KJ (kilojoule) | 千焦耳，功的单位 |
| LCE (Logistics Combat Element) | 后勤保障单元 |
| LCS (littoral combat ship) | 濒海战斗舰 |
| LPD (Landing Platform Dock) | 船坞登陆舰 |
| LTA (Lowest Astronomical Tide) | 最低天文潮 |
| M/V (Motor Vessel/ Merchant Vessel) | 商船 |
| MAC (Multiple All-Up-Round Canisters) | 多个圆形罐发射器 |
| MAGTF (Marine Air-ground Task Force) | 海军陆战队空地特遣队 |
| MARDIV (a composite word of "marine" and "division") | 美国海军陆战队陆战师 |
| MC (Main Channel) | 主用波道；主信道；主通路 |

| | |
|---|---|
| MCM (mine countermeasures) | 反水雷措施，水雷对抗 |
| MCS (Mine Countermeasure Ship) | 反水雷舰艇 |
| MEU (Marine Expeditionary Unit) | （美）海军陆战队远征分队 |
| MEW (Main Engine Watches) | 主机值班员 |
| MILCAP (Military Cash Awards Program) | 军事现金奖励项目 |
| MTI (Moving Target Indicator) | 移动目标指示器 |
| MVA (megavolt-ampere) | 兆伏安，电力设备（如变压器、电机等）容量的一种单位 |
| MW (megawatt) | 兆瓦，百万瓦特 |
| NATO (North Atlantic Treaty Organization) | 北大西洋公约组织 |
| NDAA (National Defense Authorization Act) | 《美国国防授权法案》 |
| NDS (National Defense Strategy) | 国防战略 |
| NEO (noncombatant evacuation operations) | 非战斗人员撤离行动 |
| NETC (the Naval Education and Training Command) | 海军教育训练司令部 |
| NFL (US Navy Foreign Liaison) | 美国海军对外联络处 |
| NLOS (non-line-of-sight) | 非视距 |
| NTC (Northern Theater Command) | 北部战区 |
| NWC (the Naval War College) | 美国海军军事学院 |
| OCS (Officer Candidate School) | 军官候选/培训学校 |
| OIS (Officer Indoctrination School) | 军官教化学校 |
| OMTE (Outline of Military Training and Evaluation) | 军事训练与考核大纲 |
| ONR (Office of Naval Research) | 海军研究处 |
| OOD (Officer of the Deck) | （舰）值更官 |
| OOW (Officer of the Watch) | 舰上值班军官 |
| PCU (Pre-Commissioning Unit) | 在建 |
| PDA (personal digital assistant) | 掌上电脑 |
| PLAJLSF (People's Liberation Army Joint Logistic Support Force) | 中国人民解放军联合保障部队 |
| PM (phase modulated) | 调相 |
| PNT (positioning, navigation, and timing) | 定位导航授时 |
| PRF (pulse repetition frequency) | 脉冲重复频率 |
| QMW (Quartermaster of the Watch) | 值班操舵兵 |
| RCOH (Refueling Complex Overhaul) | 加油综合检修 |

RDT&E (Research, Development, Test and Evaluation) 研究、开发、测试与评估

RF (radio frequency) 射频

RIMPAC (the Rim of the Pacific Exercise) 环太平洋联合军演

ROTC (Reserve Officers Training Corps) 美国预备役军官训练营

RUT (Realistic Urban Training exercise) 城市环境作战训练

SAR (search and rescue) 搜索和救援

SAT (Scholastic Assessment Test) 学习能力考试

SDR (software defined radios) 软件无线电

SEP (Skill Enhancement Program) 技能提升项目

SIGINT (signal intelligence) 信号情报

SLE (Service Life Extensions) 服役年限扩展

SLOCs (Sea Lines of Communication) 海上交通线

SOCCEX (Special Operations Capable Certification Exercise)

MEU认证演习

SOF (Special Operations Forces) 特种作战部队

SPT (Sound Powered Telephone) 声能电话

SSBN (Strategic Submarine Ballistic Nuclear) 弹道导弹战略核潜艇

SSGN (Strategic Submarine Guided Nuclear) 巡航导弹核潜艇

SSK (Diesel-electric attack submarines) 柴电混合动力攻击潜艇

SSN (Nuclear Powered Submarine) 核动力潜艇

STC (Southern Theater Command) 南部战区

SWATT (Surface Warfare Advanced Tactical Training) 水面作战高级战术训练

TC (Theater Command) 战区

TKMS (Thyssen Krupp Marine Systems) 蒂森克虏伯海洋系统

TRAP (Tactical Recovery of Aircraft and Personnel) 飞机和人员的战术救援

UAV (unmanned aerial vehicle) 无人飞行器

UCMJ (Uniform Code of Military Justice) 统一军事司法法典

UNCLOS (The United Nations Convention on the Law of the Sea)

《联合国海洋法公约》

VBSS (Visit Board Search and Seizure) 登船搜查和扣押

VSTOL (vertical short takeoff and landing for an aircraft) （飞机）短距离或垂直起降

WASS (Whitehead Alenia Sistemi Subacquei) 意大利WASS公司

WIG craft (Wing-In-Ground craft) 地效翼船